This book is dedicated to my parents
JOHN AND ORELIA RAWLINGS

both of whom by precept and example
taught me from my youth to love and
learn the central, foundational truths of
the Bible.

ACKNOWLEDGMENTS

It would be impossible to list all who have had some part in the shaping of this book. As I noted in the "Dedication," my parents are at the top of the list of those who first taught me to respect the Bible, to be aware of its most important truths, and to be willing to share those truths with others. I was blessed with a number of excellent Bible teachers in Sunday School who reinforced what my parents had drilled into me. Later in college and seminary, new vistas of understanding were introduced which would serve only to further buttress what I had been taught in my youth. The members and staff of my former congregations in St. Louis and Cincinnati made their contributions as well. All of those who have read parts or all of the manuscript and offered helpful suggestions and criticisms deserve special thanks. My gratitude goes out to 21st Century Press and especially to Lee Fredrickson for his valuable comments and assistance along the way. None of the foregoing persons should be blamed for any theological misstatements, omissions, or what might appear to some as questionable viewpoints expressed in the book. If faults are to be found, I alone bear the responsibility for their inclusion.

Whatever you may learn from these lessons that will make you more resolute to love and guard the truth, I will be grateful; but the credit is not mine. Paul urged Timothy to "hold fast" to the truth he personally had taught him, reminding him that he could do this only with the assistance of the Holy Spirit who lives within him (2 Tim. 1:13, 14). It is by the wisdom of the Holy Spirit that we are rendered competent to understand the great spiritual truths of Scripture; it is by His power that we are able to guard the precious deposit entrusted to us and successfully protect it against the onslaughts of a world increasingly at odds with Biblical certainty. It is my desire that these lessons will not impress you with the skill and wisdom of the author, but with the goodness and majesty of Almighty God and the power of His ever-relevant truth as revealed in Holy Scripture. To Him be the glory.

HAROLD RAWLINGS

BASIC BAPTIST BELIEFS

AN EXPOSITION OF KEY BIBLICAL DOCTRINES

21ST CENTURY
PRESS
PUBLISHING WITH PURPOSE
WWW.21STCENTURYPRESS.COM

BASIC BAPTIST BELIEFS
An Exposition of Key Biblical Doctrines

Published by 21st Century Press
Springfield, MO 65807
in partnership with The Rawlings Foundation
Wellington, Florida 33414

For information about books published by The Rawlings Foundation, write:
The Rawlings Foundation,
325 West Main St., Suite 1750
Louisville, KY 40202.

Cover Design: Keith Locke
Book Design: Terry White

ISBN 0-9766243-4-6

www.haroldrawlings.com

Visit our web-site at: 21stcenturypress.com

Printed in the United States of America

CONTENTS

AN EXPOSITION OF KEY BIBLICAL DOCTRINES

Acknowledgments 4
Introduction 9

The Scriptures

1 In What Way Does God Reveal Himself? **15**
2 How Did God Give Us the Bible? **21**
3 Is the Bible Trustworthy? **27**
4 How Do We Know Which Books Belong in the Bible? **33**
5 How is Scripture Best Understood? **37**

The True God: God the Father

6 Is it Possible to Prove the Existence of God? **45**
7 How is God Known? **51**
8 What is God Like? **55**
9 Are There Three Gods or One God in Three Persons? **61**
10 Is God the Spiritual Father of Every Human Being? **65**

The True God: Jesus Christ

11 Why Did the Son of God Become a Man? **71**
12 Was Jesus Really Born of a Virgin? **77**
13 How Do We Know That Jesus Christ is God? **83**
14 How Do We Know Jesus is the Messiah? **87**
15 Did Jesus Truly Rise from the Dead? **91**
16 Why is Jesus Called a Prophet, a Priest, and a King? **95**

The True God: The Holy Spirit

17 What is the Holy Spirit Like? Is He God? **101**
18 What is the Mission of the Holy Spirit? **105**
19 Are Baptism and the Filling of the Holy Spirit the Same? .**111**

The Devil and Other Angelic Creatures

20 How Did the Devil Originate and What is His Mission? .**117**

21 How Does One Overcome the Devil and
What Will Be His Final End? **121**
22 If Good Angels Exist, What Do They Do? **125**

Creation

23 Was the Universe Created or Did it Evolve? **131**
24 Are Humans the Product of Evolutionary Forces? **137**

The Fall of Man

25 How Did Sin Originate? **145**
26 What Are the Extent and Effects of Sin? **149**

The Atonement

27 Why Did Jesus Have to Die? **157**

Regeneration or the New Birth

28 What Does it Mean to be "Born Again?" **163**

Salvation, a Free Gift

29 In What Sense is Salvation Free? **169**

Justification

30 Is Justification By Faith or Faith Plus Works? **175**

Repentance and Faith

31 What is True Repentance? **183**
32 What Role Does Faith Play in Salvation? **187**

Sanctification

33 Are All Christians Sanctified? **195**

Eternal Security

34 Can a Saved Person Ever Be Lost Again? **203**

The Church

35 Who Instituted the Church? **211**
36 How is a Church to Be Governed? **215**

Baptism and the Lord's Supper

37 Why is Baptism a Requirement? 223
38 Why Must Baptism Be By Immersion? 229
39 What is the Purpose of the Lord's Supper? 233

Missions

40 What is the Mission of the Church? 241

The Grace of Giving

41 How is the Church to be Financed? 249

Civil Government

42 What is the Christian Attitude Toward Government? 255

The Return of Christ and Related Events

43 Can We Still Believe in the Second Coming? 263
44 When Does the Great Tribulation Occur? 267
45 What Will the Millennium Be Like? 271
46 Will Everyone Be Judged? 275

The Final State

47 How Can a Loving God Send People to Hell? 283
48 What is Heaven Like and Who Will Go There? 289

Appendix 1: Other Notable Baptist Distinctives 295
Appendix 2: Selective Glossary of Terms 298

Bibliography 317

INTRODUCTION

We live in a culture in which people increasingly base some of the most important life decisions on experience—how they *feel* about a certain situation or idea. "If it feels good, do it," is a commonly heard maxim. Even in the Christian realm, *feelings* and *emotions* are often elevated above *doctrine* in importance. Although emotions can play a powerful and positive role in the Christian's journey through life, they are far too unreliable and fluctuating to become the basis for one's belief system. The Bible does not say, "The just will live by *emotions*," rather, "The just will live by *faith*"—faith in what God has revealed in His Word. Indeed, without such faith it is impossible to please God (Heb. 11:6).

Some allege that people will no longer listen to *doctrine*. "It's too divisive," they complain. However, it is my contention that this is entirely false. Not only can theology be a captivating study ("the queen of the sciences," as it was once called), it is essential for Christians to know what they believe. The Apostle Peter confirmed this when he urged his readers to be prepared to give an *answer* (Greek *apologia*, a defense) to anyone who might raise questions about their Christian beliefs (1 Pet. 3:15). Twice in his letter to the church at Philippi, Paul speaks of his yearning to defend (*apologia*) the gospel (Phil. 1:7, 17). We are not to be silent when challenged to defend the Faith, regardless of the risks (for Paul it meant imprisonment and torture); but if we are not acquainted with the basic tenets of Christianity, we are likely to remain speechless when confronted by skeptics, either those who have a genuine interest in Christianity, or those seeking to lead us down the slippery slope of false doctrine. Furthermore, not being acquainted with the teachings of the Bible, Christians are likely to be "blown about by every wind of doctrine," frequently changing their minds about what they believe, easily duped by some clever religious charlatan who makes a lie sound like the truth (Eph. 4:13, 14).

In one sense, every Christian "does theology" regardless of whether or not they consider themselves a theologian. They may not be experts in theology; in fact, they may be very poor theologians, but they are theologians nonetheless. The word *theology* comes from two Greek words, *theos*, "God," and *logos*, "word." Hence, theology may be defined as *a word or study about God*—His being, attributes, purposes, and works. Every true Christian has some knowledge of and interest in these matters and can discuss them with some degree of skill, making them theologians. However, all of us should endeavor to be more competent theologians; in other words, to be able to confidently set forth our case about key doctrinal matters with conviction and clarity.

The purpose of this study is to meet a widely felt need for an up-to-date and concise source book on the principal teachings of the Bible from a Baptist perspective. It is not intended for scholars; rather it is to serve as a handy guidebook for laymen as well as beginning theology students, assisting them in grasping some of the foundational beliefs that distinguish Baptists. The studies are based primarily but not exclusively on the New Hampshire Confession of Faith, a summary statement of Baptist beliefs, originally drafted in 1830. After several drafting committee revisions, the New Hampshire convention board finally approved the Confession on January 15, 1833. Most modern Baptist groups in North America have adopted this Confession, or a modified version of it, and some choose to identify them as "articles of faith."

I am not naive enough to believe that all Baptists will agree with everything put forward in this book. Some will insist that I should have given more space to the sovereignty of God and election. Others may fault me for too much of an emphasis on the doctrines of grace, particularly as delineated in the chapter on "Eternal Security." Almost all Baptists of whatever persuasion are premillennialists, but not all will agree with the time the Rapture occurs, or whether there will even be a Rapture before Christ returns to establish His kingdom on earth. Some might wish for more clarification on the Lord's Supper, whether it should be open or closed. One thing all Baptists agree on is *the importance of their disagreements!* I am confident, however, that most of what is presented here will resonate with conservative Baptists throughout the world.

These lessons are designed so that one's Bible becomes a necessary tool to fully understand them. After all, what the Bible says about a matter is much more important than what any human says about it. Most of the Scripture references are not quoted, the rationale being that I felt it would be more beneficial for the reader to look up and read the references from the Bible itself. Like the Bereans in Acts 17, it should be the desire of all Bible students, when some doctrinal matter is discussed, to *search the Scriptures* to see if what they have been exposed to corresponds with what is revealed in the Bible.

Some churches may want to spend a full year in their Bible study classes going through these chapters. The basic articles of faith are subdivided into 48 chapters, each of which is headed by a question relating to the article. Pastors may desire to utilize them for a sermon series. Small group Bible studies and discipleship classes can profit from them. Additionally, they can be helpful for beginning theology students in Bible institutes, colleges, and even seminaries, here and on the various mission fields.

My fondest hope is that the information presented in these reflections will prove to be useful to individuals, churches, and institutions, the end result being the enabling of many to witness more effectively for Christ, the building up of believers in the faith, and the equipping of Christians to live out their convictions in an increasingly hostile world.

BASIC
BAPTIST
B E L I E F S

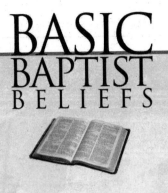

THE SCRIPTURES

We believe that the Holy Bible was written by men supernaturally inspired; that it has truth without any admixture of error for its matter; and therefore is, and shall remain to the end of the age, the only complete and final revelation of the will of God to man; the true center of Christian union and the supreme standard by which all human conduct, creeds and opinions should be tried. By "The Holy Bible" we mean that collection of sixty-six books, from Genesis to Revelation, which, as originally written, does not only contain and convey the Word of God, but IS the very Word of God. By "inspiration" we mean that the books of the Bible were written by holy men of old, as they were moved by the Holy Spirit, in such a definite way that their writings were supernaturally and verbally inspired and free from error, as no other writings have ever been or
ever will be inspired.

CHAPTER 1

IN WHAT WAY DOES GOD REVEAL HIMSELF?

No book has been so loved, so hated, and so revered as the Bible. Millions have died for their faith in this Book. It has inspired man's greatest, noblest acts, and been blamed for his most reprehensible deeds. Wars have been waged over the Bible, revolutions have been nurtured in its pages, and kingdoms have crumbled through its ideas. People of all viewpoints search its pages for words to justify their deeds.

One salient fact that makes the Bible worthy of one's consideration is that it is the most widely circulated book in all history. According to the 1988 edition of the Guinness Book of World Records, an estimated 2,500,000,000 copies were printed between 1815 and 1975. That is an enormous figure. No other book in history has come close to the Bible in circulation figures. Besides that, the Bible can now be read, in its entirety or in part, in more than 2,303 languages (as of 2003). The American Bible Society reports that it is now accessible to 98 percent of the population of our planet. Imagine the huge effort involved in producing so many translations. No other book has received such attention.

The Bible's uniqueness does not come from its political, cultural, and literary influence, but from its source and subject matter. It is God's revelation of Himself to His creatures. The word *"revelation"* may be defined as "a supernatural communication from God to humans, either oral or written." The term is usually understood to refer to a written communication.

Throughout history some have questioned God's existence, while many have confidently asserted that He exists and that He *has* taken the initiative to reveal Himself and make known to us the hidden designs of His will. His purpose is that, through Christ and with the help of the Holy Spirit, we might have access to the Father and come to share in the divine nature.

Actually God reveals Himself on two levels of knowledge. His first witness is in the world of creation, which is sometimes referred to as *general* or *natural revelation*; and He has also revealed Himself through *special revelation*.

GENERAL REVELATION

General revelation is universal in its scope and includes all that God has revealed in the world around us.

Creation is one way God has chosen to reveal Himself.

One key passage of Scripture conclusively demonstrates this. It is found in Psalm 19:1-6. The Psalmist expressly declares that the heavens, the expanse of the universe, day and night, continually provide evidence of God's existence and reveal His glory. No place on earth is deficient of this knowledge. Nature speaks a universal language. This knowledge is available to everyone and appeals to reason. Even blind people can feel the warmth of the sun, smell the aroma of a rose, hear the melodious sounds of nature, and taste the delectable foods God has provided for our health and enjoyment. All of these things witness not only to the existence of God, but to His greatness, His goodness, and His glory.

Moreover, everywhere in nature we find *order* and *design*. To try to explain order and design as the result of chance is foolish (Ps. 14:1). No one would ever seriously maintain that a watch simply came into being, that the metal out of which it is made happened to form itself into the shape of a watch, that the numerals on the face of the watch just happened to form themselves in the sequence of one to twelve and locate themselves in mathematical precision just so far from one another as to allow the hands of the watch to move (again by chance) precisely this fraction of an inch every minute. Even if one allowed millions of years for all this to have happened, one could not reasonably claim that anything as orderly and complex as a watch was produced by blind chance.

If this is true of a watch, what is to be said about the earth, the planets, the solar system, and the universe itself? Everywhere in nature there is *order* and *design*. Everywhere we find *the laws of nature*. Only a living, intelligent being could have designed the universe. This being we call God. Nature provides evidence that such a being exists.

Paul explicitly declares that no one—not even those who have never heard of the Bible or of Christ—has an excuse for not recognizing the existence of God and honoring Him as the Creator of all things (Rom. 1:18-20). However, because many reject and pervert the knowledge revealed to them in creation about the true God, His wrath is revealed against them (Rom. 1:21-32). Moreover, he asserts that it is a deliberate ignorance. They had the knowledge available to them but did not see fit to acknowledge God (vs. 28). The truth was accessible to them, but they suppressed it and embraced a "lie" in preference to it. Therefore "God gave them up" to the consequences of their choice. We can readily see the results of such skewed thinking in our modern world. Shameful perversions are now regarded as normal human behavior, and those who refuse to endorse such conduct are considered "homophobic" or "ignorant religious fanatics."

The very existence of humans provides evidence of a Creator.

How can humans—moral, intelligent, and living beings—be explained apart from a moral, intelligent, and living God? C. S. Lewis in his book, *Mere Christianity*, observes that all people have a sense of fairness or "fair play" which points to someone (God) who is the source of this universal moral "law" or principle.

Evolution fails in its effort to explain the existence of the soul, the conscience, or the religious instinct, all of which distinguish human beings from the animal kingdom. The complexity of humans demands a more rational explanation than that they evolved from a one-celled organism and are the result of a mere chance of fate. Besides, where did the energy originate to make the one-celled organism? A mind untainted by evolution almost always concedes that human beings are the product of a divine Creator.

All of creation testifies to the reality of a Creator, and yet the world around us sometimes gives mixed signals, presenting questions as well as answers. The same sunshine that testifies of a loving Creator can turn the earth into a parched desert, bringing starvation. The same rain that refreshes can turn into a raging flood that destroys and drowns indiscriminately. And human beings, as wonderfully versatile and ingenious as they are, often display jealousy, envy, anger, and even hatred that lead to murder. The world around us reveals a conflict between good and evil, but does not explain how and why the conflict started, who is fighting, why, or what the ultimate verdict will be.

SPECIAL REVELATION

God has used various means to make known His will to mankind.

Some of these are: signs (Moses' rod), dreams and visions (Joseph's, Pharaoh's, Peter's, etc.), face-to-face encounters (as Moses had), the urim and thummim (these were possibly two stones placed inside the pouch of the breastplate worn by the high priest which were used, like the lot, to determine God's will), visions, miracles, angels, events, theophanies (the appearance of the Angel of the Lord who communicated the divine message to the people); and, of course, Jesus Christ Himself, also called *the Word.*

God has used the Bible to reveal His will.

This is the most important of all the means God uses today to communicate with humans. All that we know about the life of Christ appears in the Bible, though not all that He said was recorded in Scripture (John 21:25).

Because *sin* has obscured God's revelation in *creation,* limiting man's ability to properly interpret God's testimony, it is necessary that God reveal Himself in a more direct and discernable way. Hence, through both the Old and New Testaments He discloses Himself to us in a specific way, leaving no doubt about His character and will.

The Bible declares the truth about God and reveals Him as a person. It exposes the human predicament, and reveals God's solution. It presents us as lost, separated from God, and reveals Jesus as the one who seeks us out and brings us back (reconciles us) to God (Luke 19:10; Eph. 2:14-18). The truth about God is found in the person of Jesus Christ, the embodiment of all truth (Eph. 4:21) and the central figure of Scripture. The Old Testament sets forth the Son of God as the Messiah; the New Testament reveals Him as Jesus, the Savior and Coming King.

The theme of God's love, particularly as seen in Christ's sacrificial death on the cross—the grandest truth of the universe—is the focus of the Bible (John 3:16). All major Bible truths, therefore, should be studied from this perspective.

CHAPTER 2

HOW DID GOD
GIVE US THE BIBLE?

The most crucial matter in reference to the Bible is its origin. In other words, did God produce the Bible, and if so, *how did He do it?* Paul affirmed that all of Scripture was given to us by God (2 Tim. 3:16). The distinguishing characteristic of the Bible is its divine inspiration. Acting as the principal Author, God moved ("inspired") the human authors of the Scriptures to understand and write precisely what He wished them to write. The Greek word *theopneustos,* translated as "inspiration," literally means "God-breathed." God "breathed" truth into men's minds. They, in turn, expressed this truth in the words found in the Bible. Inspiration, therefore, can be defined as the mysterious process by which God communicated His eternal truth through human writers without sacrificing their individuality, personality, or style. The result of this divine-human partnership is that God's truth was recorded without error in the original manuscripts.

The word "inspiration," however, means different things to different people. Some will acknowledge that the Bible is inspired, but their concept of inspiration is altogether different from that of the Apostle Paul. Some define the Bible as a human production which may at certain times and under certain circumstances become the Word of God to the reader. By that definition they would agree that the Bible is inspired. Others insist the Bible is inspired in the same way the works of Shakespeare were inspired. They use the word "inspired" in a general sense. For example, someone might say,

"That songwriter was certainly inspired." Given that meaning, even the liberal theologian will admit the Bible is inspired. But that is not what Paul meant. He meant that the writers of Scripture were so influenced by God, and their thought processes so illuminated by His Spirit that what they wrote were the very words of God.

THE PROCESS OF INSPIRATION

It is perhaps needless to say that the Bible was not actually written by the hand of God (although there is one instance of God writing His exact words—the *Ten Commandments*, Ex. 31:18; Deut. 10:4-5). However, abundant evidence exists that what is found in the sixty-six books of the Bible are the exact words God meant to be there. The inspiration came from God to human personalities to give to us the Bible. Forty different individuals wrote over a period of some 1,500 years as God inspired them.

The process of inspiration is disclosed in two significant New Testament passages. The first one we have already considered: 2 Timothy 3:16. If Paul had said, "*Certain portions of Scripture are inspired by God*," it would have been left to each individual or church to determine which parts were inspired. This would make human reason the test and judge of what is inspired and what is not.

We must assume that those who insist that the Bible is inspired only in spots are themselves inspired to "spot the spots" that are inspired. But as we know all too well, human reason is not always a reliable standard for determining what is truth and what is falsehood. Paul clearly intended to convey the message that *God inspired all of Scripture*, not just certain parts here and there.

The second passage is 2 Peter 1:21. According to the Apostle Peter's words, divine revelation was given by inspiration of God to holy men who where then "*moved*" by the Holy Spirit to write the very words of God. The word "*moved*" implies that these men were carried along as if by a strong current or mighty influence.

This distinctly teaches that the Bible was not written at the initiative or whim of human beings, but by those who were moved upon, yes, even driven along, by the promptings of the Holy Spirit. They wrote in obedience to the divine command and *were kept from all error*, whether they revealed truths previously unknown or recorded truths already familiar.

Inspiration is not dictation.

In some instances writers were commanded to express the exact words of God, but in most cases the Holy Spirit controlled the authors' thoughts and judgments, permitting them to express themselves in terms reflecting their own language patterns and style. The Old Testament was written in Hebrew, except for brief sections in Aramaic, and the New Testament was written in Greek. By allowing the authors (most of whom were not among the literary elite) to use a vocabulary familiar to them, suggests that *God set the pattern that His Word should be in the common idiom of the day.*

The Bible, then, is divine truth expressed in human language.

A parallel exists between the incarnation of Jesus and the Bible: Jesus was God in human flesh—God and man combined, deity and humanity in one (John1:14). Even so the Bible is the divine and human combined (2 Peter 1:21). This divine-human combination makes the Bible unique among literary works.

THE EXTENT OF INSPIRATION

Does the Bible only *contain* the Word of God, or is it appropriate to say the Bible *is* the Word of God? Is inspiration confined only to the Bible's important doctrines and spiritual lessons, or is all of Scripture (even the historical parts) the Word of God?

**The Bible is the Word of God in its entirety
and all the words of Scripture are inspired.**

This is called *plenary* as well as *verbal* inspiration. These two words imply that the biblical authors were not simply inspired in their general ideas, but in *the very words they used* (verbal inspiration); and inspiration extends to the *whole* Bible (plenary inspiration), not merely to certain parts. This is not to say that all parts of the Bible are equally useful or significant, anymore than a finger is as important as the heart. But just as all parts of the body are useful, so all parts of the Bible make an essential contribution to the total message.

Inspiration does not extend to translations of Scripture.

No translation is inspired in the same sense as the originals. However, God has preserved His Word and will continue to do so, which means we can rest confidently in the promise that God's Word will endure forever (I Pet. 1:23-25).

TRADITIONS AND NEW REVELATIONS

We do not believe that God has added or ever will add anything to His revelation in His Word (See Rev. 22:18,19). Tradition may have its place and can be a valuable tool at times in enhancing one's understanding of the Scriptures, but it should never be deemed equivalent to inspired Scripture or used as the basis for the formulation of doctrine.

Those who claim to be recipients of special revelations are on dangerous ground as well. If what they claim is true and the prophecy they receive is directly from God, their message should receive the same credibility as the writings of the Apostles. Our answer to this is that *the Bible is complete and entirely sufficient as is.* All that we presently need to know about God and the salvation He offers us is revealed in the sixty-six books of the Bible. To believe otherwise is to open a Pandora's box and advance the cause of false religions.

THE MESSAGE OF THE BIBLE

Since the Bible is our infallible guidebook, and because our belief and conduct are to be governed by what it teaches, let us see what those things are to which we should give attention above everything else:

The Bible reveals God's plan of salvation.

The Scriptures teach what God has done and is doing for the salvation of mankind. Many people are confused and have been mislead about how to rightly connect with God. They believe that salvation is attained by performing some type of meritorious work—giving money to worthy causes, living an upright life, keeping the commandments, etc. The Bible clearly teaches that salvation only comes to the one who has a personal relationship with Jesus Christ (Acts 4:12; 2 Tim. 3:15).

The Bible reveals our need to accept God's salvation.

Knowing the right way is not enough. The Bible is explicit about what one must *do* in order to be saved (Acts 16:25-34; John 1:11-12; Rom. 10:13).

The Bible reveals our condition in the life to come.

Some frantically search for answers to what will transpire in the future. Sadly, they search in all the wrong places. They consult fortunetellers, the paranormal, and religious cults, but Scripture explains the foolishness of such practices (Isaiah 8:19; Luke 16:29-31).

In contrast to the doubts, uncertainty, and despair of human speculation, the Bible gives a true and trustworthy message about the life to come. To escape the judgment of God and enjoy an eternal home in Heaven, a person must accept Jesus Christ as the one who paid for his or her sins on the cross (Matt. 7:13-14 & John 14:1-6).

CHAPTER 3

IS THE BIBLE TRUSTWORTHY?

The Bible is the central textbook of the Christian Faith. If it is only a record of the struggle of the Jewish people in their quest for God, it cannot be the Word of God as the term is generally understood in the Christian community. If it is only a good book that proposes useful moral and spiritual truths but contains many historical and scientific errors, we have no right to call it a "holy" book. It would be no better than other books that put forward moral and spiritual principles.

On the other hand, if we claim it is the authentic Word of God, how can we be sure those claims are reliable? If the Bible is to be trusted as the very Word of God, what are some of the evidences that will assure us that it is what it professes to be?

THE TESTIMONY OF JESUS CHRIST
AND THE APOSTLES

Time and again, Jesus and his apostles testify that the Scriptures are the Word of God (Matt. 5:17-19; Luke 24:27, 44; 1 Cor. 2:9; 2 Tim. 3:15-16). Many unbelievers consider Jesus the wisest and best man who ever lived. But if He deliberately deceived the people by making appeals to the Old Testament when He knew it was filled with myths and fables and was totally unreliable, He was *not* a good man, and He certainly could not be evaluated as wise. If Jesus cannot be trusted here, where can He be trusted?

THE TESTIMONY OF THE HOLY SPIRIT

Every believer has the Holy Spirit living within his or her person (Rom. 8:9). The believer's body is the temple or dwelling place of the Holy Spirit. The Spirit witnesses to the truth of Scripture, convincing us that the Bible is the Word of God (John 16:13-15; 1 Cor. 2:13-15; 1 John 5:6). Those who persist in denying that the Bible is the Word of God, are giving undeniable evidence that the Spirit of God does not reside in them.

THE TESTIMONY OF MANUSCRIPT EVIDENCE

We do not have the original manuscripts of the Bible, but we have almost 6,000 known Greek manuscripts of the New Testament. The textual variants that exist between these manuscripts do not endanger one essential doctrine of Scripture.

Not as many Old Testament manuscripts exist as do New Testament manuscripts, but with the discovery of the Dead Sea Scrolls, a number of Old Testament documents have been found that scholars date before the time of Christ. Every manuscript discovery so far has only verified the reliability of the Scriptures as we now know them. The Jewish scribes who reproduced copies of the Old Testament Scriptures were so meticulous in their handling of the sacred text that we may be reasonably certain that very few mistakes ever blemished a single page.

Sir Frederic G. Kenyon, the former director and principal librarian of the British Museum, said: "The Christian can take the whole Bible in his hand and say without fear or hesitation that he holds in it the true Word of God, handed down without essential loss from generation to generation throughout the centuries."

THE TESTIMONY OF THE BIBLE'S LIFE-GIVING POWER

It promises a transformed life to those who repent of their sins and put their faith and trust in Jesus Christ as Lord and Savior (2 Cor. 5:17). Over the centuries this promise has been fulfilled countless times. Many can echo the words of the hymn writer:

> What a wonderful change in my life has been wrought,
> Since Jesus came into my heart.
> I have light in my soul, for which long I had sought,
> Since Jesus came into my heart.

It promises peace to those who are troubled (John 14:27; Acts 10:36; Phil 4:7).

One vital quality missing in the lives of many in our modern world is the element of peace. This lack of inner peace and satisfaction drives many people to drugs, alcohol, immorality, and other destructive habits. The Psalmist proclaimed that those who love the Word of God have *"great peace"* (Ps. 119:165). Jesus reminded us that in the world we will have trouble, but peace is to be found in Him (John 16:33). This promise of peace has found fulfillment in the lives of believers since Jesus first proclaimed the guarantee.

It promises that God will supply the material, physical, and spiritual needs of His children (Phil. 4:19; Matt. 6:25-34).

These needs have been abundantly supplied wherever and whenever God's children have met His requirements.

It promises to be food for the soul.

Our innermost being craves communion, guidance, and fellowship with God. The Bible was given to mankind to satisfy this longing for light concerning things present and things to come. It is a guide from the present into the great eternal (Ps. 119:105; John 14:1-3).

The Bible never fails to do as it promises.

Millions can testify that the Bible has done exactly what it promised it would do. Those who, in faith, are willing to put the Bible to the test will discover that its promises are always reliable; its claims are trustworthy (John 7:17).

THE TESTIMONY OF FULFILLED PROPHECY

No one but God can foretell the future with certainty. If it can be shown that the Biblical writers often accurately foretold events before they occurred and before anyone could have known what would happen, it offers proof that the Bible came from God.

The Old Testament is replete with prophecies relating to the ministry and person of Jesus Christ.

Prophecies concerning Jesus' birth and early childhood:
• Born of the seed of a woman (Gen. 3:15; Luke 1:30-35; Gal. 4:4);

- Of the line of Abraham, through Isaac and Jacob, not Ishmael and Esau (Gen. 21:12; 22:18; Matt. 1:1, 2; Luke 3:23, 34);
- Of the tribe of Judah and the family of David (Gen. 49:8-12; Jer. 23:5; Matt. 1:1-6; Luke 3:23, 31, 33; Rev. 22:16);
- Born at Bethlehem (Micah 5:2; Matt. 2:1; Luke 2:4-7);
- Born of a virgin (Isa. 7:14; Matt. 1:18, 24, 25; Luke 1:26-35);
- The escape to Egypt (Hosea 11:1; Matt. 2:13-15).

Prophecies concerning Jesus' nature and ministry:
- His pre-existence (Micah 5:2; John 17:5; Col. 1:16, 17);
- Shall be Immanuel—"God with us" (Isa. 7:14; Matt. 1:23);
- Preceded by a forerunner (Isa. 40:3; Mal. 3:1; Matt. 3:1-3);
- His ride into Jerusalem on a donkey (Zech. 9:9; Luke 19:35-37);
- His betrayal, trial and crucifixion, death, burial (Ps. 41:9; Ps. 22:1, 14-18; Isa. 53);

It has been estimated that more than 300 prophecies have been fulfilled in the person and ministry of Jesus Christ. Those that are yet unfulfilled pertain to his Second Coming and reign, which is still future.

THE TESTIMONY OF ARCHAEOLOGY

During the nineteenth century, many liberal theologians commonly treated the Bible as a book of legends and myths. Many of its events and characters were regarded as fictitious. For instance, some charged that Moses could not have written the first books of the Bible since writing was not invented at that early date. Today, archaeology has refuted the skepticism of the critics and confirmed the reliability of biblical history.

The noted Jewish archaeologist, Nelson Glueck, affirmed that "no archaeological discovery has ever controverted a biblical reference. Scores of archaeological findings have been made which confirm in clear outline or exact detail historical statements in the Bible." Yale scholar Millar Burroughs adds, "More than one archaeologist has found his respect for the Bible increased by the experience of excavation in Palestine."

Archaeology refutes the critics' contentions that the Bible is inaccurate and fallible. On the contrary, its discoveries have done much to prove that the biblical records are true.

CONCLUSION

The Bible is the only book that both claims and proves to be the Word of God. It even accurately predicts its own future—it will *"stand forever,"* and will *"never pass away"* (Isa. 40:8; Matt. 5:18; Matt. 24:35; 1 Pet. 1:25). Century after century it lives on in spite of the many enemies who foolishly predict its demise.

However, even in the face of evidence such as the above, many will not open their hearts to the truth of God. Essentially the problem is a spiritual one. Only when one permits the light of the gospel to shine into one's heart will the Bible be regarded as the very Word of God (2 Cor. 4:3-4).

CHAPTER 4

HOW DO WE KNOW WHICH BOOKS BELONG IN THE BIBLE?

The Bible has far and away been the best-selling and most influential book in history and has been translated into more languages than any other book. Some suggest the Bible is the history of man striving after God. The Christian viewpoint is that the Bible is the written Word of God, directly inspired by God as no other book has ever been or ever will be and is the history of God reaching out to man. Our English word "Bible" comes from the Greek words *biblos* and *biblion*, which mean "book." The term "scriptures" (writings) is the title most often used in the Bible itself (2 Tim. 3:15, 16). It is also called "the Word of God" (Heb. 4:12).

The Bible is not merely a book among books; it is *the Book of Books*. It is the source book of our knowledge of God, the guidebook to everlasting life. The Bible is a library of sixty-six books made up of two parts, the Old Testament (39 books) and the New Testament (27 books). The word *testament* means "covenant" or "agreement." As we have already observed, the Old Testament was originally written in Hebrew (except for brief sections in Daniel and Ezra that were written in Aramaic), and the New Testament was written in Greek. The study of the "Canon of Scripture" is vital, because it deals with which writings belong in the Bible and which do not.

THE MEANING OF THE TERM "CANON"
* The word *canon* comes from the Greek word *kanon* which means

a reed or measuring rod; hence, a norm or rule. In the fourth century A.D. it came to be used of the Bible to indicate all the books that together make up the authentic Word of God.

- Today when we speak of the "Canon of Scripture" we mean those sixty-six books that comprise the Bible.

- The word *canon* also implies that the collection of canonical books contains the rule of faith and practice for the believing Christian.

THE OLD TESTAMENT CANON

To have a place in the Old Testament, a book must have been written, edited, or endorsed by a prophet. A prophet was one who declared what God had disclosed, and his prophecies were recognized as authoritative (2 Pet. 1:21).

Moses recorded every word the Lord spoke, then read this *Book of the Covenant* to the people (Ex. 21-23; 24:4, 7).

Joshua's farewell address was written "*in the book of the law of God*" (Josh. 24:26). The law was always considered to be from God (Deut. 31:24; Josh. 1:7, 8).

Samuel spoke concerning the manner of the kingdom and "*wrote it in a book*" (1 Sam. 10:25).

The expression, "*God said,*" is repeated numerous times in the Old Testament (See Gen.1). "*The Lord said to me,*" "*The Lord spoke to me,*" "*The word of the Lord came to me,*" are familiar utterances of the prophets (Isa. 1:2; Jer. 1:2; Hos. 1:1; Jonah 1:1; Mic. 1:1; Zeph. 1:1; Hag. 1:1; Zech. 1:1).

It is important to remember that the Old Testament was more than a thousand years in the making—the oldest parts being written by Moses (the law), and the latest (many of the prophets and writings) after the Babylonian exile.

Jesus affirmed the Old Testament Canon of Scripture, regarding it as an inspired record of God's activity among His chosen people. He repeatedly appealed to the Scriptures as authoritative (Matt. 19:4; 22:29; Luke 24:27, 44; John 5:39).

The early church maintained this same attitude towards the Old Testament. Paul affirmed the full inspiration and canonicity of the Old Testament scriptures (2 Tim. 3:15-16).

There are some 250 quotes from the Old Testament books in the

New Testament (only Esther, Ecclesiastes, and the Song of Solomon are not quoted). No quotes are to be found from the *Apocrypha**. Josephus (A.D. 37-100) acknowledged that the Jews held as sacred *only* twenty-two books, which are the same as our thirty-nine books. What may be said with certainty is that well before the New Testament era, the Old Testament canon of 39 books was fixed in the form in which we now know it.

THE NEW TESTAMENT CANON

The early church had a canon from the very first—the Old Testament Scriptures and the tradition of the works and teaching of Jesus. At first the latter was only in oral form. The Gospels and Epistles were gradually collected and used as Scripture, a process accomplished by the third quarter of the second century. It is important to understand that the books were inspired when first written. The delegates only attested at the Council of Carthage (A.D. 397) what was already true—that the twenty-seven books as we have them today in the New Testament are inspired Scripture.

To have a place in the New Testament, a book must have been written by an apostle or a companion of an apostle (Mark was a companion of both Peter and Paul; Luke was a companion of Paul).

Jesus promised the apostles that the Holy Spirit would bring to their remembrance what He taught them while on earth (John 16:12-15; Matt. 10:20; John 14:25-26).

The apostles spoke and wrote with divine authority (1 Cor. 2:9-13; Gal. 1:11-12).

Peter acknowledged Paul's epistles as being *"scripture"* (2 Pet. 3:15-16).

The New Testament books were read in the churches (1 Thess. 5:27); they were circulated among the churches (Col. 4:16; 2 Pet. 3:15, 16); and the churches were warned against forgeries (2 Thess. 2:2).

WHAT THIS TEACHES US

Non-canonical writings, whatever merits may be claimed for them, have no place in Scripture because they are not inspired by God.

Because the canon is closed, this leaves no room for additional revelations such as those allegedly given to Mohammed, Joseph

Smith, Mary Baker Eddy, Ellen G. White, the pope, charismatics, etc.

God inspired the Canon of Scripture; hence, we may approach the Bible with the utmost confidence that it is reliable and worthy of our complete trust and allegiance.

Only by frequent exposure to Scripture can faith be nurtured (Rom. 10:17).

*It was not until A.D. 1546, at the Council of Trent, that the Roman Catholic Church officially declared the *Apocrypha* to be part of the canon. Some of these books contain support for the Catholic teaching of prayers for the dead (2 Maccabees 12:45) and justification by faith plus works. The writings of the *Apocrypha* should not be regarded as Scripture because they do not claim for themselves the same kind of authority as the Old Testament writings. They were not regarded as Scripture by the Jews, and they were not considered authentic Scripture by Jesus or the New Testament writers. The early English translators considered them to be valuable for devotional and historical purposes but did not regard them as authentic Scripture. Almost all English Bibles through the eighteenth century (including the KJV) included them between the Testaments, rather than intersperse them between the Old Testament books as Roman Catholics did.

CHAPTER 5

HOW IS SCRIPTURE BEST UNDERSTOOD?

Bible scholars refer to the discipline of Scriptural interpretation as "hermeneutics." It comes from the Greek *hermeneia*, which means to "interpret" or "translate." The Bible is God's message to us. He did not send it in code to keep it a secret. He did not make it so difficult that only theologians and specialists could understand it. God wants us to read and understand the Bible far more than any of us want to read and understand it. We just need to grasp a few principles to make sense of God's Word.

The goal of interpretation is threefold:
1. *To discern God's message;*
2. *To avoid or dispel misconceptions or mistaken conclusions about the Bible;*
3. *To be able to apply the Bible message to our lives.*

We live in a day of abuse: physical abuse, sexual abuse, emotional abuse, and verbal abuse. There is also such a thing as *biblical abuse.* By that is meant, being deceived by someone's improper application or interpretation of Scripture. It is not at all uncommon to hear someone twisting Scripture, forcing it to mean something the author did not intend. Those unfamiliar with Scripture begin to believe the misleading interpretation with all their heart, only to discover later that both the interpretation and the application were false and harmful to their spiritual well-being.

Here are some basic principles to assist in helping one correctly understand the Bible and grasp its essential message.

LOOK FOR THE AUTHOR'S INTENDED MEANING

To properly interpret the Bible you must look for the author's original meaning rather than impose your own meaning on a text. Each biblical passage has a precise meaning intended by its author. The reader's task, with the assistance of the Holy Spirit, is to discover that meaning.

Discover who the author is as well as his intention.

Even when you know the name of the human author (Moses, John, Paul, etc.), you have no direct access to him. A secret to uncovering the meaning of a passage is to put yourself in the time period when the author first wrote and ask what he meant to tell us. In other words, put yourself into the skin of a Jewish person living 2,000 or more years ago in the Middle East, while at the same time making the appropriate application for your own life today.

Depend on the Holy Spirit to illuminate the passage.

The meaning of a passage ultimately resides in the intention of its real author, the Holy Spirit of God (2 Peter 1:20, 21). *Illumination* is the work of the Holy Spirit who brings light to the words of the Bible as we read them (Luke 24:45). Jesus promised He would send the Holy Spirit to assist believers in understanding the truth of Scripture (John 16:13). Each time you approach Scripture, pray that your eyes may be opened that you may be able to grasp the wonderful truths God has made available to you in His Word (Ps. 119:18).

Approach the Bible with an attitude of humility.

James reminds his readers that an attitude of humility is essential if one is to receive and benefit from the Word (James 1:21). To receive the Word with "humility" means being willing to hear of our faults and weaknesses, receiving the news not only patiently but with gratitude, desiring also to be transformed by the doctrines and precepts we encounter in the Word. The Bible never yields its secrets to a haughty, "know-it-all" attitude.

READ THE PASSAGE IN CONTEXT

By *context* is meant *what goes before and what comes after a passage.* As your knowledge of the Bible increases, you will begin to see words and sentences in relation to the whole book, not just the one passage you might be reading.

As with all literature, you must get a grasp of the whole Bible in order to appreciate and understand its different parts. For instance, when reading in Romans 6 about sin, you can better understand what is said by having an understanding of how Paul's teaching on sin fits in with the message of Genesis.

You must exercise caution when reading little bits and pieces of Scripture. Imagine reading Paul's words in 1 Corinthians 7:27 without taking into account its context: "*Are you unmarried? Do not look for a wife!*" Taken by itself it would appear that Paul is advocating celibacy as a rule for every man.

When you want to find out what the Bible is teaching, read the entire chapter (and at times the entire book), not just a single line. Find out who is talking to whom. Read what precedes and what follows. The only way to make sense of a story is to *know the context* of the story.

The ultimate context of any Bible passage is the whole Bible. How does one learn to read in context? *By reading entire books at one sitting.* If you can sit down for two or three hours to read a novel, try the same with Genesis or John or Ephesians. In all books of the Bible that you may read, you should have a sense of the whole book as you study its various parts. Ask yourself, "How does this passage fit into the message of the whole book, even the whole Bible?"

Your ability to read the Scriptures in context will increase greatly as you spend more time reading God's Word. You might start by reading Colossians all at one sitting.

IDENTIFY THE TYPE OF LITERATURE

The Bible is filled with various literary types. From Genesis to Revelation we encounter history, poetry, metaphor, hyperbole, and various figures of speech. Knowing the type (or genre) of literature you are reading is essential to understanding it. Different genres evoke different expectations and interpretive strategies.

For example, when Jesus declares that a camel can pass through the eye of a needle more easily than a rich person can enter the kingdom of God (Matt. 19:24), He is employing *hyperbole* or overstatement. He did not mean it was impossible for rich people to be saved, just difficult. Another *hyperbole* is found in Matthew 5:29-30, when Jesus says if your right eye causes you to sin, jerk it out and throw it away. Of course, Jesus did not in this instance intend for His words to be taken literally.

Psalm 98:8-9 contains another type of literature—*poetry*. "*Let the rivers clap their hands; let the hills sing together before the Lord.*" Poets use beautiful expressions to convey wonderful ideas. Poetry is not always to be taken literally, for rivers do not clap their hands nor do hills sing.

On the other hand, much of Scripture is to be taken literally. A good rule of thumb for Scriptural interpretation is: "When the plain sense of Scripture makes common sense, seek no other sense. Take every word at its usual, literal meaning, unless the word, when studied in the light of its context, indicates otherwise."

IDENTIFY THE MAIN TRUTH

It is a mistake to try to find deep, secret, hidden meanings in obscure details of the Bible while ignoring the main point that is being made.

Origen, an influential third-century theologian, believed that the literal meaning of Scripture was not as important as the allegorical. He searched for hidden meanings. This allowed him to make the Scripture say what he wanted it to say.

Some believe that the grand purpose of Jesus' ministry was to set an *example* for His followers to emulate. Those who advocate this belief completely ignore the verses that set forth the *main purpose* for His appearance in the world, and that was to become the sin-bearer for all the lost and hurting people of the world who would believe on Him (See Mark 10:45, Luke 19:10, and John 1:1-13).

LET THE BIBLE INTERPRET ITSELF

Many of the questions that crop up and cause concern or confusion when one reads Scripture are most often answered elsewhere in the Bible.

Commentaries on the Bible can be very helpful, but you must remember that *the Bible is its own best interpreter.*

SEEK THE FULL COUNSEL OF SCRIPTURE

Though the Bible is an anthology of many books, it is also *one* Book. While it has many stories to tell, they all contribute to a single Story. This principle has a number of important implications:

Never base doctrine on an obscure passage of Scripture. The most important teachings of the Bible are stated more than once.

If one obscure passage teaches something that other passages seem to contradict, you must understand the former in light of the latter. In other words, you must determine the meaning of the obscure passage by examining the clear teaching of other parts of Scripture that bear on the same subject.

Reading Scripture in the light of the whole message—the whole counsel of God—not only prevents erroneous interpretations, it gives one deeper insight into the Word of God.

INVESTIGATE WHAT OTHERS SAY

Christians have been studying the Bible for over 2,000 years. They have discovered the answers to almost all of our questions. They have dealt with the misunderstandings.

Many helpful Bible study tools are now available. A Bible dictionary, a one-volume commentary, and a Bible handbook would be valuable additions to any Christian's library. Even a regular dictionary is useful when reading the Bible.

Furthermore, you should take advantage of the opportunities available to you to learn more about the Bible—such as being part of a Sunday Bible study class or a neighborhood Bible study sponsored by your church. Another suggestion is to take notes when the pastor delivers a message or the Bible study teacher teaches. We often quickly forget what we hear.

CONCLUSION

Finally, as we have previously noted, you should bathe your Scripture reading in prayer and ask the Holy Spirit to open your eyes to the truth found in the Word. Without the assistance of the Spirit you cannot fully understand the spiritual message of God's Word (1 Cor. 2:6-16).

Be systematic in your approach to Bible study. Set aside a certain time of day for your appointment with God, whether it is ten minutes, fifteen minutes or longer.

The Word of God alone can keep one from error and provide an objective criterion by which to determine the truth or falsity of the ideas we are constantly exposed to in our modern society (2 Tim. 3:16, 17).

BASIC BAPTIST BELIEFS

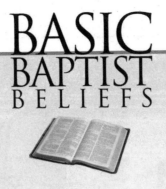

THE TRUE GOD
GOD THE FATHER

We believe that there is one, and only one, living and true God, an infinite, intelligent Spirit, the maker and supreme ruler of heaven and earth; inexpressibly glorious in holiness, and worthy of all possible honor, confidence and love; that in the unity of the Trinity there are three persons, the Father, the Son and the Holy Spirit, equal in every divine perfection, and executing distinct but harmonious offices in the great work of redemption.

CHAPTER 6

IS IT POSSIBLE TO PROVE THE EXISTENCE OF GOD?

Humans propose many different ideas about God. These ideas are related to one's world-view. All the possible world-views can be divided into the following:

1. *Theism.* There is a personal God, Creator, Preserver, and Ruler of all things.
2. *Deism.* There is a God, but He is beyond the world and not actively supporting it. God created the world, but it now runs on its own.
3. *Pantheism.* God is identical with the world.
4. *Atheism.* There is no God in or beyond the world.
5. *Infidelity.* A doubt of or disbelief in the existence of God.
6. *Agnosticism.* A denial that God can be known.

THE GROUNDS FOR BELIEF IN GOD

The Scriptures do not attempt to prove God's existence, but everywhere either assume or affirm it (Gen. 1:1; Isa. 45:5; John 1:1). The Scriptures declare that the knowledge of God is universal (Ps. 19:1-6; Rom. 1:19-21, 28, 32).

God has stamped this fundamental truth in the heart of humans, so that *nowhere on earth is He without witness.* All around the world, even among the most primitive tribes, there is this elemental awareness of God. Atheists are a tiny minority among the various nations of the world.

However, the Bible does not recognize this universal "God consciousness" as an adequate basis for a saving relationship with God. The Bible says humans must approach God by *"faith."* Those who come to God must believe that He actually exists and that He rewards those who earnestly seek Him (Heb. 11:6).

THE PROOFS OF GOD'S EXISTENCE

The Bible explicitly states that no one but a *"fool"* will deny the fact of God (Ps. 53:1). It takes more faith to believe that all living things sprang into existence accidentally—the result of a chance of fate—than to believe that behind all of creation is a living, all-powerful, infinite God.

Some unbelievers contend that scientists have proven there is no God. Science is incapable of proving the non-existence of anything. When people use science to try to disprove the existence of God, they are misusing science.

Because scientists are generally regarded as experts on all technical matters, if one of them asserts that God does not exist (it should be noted that many scientists are not atheists or agnostics), many of the gullible are snared by this unproven contention. But simply asserting the non-existence of God is not proof or evidence of the claim. Some scientists have foisted this cliché on the public, acted as if they have said something really profound, when all they have done is present an unfounded opinion.

If it is impossible to prove God's existence, how do they know this? Are there any proofs that demonstrate it is impossible to prove God's existence? An interesting observation about the assertion that it is impossible to prove the existence of God is that this is an absolute statement. The irony is that many who make this absolute statement also contend there are *no* absolutes.

Over the years, great Christian thinkers have sought to prove the existence of God from things within the world. Their contention is that the arguments for His non-existence are not compelling, or that to believe in the existence of God is not an act of intellectual suicide. The following are some of those proofs, which, taken together, furnish a validation of our conviction that there is a God.

Universal belief in the existence of God.

Humans everywhere believe in the existence of a Supreme Being or beings to whom they are morally responsible and to whom an atoning sacrifice needs to be made. This universal belief is innate and comes from within man.

The argument from cause.

This argument asserts that the existence of the world requires a Supreme Being to account for it. That the world did not come into being of itself seems obvious. No one believes that nails, brick, mortar, wood, drywall, or paint could form into a house by themselves. A designer of infinite power and wisdom built this world and all within it. That the first Cause must have been an intelligent Being is proven by the fact that humans are intelligent beings themselves (Heb. 3:4).

The argument from design.

As we have previously observed, a watch proves not only a designer and a maker; it is made for a purpose. A thoughtful, designing mind developed the watch. Its existence could never be explained by chance. By the same token a universe manifesting design implies a designer. All of science is based on the premise that every effect has a cause, which is incentive enough to believe that there had to be a *First Cause*.

Isaac Newton, one of the premier scientists of all time and a devout Christian, was a firm believer in the argument from design. The evidence of intricate order and complexity in the universe confirmed his certainty in the existence of an intelligent Designer. He said, "When I look at the solar system, I see the earth at the right distance from the sun to receive the proper amounts of heat and light. This did not happen by chance." It is much more reasonable to believe that our universe is the product of intelligent design than it is to believe that it is a result of chance.

The moral argument.

Morality is an essential part of the human experience. Humans have an intellectual and moral nature, a sense of right and wrong. Where did we get this standard of right and wrong? The answer suggests the existence of a personal God. If there is no God, there is no logical ground for our morality. The rejection of God logically implies the elimination of absolute morality.

Writing to the Christians at Rome, the Apostle Paul confirms the reality of the moral argument (Rom. 2:15). Every person has a conscience, a moral awareness of the vast difference between good and evil; they have a sense of justice and equity, honor and purity, love and generosity. This "moral sense" has been present in every people, age, and culture known to history and anthropology. It is this inner impulse that stimulates obedience to parents, compassion to the despondent, and preservation of public peace and order. It inhibits murder, stealing, lying, perjury, moral impurity, and a host of other evils. Admittedly, these sins are present in our world, but the vast majority of humans are not criminals, deserving to be incarcerated.

Conscience is that candle of the Lord that commends what is well done and reprimands when one does what is wrong.

CONCLUSION

All the above evidences confirm that God really exists and that there is enough evidence for a person who wants to believe, but no evidence is convincing for the person who refuses to believe. Someone wisely said, "Those who know God do not need proof. Those who reject God do not want proof."

Blaise Pascal (1623-1662), mathematical prodigy, physicist, inventor, and literary stylist, was one of the remarkable geniuses of Western intellectual history. Among other discoveries, he devised the first calculating machine. After his conversion to Christianity in 1654, Pascal set about preparing an *Apology* [defense] *for the Christian Religion*. The work was never finished, for Pascal died at the age of thirty-nine, leaving only a set of remarkable notes, later published as *Pensees*. The work undertakes to put the case for Christianity up against the rationalism and skepticism of some of the leading thinkers of his day.

Pascal's contention is that God is to be known by faith—faith in His Son, Jesus Christ; but the evidences for validating Christianity are great: fulfilled prophecy, miracles, the witness of history, and the power of Scripture to transform lives.

Pascal proposed what later became known as *Pascal's Wager*.

Because he believed that logical reasoning by itself cannot prove the existence of God, he proposed a "wager." And so we are asked: Where are you going to place your bet? If you place it with God, you lose nothing, even if it turns out that God does not exist. But if you place it against God, and you are wrong and God does exist, you lose everything: God, eternal life, Heaven, infinite gain.

Dostoevsky said, "If there is no God, then all is permitted." Everyone, with impunity, does what is right in his own eyes.

CHAPTER 7

HOW IS GOD KNOWN?

Few of the spectators who watched Jesus die on the cross recognized who He really was. Among those who did was the dying thief who acknowledged Jesus to be *a king with a kingdom*—another way of admitting He was *Lord* (Luke 23:42). Another was the Roman soldier who declared Him to be *the Son of God* (Mark 15:39).

The Apostle John wrote that Jesus presented Himself to His own people as their Savior and Messiah but they refused to admit who He really was (John 1:11). When penning those words, he was thinking not merely of Israel but of every generation that has lived. Except for a minority of those who have populated the world throughout the centuries, all humanity, like that raucous crowd at Calvary, has failed to recognize in Jesus Christ their God and Savior. This tragic failure shows that humanity's knowledge of God is radically deficient.

The many theories attempting to explain God, and the many arguments for and against His existence, show that human wisdom cannot penetrate the divine. Depending on human wisdom alone to learn about God is like using a magnifying glass to study the constellations. Hence, to many, God's wisdom is a *"hidden wisdom"* (1 Cor 2:7). To them, God is a mystery. Paul wrote that none of the rulers of this age understood the nature of God, because if they had known, they would not have crucified Jesus (1 Cor. 2:8).

One of the most basic commandments of Scripture states that we are to love God with all our heart, soul, and mind (Matt. 22:37; cf.

Deut. 6:5). We cannot love someone we know nothing about, yet we cannot by searching find out the deep things of God (Job 11:7). How then can we come to know and love the Creator?

GOD CAN BE KNOWN

If we are to know God, it is necessary that He reveal Himself to us. We have already seen that God has revealed Himself through nature. Paul says that what can be known about God is obvious because God has made it plain to all mankind (Rom. 1:19, 20). Creation reveals God to those who open their eyes to the truth.

However, realizing that sinful people often misunderstand and distort the revelation of God found in nature (Rom. 1:18, 21, 25), it was necessary for God to go a step beyond and communicate to us through a written record of His will for His creatures. Hence, God, in His love and compassion, reached out to us through the Scriptures. The Bible reveals that Christianity is not a record of man's quest for God; it is an account of God's revelation of Himself and His purposes for all mankind.

GOD CAN NEVER BE FULLY UNDERSTOOD

Because God is infinite and we are finite, we can never fully fathom all there is to know about God. The Psalmist declares that God's greatness is beyond human comprehension (Ps. 145:3). His understanding of things cannot be measured (Ps. 147:5). When David reflected on the knowledge of God, he admitted it was too wonderful for him to grasp (Ps. 139:6).

Paul, like David, spoke of the incomprehensibility of God when he affirmed that no one understands the things of God except the Spirit of God (1 Cor. 2:11). Writing to the Roman Christians, he extolled the depth of the riches, wisdom, and knowledge of God, and admitted how impossible it is for us to understand His decisions and His ways (Rom. 11:33). These qualities of God are beyond our capacity as humans to fully understand.

Even in our glorified bodies in the heavenly world, with our perception much more sophisticated than now, we will never grasp all there is to know about God. We will never stop growing in our knowledge of God. This will be one of the many pleasures we will enjoy in the next life, to be ever expanding in our comprehension of our heavenly Father.

It should be considered a delightful challenge to us during our brief sojourn in this world to daily increase in our knowledge of God through diligent study of His Word. In his sermon titled "The Christian Pilgrim," Jonathan Edwards wrote: "The enjoyment of [God] is the only happiness with which our souls can be satisfied. To go to Heaven, fully to enjoy God, is infinitely better than the most pleasant accommodations here. Fathers and mothers, husbands, wives, or children, or the company of earthly friends, are but shadows; God is the substance. These are but scattered beams, but God is the sun. These are but streams; but God is the ocean."

OBTAINING A SUFFICIENT KNOWLEDGE OF GOD

Even though we cannot know all there is to know about God, we can know many true things about Him.

Knowing God involves the whole person, not just the intellect.

Hence, there must be a responsiveness to the Holy Spirit (Rom. 8:14), and a willingness to do God's will (John 7:17; cf. Matt. 11:27).

Unbelievers cannot understand God (1 Cor. 1:20-21).

In these verses Paul indicates that the world cannot know God through human wisdom, for God has made foolish the wisdom of this world. Indeed, the wisdom of the world is foolishness to God (3:19). But this condition is overcome when the Holy Spirit begins to work within us (2:9-13). Only with the Spirit's aid can humans understand God.

In our search for a true understanding of God, **we must submit to the authority of His Word.** Since the Bible is its own interpreter, we must subject ourselves to the principles and methods its provides. Without these Biblical guidelines we cannot know God.

Why did so many of the people of Jesus' day fail to perceive who He really was? Because they refused to subject themselves to the guidance of the Holy Spirit through the Scriptures, they misinterpreted God's message and crucified their Savior. Their problem was not one of intellect. It was their closed hearts that darkened their minds, resulting in eternal loss.

HOW TO KNOW GOD PERSONALLY

It is one thing to know the right facts about God—for instance that He is the *creator* (Gen. 1:1), He is *love* (1 John 4:8), He is *spirit* (John 4:24); it is another thing to know Him personally.

God's greatest expression of love came through His willingness to send His Son, Jesus Christ, into the world to become fallen humanity's redeemer (John 3:16). It is through Jesus that we can know the Father. John the Apostle states that the Son of God came to give us the capacity to know God (1 John 5:20).

Jesus said the way to have eternal life is to know the only true God; and the way to know this one and only true God is to believe on His Son whom He sent into the world (John 17:3).

This is *good news*. Although it is impossible for our finite minds to know all there is to know about God, the Scriptures afford a practical knowledge of Him that is sufficient for us to enter into a saving relationship with Him.

CHAPTER 8

WHAT IS GOD LIKE?

We have seen that belief in God is a reasonable belief, so reasonable in fact that only a fool denies God's existence (Ps. 14:1). With the Hebrews, however, the problem was not atheism but polytheism; not, does God exist, but which God exists? And so it is in our time. Because nearly everyone believes in a god of some kind, we need to consider not only the existence of God ("Is there a God?"), but the character of God ("What is God like?").

Just as the Bible nowhere attempts to establish the existence of God, so it proposes no definition of His person. The Hebrews were prohibited from making any graven image of God, and they made no effort to restrict God to a definition. However, we do have a significant description of Him in the conversation between Moses and the Lord at the burning bush in the Sinai desert. Moses inquired of the Lord what he should tell the children of Israel when they ask him who sent him on his mission. The Lord instructed Moses to tell them that *I AM* had sent him (Exod. 3:13-14).

This mysterious description of God demonstrates that a complete definition of Him is fundamentally impossible. Just as a graven image of God cannot depict Him, so a definition of God cannot explain Him. After we have said all we can about God, there remains a great element of mystery (Isa. 55:8, 9).

Nevertheless, God has made a true disclosure of Himself. He has revealed Himself in such a way that we may truly know Him, even though we may not comprehend Him fully.

THE ESSENCE OF GOD

He is spirit (John 4:24).

If God is spirit, He is incorporeal; that is, He has no physical body, one that is visible to the human eye. But what about the expressions that represent God as having bodily parts (Heb. 1:10; 1 Kings 8:29; Neh. 1:6)? They are symbolic representations which serve to make God real and to express His various activities, powers, and interests.

John said that no human has seen God at any time (John 1:18). Paul calls Him *"the invisible God"* (Col. 1:15; 1 Tim. 1:17). However, spirit beings can manifest themselves in visible form. Jacob said, after wrestling with the angel of the Lord at Peniel, *"I have seen God face to face"* (Gen. 32:30). *"The angel of the Lord"* was a visible manifestation of deity (Gen. 16:7-14; Ex. 3:2-6; Judg. 6:11-23). Jesus said that anyone who had seen Him had seen the Father (John 14:9).

Scripture teaches that the redeemed will one day see God (Ps. 17:15; Matt. 5:8; Heb. 12:14; Rev. 22:3, 4). In our glorified bodies, our power of sight will be totally altered and enhanced, and we will be able at last to actually see God, seated on a throne, high and lifted up.

He is the living God.

One of the noteworthy Biblical descriptions of God is that He is *living*. He is not some impersonal force or cosmic energy. At least twenty-eight times in the Bible God is said to be the *"living God."* For example, one of the reasons David was so outraged over Goliath was that this Philistine had defied *"the armies of the living God"* (I Sam. 17:26, 36).

The Psalmist expressed his great spiritual desire with such words as, *"My soul thirsts for God, for the living God"* (Ps. 42:2). In numerous places throughout the New Testament the same truth is repeated (Matt. 16:16; Acts 14:15; Rom. 9:26; Heb. 3:12; Rev. 7:2).

He is a person.

Scripture represents God as possessing the characteristics of personality: self-consciousness (Ex. 3:14; 1 Cor. 2:10); intellect (Gen. 18:19; Acts 15:18); volition (Gen. 3:15; John 6:38). He is described as speaking (Gen. 1:3); seeing (Gen. 11:5); hearing (Ps. 94:9), grieving (Gen. 6:6); repenting (Gen. 6:6); being angry (Deut. 1:37); jealous (Ex. 20:5); and compassionate (Ps. 111:4).

He is the eternal, self-existing one.

Like a circle, God has no beginning and no end. He is called *"the Eternal God"* (Gen. 21:33). He is not limited by time. In fact, He was before time began and is the cause of time. He was, He is, He will be. The Psalmist addresses God in personal terms and affirms His eternal existence and infinite power (Ps. 90:2).

THE ATTRIBUTES OF GOD

Implicit in the Christian's understanding of God is the confidence that He is all sufficient and altogether adequate to meet the needs of His creation.

He is Omnipotent.

He is all-powerful and capable of doing whatever is consistent with His character (Gen. 18:14). It was described in the Old Testament by the sacred name El, especially in the composition of El shaddai (God Almighty), and says that nothing is impossible with God. However, omnipotence does not imply that God can do everything conceivable. For example, He cannot lie, He cannot change, He cannot be unfaithful, He cannot do something irrational, such as creating a rock bigger than He can lift. He is only capable of doing what is consistent with His own character and necessary to His government of the universe (Dan. 4:17, 25, 35; Matt. 19:26; Rev. 19:6).

The discovery of the incredible immensity of our universe, where distances are measured in light-years, has given us a new understanding of the omnipotence of God.

He is sovereign. The Biblical term "Lord," used by the Jews in place of the unutterable name for God, YHWH (translated *Jehovah* or *Yahweh*), implies particularly the sovereignty of God. **It might even be said that the sovereignty of God is the principal doctrine of the whole Bible.** This idea of God as king assumes that He is the ruler over the whole universe, material and spiritual, and has a moral claim on the lives of all His creatures (Mark 12:28-30). If there is but one God, then He must be the God of all the earth. All other so-called gods are false and are to be repudiated (Ex. 20:1-3; Matt. 4:10).

He is the creator and sustainer of all. He is the One who made the universe and keeps it going (Gen. 1:1; John 1:3; Heb. 1:1-3). If we ask *how* God created all things, we learn that it was by the power of His word (Ps. 33:6, 9). God spoke and it was done. If we ask how God *sustains* all things, we learn that all things hold together and are kept intact by His powerful Word (Col. 1:17; Heb. 1:3).

He is Omniscient.

Because He is all-knowing, his wisdom and knowledge are infinite (Ps. 139:2-4; 147:5; 1 John 3:20). His knowledge of the future is limitless (Isa. 46:9-10). He is even aware of the minute details of our lives (Matt. 6:8; 10:30).

A contemporary movement involving a small but influential group of theologians proclaims that God has imposed upon Himself certain limitations that restrict His ability to know all things. In other words, God is unable to always predict the future and sometimes changes His mind. It is called "Openness Theology." Thankfully, most such theological aberrations, like passing fads, come and go rather quickly.

How God can comprehend so vast an amount of knowledge is beyond the reach of man's intellectual capacity. One can only stand amazed in the presence of such matchless wisdom (Rom. 11:33).

He is Omnipresent.

He is everywhere present in creation at the same time. Because God is spirit (John 4:24) and not constrained by a physical body, he is unrestricted with respect to space. If God has brought all things into existence by His creative power and sustains the entire universe through His wisdom and might, it follows that wherever His creatures are, there He is also (Acts 17:28).

No matter how far humans may range in the universe, either on this planet or in space, they will find the presence of God (Ps. 139:7-10).

THE MORAL ATTRIBUTES OF GOD

He is holy.

The Lord is called "*the Holy One*" some thirty times in Isaiah alone. It is the attribute by which He is especially known in the Old

Testament (Lev. 11:44ff; Josh 24:19; Ps. 22:3). Because of God's holiness and man's sinfulness, humans must approach Him through the merits of another, else they cannot approach Him at all. But Christ has made such access possible (Rom. 5:2; Heb. 10:19ff).

He is love (1 John 4:8, 16).

He created the world in order to show forth His glory and to share His love with the beings He created. The Apostle John gives us a brief but vivid description of the *extent* of God's love in John 3:16.

He is just.

God is impartial and equitable in all His dealings with His creatures (Deut. 32:4; Rev. 15:3). We have to balance out God's justice with His other attributes. Because of His justice, God is obligated to punish evildoers. Because of His love, patience, and goodness, He wants no one to perish, but everyone to come to repentance (2 Pet. 3:9).

CONCLUSION

God is the One limitless, almighty, all-knowing Spirit. He does not need anything or anyone outside of Himself. He depends on nothing and on no one, but all things depend on Him. Knowing these truths about God should motivate us to worship Him with greater fervency, remembering that throughout eternity we shall be in His presence extolling His virtues.

CHAPTER 9

ARE THERE THREE GODS OR ONE GOD IN THREE PERSONS?

According to the Bible there is only one true God. The *Shema* is recited every Sabbath in Jewish synagogues around the world: *"Hear, O Israel: The Lord our God is one Lord"* (Deut. 6:4). This is a strong declaration of the oneness and uniqueness of God. The Bible teaches a strict monotheism, and definitely excludes every form of dualism and polytheism. Dualism teaches the existence of two mutually hostile divine beings, one representing everything good and beneficial to mankind, the other representing everything that is sinful and evil. Polytheism is the belief in more gods than one. The true God is not one among many, or even the best among many; He is absolutely unique, the *only* God.

In this chapter we consider the mystery of the Trinity and what it means to believe there are three Persons equal in majesty and power, undivided in splendor, yet one Lord, one God, ever to receive our undivided loyalty and praise. To believe in the Trinity is to believe that there is only one God, and yet there are three distinct Persons, the Father, the Son, and the Holy Spirit who possess eternally the same divine nature.

Because Christians believe in the Trinity, that God is one, yet in that one being are three distinct persons, many accuse them of believing in three Gods. Explaining the Trinity is not easy, but there can be no question that an unbiased study of Scripture reveals that there is a plurality of beings within the Trinity.

To say that something is mysterious or difficult is not the same as to say that it is not true. It is wrong to say the Trinity does not exist simply because it is beyond our comprehension. Very few people understand quantum physics. The theories and concepts of quantum physics are too complex for most people. In fact, some of the theories seem ridiculous or totally illogical to the untrained eye. Yet, quantum physics is used every day to make our lives better. We must be careful not to discredit something simply because we do not understand it.

Although the word *Trinity* is not found in the Bible, the concept is plainly taught.

THE TRINITY IN THE OLD TESTAMENT

There are occasions where God refers to Himself in plural terms (Gen. 1:26; 3:22; 11:7; Isa. 6:8). The Apostle John affirms the Isaiah passage refers to Jesus (John 12:41).

There are references to the Angel of the Lord who is identified with, yet distinct from, God (Gen. 16:7-13; Ex. 3:2-6; Judges 13:2-22).

The Old Testament refers to the Spirit of God as God's personal agent (Gen. 1:2; Neh. 9:20; Ps. 139:7).

There are prophecies that identify the long-awaited Messiah with God (Ps. 2; Isa. 9:6f.).

THE TRINITY IN THE NEW TESTAMENT

Several New Testament passages imply or state that God is a trinity (Matt. 3:13-17; 28:19; John 14:15-23; Acts 2:32, 33; 2 Cor. 13:14; Eph. 1:1-14; 3:16-19). Each person of the Trinity is asserted to be divine.

The Father is God.

Of the Father, Jesus says that He is *"the only true God"* (John 17:1-3). Paul affirms that there is but one God, the Father (1 Cor. 8:6). He is a person distinct from the Son (John 3:16; Gal. 4:4). In Galatians 4:6, He is distinguished from the Son and the Spirit.

The Son is God.

If Jesus of Nazareth is anything like the Gospel writers say He was like, then He was more than an ordinary man. Here was a man who, though He ate, drank, slept, and became tired as ordinary mortals do, also multiplied wine and food, gave sight to the blind, healed incurable diseases, stilled storms, cast out demons, and even raised people from the dead. Either those writers were deluded or deliberately deceptive, or they described someone who was unlike any person who has ever lived. The answer is, He is God. He claimed to be God and His disciples were convinced of His claims, not merely because of what He taught or ascribed to Himself, but because of His miracle-working powers.

The New Testament establishes the truth that Jesus is God: first, by direct statements; second, by statements that imply His deity; and third, by use of quotations that, in the Old Testament, refer to Jehovah (*Yahweh*).

Jesus is called Immanuel, which means, *"God with us"* (Matt. 1:23). According to John 1, Jesus is referred to as the *Word*, and is said to have been with God from all eternity; in fact, He was not only *with* God, He *was* God (John 1:1). He claimed that whoever had seen Him had seen the Father (John 14:9).

Jesus said that He and the Father were one (John 10:30). His enemies knew exactly what He meant because they took up stones to stone Him for blasphemy. They insisted in their blindness that, though He was a mere man, He was making Himself God (John 10:33).

Jesus repeatedly called Himself by the name or designation reserved for God. He affirmed to His enemies that before Abraham was born, *"I AM"* (John 8:58; cf. Exo. 3:13,14). In Isaiah, Jehovah is the First and the Last, a title that, in the book of Revelation, is given to Christ (Isa. 44:6; Rev. 1:17).

Jesus said He was God, and that is what the disciples who wrote the New Testament proclaimed Him to be. Jesus was not just a great and good man sent from God, nor a prophet, nor an angel. When we encounter this Man, we meet God. If we want to know who God is and what God does, we have to look at Jesus Christ.

The Holy Spirit is God.

Jesus spoke of the Holy Spirit in terms that cannot be misunderstood. He told His disciples that He would ask the Father to send someone to replace Him who would do for them exactly what He had done for them while on earth (John 14:16). Jesus used the Greek word "*Paracletos*" ("one called alongside to help") to describe the Holy Spirit's mission. "*Paracletos*" is also used of Christ Himself in John's first epistle. Christ is described as our "advocate," the one who speaks to the Father in our defense (1 John 2:1). Jesus called the Holy Spirit "*the Spirit of truth*" (John 14:17), while referring to Himself as "*the truth*" (14:6).

Ananias and Sapphira were rebuked for endeavoring to deceive the Apostle Peter about their gift to the church. Peter asked them why they had lied to the Holy Spirit. He then explained the gravity of the attempted deceit, warning them that they had not lied to men but to God (Acts 5:3, 4, 9). The Holy Spirit in this passage is equated with God.

Once we acknowledge God the Father and God the Son to be fully God, the Trinitarian expressions in verses such as Matt. 28:19 ("*baptizing them in the **name** of the Father and of the Son and of the Holy Spirit*") assume significance, because they show that the Holy Spirit is regarded as being equal with the Father and the Son. The unity of the Trinity is underscored by the use of the singular word *name* rather than *names*.

CONCLUSION

We conclude then that the three persons of the Trinity, though distinct, are equally divine and equally God in every way. The truth may be difficult for humans to grasp, but that is what the Scriptures teach about God. Many have tried to find ways of expressing at least something of the mystery of the Trinity by analogy with things with which we are familiar. For instance, just as two people—a man and woman—become one in the marriage relationship, though remaining two distinct individuals, so these three separate Persons—Father, Son, and Holy Spirit—are *one* in the divine relationship we call the Trinity. Nevertheless, all human analogies are inadequate in expressing the mystery of the Trinity. In the final analysis, our faith in this vital truth rests upon what is revealed about it in the Word of God.

CHAPTER 10

IS GOD THE SPIRITUAL FATHER OF EVERY HUMAN BEING?

The fatherhood of God is one of the most comforting truths of the Bible. Often God is caricatured as an aloof, mysterious, mean-spirited figure, out to severely punish all who disobey Him. Conversely, others depict Him as a benign, easy-going, grandfatherly type who overlooks human foibles and withholds punishment for even the worst offenses. Jesus taught us differently. He often referred to God as "*Father,*" depicting Him as a father who is patient and loving but just, who only punishes as a last resort. He is someone who is interested even in the insignificant details of our lives—exactly as we would imagine a good human father to be.

Those who maintain that God is the spiritual Father of the whole human race, though they may be well-meaning, misrepresent the concept of the fatherhood of God. This commonly held belief is sometimes referred to as "the universal fatherhood of God." Whereas God is the creator of all, hence the Father of all, He is not the spiritual father of every human being. The Bible clearly teaches that He is the spiritual Father only of those who believe on Jesus Christ as Savior and Lord (Gal. 3:26).

GOD THE FATHER IN THE OLD TESTAMENT
The Old Testament does not develop the concept of the fatherhood of God as fully as the New Testament; nevertheless, God's fatherhood is revealed there in ways that leave no doubt as to His paternal nature.

He is a God of mercy.

"Mercy" is defined as kind and compassionate treatment of an offender, an enemy, or a person under one's power. Though no sinful human being has ever seen the Father—we have no photograph or painting of His features—He has demonstrated His character by His gracious acts and by the word pictures we have of Him in the Bible (Ex. 34:6, 7; cf. Heb. 10:26, 27). Yet, mercy does not blindly pardon, but is guided by the principle of justice. Those who reject God's mercy reap His punishment.

He is a redeemer God.

"Redeem" means to "buy back." God's miraculous delivery of the children of Israel from Egyptian bondage is the backdrop for the entire Old Testament and an example of His longing to be our Redeemer. God is not a distant, detached, uninterested person, but like a good father, very much involved in the affairs of His children (Isa. 44:21, 22). The Psalms particularly demonstrate the depth of God's loving involvement with His children (Ps. 8:3, 4; 18:1, 2; 22:24).

He is a God of refuge.

David saw God as One in whom we can find refuge—very much like the six Israelite cities of refuge, which harbored innocent fugitives (Ps. 27:5; 46:1; 125:2; 62:8; 86:15). A caring father provides a secure refuge for his children.

He is a God of forgiveness.

After his sins of adultery and murder, David was comforted by the assurance that God is wonderfully forgiving (Ps. 51:1, 2). While it is true that David paid dearly for his transgressions, he came to the realization that just as an earthly father has compassion on his children, so God has compassion on those who fear and honor Him (Ps. 103:11-14).

He is a God of goodness.

What a great picture we have of the fatherhood of God in Psalm 146:7-9. God gives justice to the oppressed, food to the hungry, freedom to the prisoners, sight to the blind, lifts burdens, loves the righteous, protects foreigners, cares for orphans and widows, and frustrates the plans of the wicked.

He is a God of faithfulness.

God is depicted as loving Israel in spite of their constant backsliding. The book of Hosea poignantly illustrates God's faithfulness in the face of flagrant unfaithfulness and rejection. God's continuing forgiveness reveals His fatherly character of unconditional love (Isa. 41:9, 10). In spite of Israel's unfaithfulness, God tenderly promised forgiveness if they would humbly acknowledge their guilt (Lev. 26:40-42; cf. Jer. 3:12; Isa. 44:21, 22).

He is a Father.

When addressing Israel, Moses referred to God as their Father who created them and gave them an inheritance (Deut. 32:6). Isaiah acknowledged God as Father (Isa. 64:8). God referred to Himself as "*Father*" (Mal. 1:6).

GOD THE FATHER IN THE NEW TESTAMENT

The God of the Old Testament does not differ from the God of the New Testament. Some have sought to pit the God of the Old Testament against the God of the New, claiming that the former is a God of vengeance, whereas the latter is a loving, merciful Father. While this may at times appear to be true, it is a misconception. They are one and the same. God the Father is revealed as the originator of all things, the father of all true believers, and in a unique sense the father of Jesus Christ.

He is the Father of all creation.

Paul identifies the Father, distinguishing Him from Jesus Christ (1 Cor. 8:6). Paul also affirms that the Father is the creator of heaven and earth, and the one from whom every family in heaven and earth derives it name (Eph. 3:14, 15).

He is the Father of all believers.

In the New Testament, this spiritual father-child relationship exists between God and the individual believer, not between God and the nation of Israel. Through the written Word, the Scriptures, Jesus and His apostles provide the guidelines for this relationship, which is established through the believer's acceptance of the Lord Jesus Christ (John 1:12, 13).

Through the redemption Christ has provided, believers are adopted as God's children. The Holy Spirit facilitates this relationship, enabling believers to cry out, *"Abba, Father!"* (Gal. 4:5, 6; Rom. 8:15, 16).

Jesus reveals the Father.

Jesus provided the most profound view of God the Father when He came in human flesh as God's self-revelation (John 1:1, 14). No other name for God (*"Father"*) was so often on His lips. The apostle John affirmed that Jesus has shown us who the Father really is (John 1:18). Jesus declared in no uncertain terms that those who had seen Him had seen the Father (John 14:9). *To know Jesus is to know the Father.*

When we see Christ feeding the hungry (Mark 6:39-44), granting hearing to the deaf (Mark 7:32-37), giving speech to the speechless (Mark 9:17-29), opening the eyes of the blind (Mark 8:22-26), curing the sick (Luke 5:12, 13), raising the dead (Mark 5:35-43), forgiving sinners (John 8:3-11), and casting out demons (Matt. 15:22-28), we see the Father in action. Jesus knew that revealing the love and compassion of His Father was the key to bringing people to repentance (Rom. 2:4).

The fatherhood of God is vividly represented in many of the parables Jesus told, especially those in Luke 15. God the Father not only welcomes the repentant sinner as he returns (Luke 15:11-20), but actually goes out to seek him (Luke 15:3-7).

But it is Calvary that gives us the deepest insight into the Father. The Father, being divine, suffered the pain of being separated from His Son, in life and death, more acutely than any human father ever could. And He suffered *with* Christ in like measure. What greater testimony about the Father could be given! The cross reveals, as nothing else can, the truth about the Father (1 John 4:9, 10; Rom. 5:10).

CONCLUSION

Because God is our Father, we are assured of His kindness and care. We are confident that we are His sons and daughters through the inner witness of the Holy Spirit, and that He is personal, approachable, and merciful. We are given the unique privilege of enjoying intimate, personal fellowship with our heavenly Father through Jesus Christ.

BASIC
BAPTIST
B E L I E F S

THE TRUE GOD
JESUS CHRIST

We believe that Jesus Christ is absolute Deity, the eternal Son of God who became man without ceasing to be God; that in His incarnation, He was conceived by the Holy Spirit and born of the Virgin Mary; that although possessing a human as well as a divine nature, He was totally without sin; that He voluntarily laid down His life, the Just for the unjust, making it possible for mankind to be saved; that He rose bodily from the dead with a glorified body on the third day, and after forty days ascended into Heaven where He is exalted at the right hand of the Father; that He is now our Intercessor and Advocate, the only true Mediator between God and man; that One day He will return in power and great glory to judge the world and to consummate His redemptive mission.

CHAPTER 11

WHY DID THE SON OF GOD BECOME A MAN?

Some two thousand years ago there lived a man whose influence on the world is unique in history. He was born in an obscure Middle Eastern village with none of the material advantages that wealth and social position can give. His brief career spanned only thirty-three years and was confined to an area of a few hundred miles. None of His activity occurred in one of the great centers of civilization. His life did not end on a note of triumph; He suffered the shameful death of crucifixion.

Yet today, over twenty centuries later, this man is worshipped by two billion people in every country of the world as the Savior of mankind. Through the centuries since His death, millions have died as martyrs to His cause, and millions more have gladly renounced all that the human heart holds dear, home, family, riches, and friends, to carry His name to the far reaches of the earth. He is loved throughout the world as no other man has been loved. His teachings have enriched, changed and comforted the lives of men and women wherever those words have circulated. Yet there is no person who is held in greater contempt.

What is it that makes Jesus Christ unique among all the people of history? What accounts for the influence He has had and still has on the world? The answer, of course, is that Jesus Christ was not merely a great teacher and religious leader. He is the Son of God. He is the Redeemer promised by God who brought the hope of salvation to the human race; and, by His death on the cross, ransoms all who put their trust in Him.

God's plan to rescue fallen humanity is made plain in the Bible. Long before the world began, His Son was chosen as the sacrifice for sin to be the hope of the human race (I Pet. 1:18-20). He was to bring us back to God and provide deliverance from sin through the destruction of the works of the Devil (1 Pet. 3:18; Matt. 1:21; 1 John 3:8).

Sin severed Adam and Eve from the source of life, resulting in their spiritual death and assuring their physical death as well (Rom. 5:12). Their act of disobedience resulted in a posterity that was contaminated with a sin nature and shackled with the sentence of death. In order to restore us as children of God, the Son of God had to become a man. Immediately after Adam and Eve sinned, God gave them hope by promising that there would be enmity between the serpent and the woman, between his seed and hers. In the cryptic prophecy of Genesis 3:15, the serpent and its offspring represent Satan and his followers. The woman and her seed symbolize the Savior of the world and His followers. This statement was the first assurance that a Savior would come and the conflict between God's Son and Satan would end in victory for the Son of God.

A SYMBOLICAL REPRESENTATION OF SALVATION

After sin entered, God instituted animal sacrifices to illustrate the mission of the Savior to come (Gen. 4:4). This symbolic system dramatized the manner in which God the Son would pay the penalty for human sin.

After Israel's exodus from Egypt, the sacrificial offerings were conducted in a tabernacle as part of a covenant relationship between God and His people. Built by Moses according to specifications given to him by the Lord Himself, the sanctuary and its services were instituted to illustrate the plan of salvation (Ex. 25:8, 9, 40; Heb. 8:1-5).

To obtain forgiveness, a repentant sinner brought an animal that had no blemishes—a picture of the sinless Savior. The sinner would then place his hand on the innocent animal and confess his sins (Lev. 1:3, 4). This act symbolized the transfer of the sin from the guilty sinner to the innocent victim, depicting the substitutionary nature of the sacrifice. Because there is no forgiveness without the shedding of blood (Heb. 9:22), the sinner then killed the animal, making the deadly nature of sin obvious.

The New Testament recognizes Jesus Christ, the Son of God, as *the Lamb of God* who takes away the sin of the world (John 1:29). Through the shedding of His blood, He obtained for the human race redemption from the penalty of sin (1 Pet. 1:19).

PREDICTIONS ABOUT A SAVIOR

God promised that the Savior would come through Abraham's line (Gen. 22:18; cf. 12:3). The prophet Isaiah said He would come as a male child, and would be both human and divine (Isa. 9:6). Bethlehem would be His birthplace (Micah 5:2). The birth of this divine-human person would be supernatural (Isa. 7:14; cf. Matt. 1:23). This Redeemer would ascend the throne of His father David and one day establish an everlasting government of peace (Isa. 9:7).

Before Jesus' birth at Bethlehem almost 2,000 years ago, He was "*in the form of God*," that is, the divine nature was His from all eternity (John 1:1; Phil. 2:6, 7). In taking the form of a slave, He laid aside divine prerogatives. He became a human in order to carry out the Father's will (John 6:38; Matt. 26:39).

JESUS CHRIST WAS TRULY HUMAN

The Bible clearly teaches that Jesus Christ had a human nature. The acceptance of this teaching is crucial (1 John 4:2, 3). Christ's human birth, development, characteristics, and personal testimony provide evidence of His humanity.

His human birth.

The Bible declares that the Word became flesh and lived among us (John 1:14). The word "*flesh*" means "human nature." Because the Holy Spirit conceived Him, He was fully God. Because He was born of a human mother, He was fully man. This manifestation of God in human form is called "*the mystery of godliness*" (1 Tim. 3:16).

Christ's genealogy refers to Him as the son of David and the son of Abraham (Matt. 1:1). As evidence of His human nature, He was born of the seed of David (Rom. 1:3; 9:5), and was the son of Mary (Mark 6:3). He could claim true humanity through His mother. (Chapter 12 describes the significance of His virgin birth.)

He was called a man.

John the Baptist and Peter refer to Him as a man (John 1:30; Acts 2:22). Paul speaks of Christ as a man (Rom 5:15). The one mediator between God and men, is the *"man Christ Jesus"* (1 Tim. 2:5). In addressing His enemies, Christ refers to Himself as a man (John 8:40).

Jesus' favorite designation for Himself, one He used 77 times, was *"Son of man"* (Matt. 8:20; 26:2). The title *"Son of God"* focuses attention on His relationship within the Trinity. *"Son of man"* emphasizes His solidarity with the human race through His incarnation.

His human characteristics.

In all things Christ was made *like* His fellow human beings (Heb. 2:17). His human nature possessed the same mental and physical susceptibilities as the rest of humanity: hunger, thirst, weariness, and anxiety (Matt. 4:2; John 19:28; 4:6; cf. Matt. 26:21; 8:24).

In His ministry to others He revealed compassion, righteous anger, and grief (Matt. 9:36; Mark 3:5), all human emotions. At times He felt troubled and sorrowful, and even wept (Matt. 26:38; John 12:27; 11:33, 35; Luke 19:41). His life of prayer expressed His complete dependence on God (Matt. 26:39-44; Mark 1:35; 6:46; Luke 5:16; 6:12). And Jesus experienced death (John 19:30, 34).

Nevertheless, when the Bible reports that the Son of God became a human being (Phil. 2:7), in no way is this meant to imply that He was sinful or participated in sinful acts or thoughts as ordinary humans do (see Heb. 4:15).

THE NECESSITY OF CHRIST'S TAKING HUMAN NATURE
To be the high priest for the human race.

As Messiah, Jesus had to occupy the position of high priest or mediator between God and humans (Zech. 6:13; Heb. 4:14-16). This function required human nature. Christ met the qualifications: (1) He could have compassion on those who were weak because He was subject to weakness (Heb. 5:2). (2) He is able to help those who are tempted because He was tempted (Heb. 2:18; 4:15).

To give His life for the sins of the world.

Christ's divine nature cannot die. In order to die, Christ had to have a human nature. He became man and paid the penalty for sin, which is death (Rom. 6:23; 1 Cor. 15:3).

To be our example.

To set the example as to how people should live, Christ lived a sinless life as a human being. As the second Adam, He dispelled the myth that humans cannot obey God's Word and have victory over sin. Where the first Adam fell, the second Adam gained the victory over sin and Satan and became both our Savior and our perfect example. In His strength, His victory can be ours (John 16:33; Phil. 4:13).

Though believers can never be perfect in the same sense Jesus was perfect, through His example and the power of the Holy Spirit who lives within us, no temptation is irresistible. We can trust God to give us the strength to endure and overcome it (1 Cor. 10:13).

CHAPTER 12

WAS JESUS REALLY BORN OF A VIRGIN?

Two thousand years ago, an extraordinary event took place in a remote Middle Eastern village that would radically change the future of the world. God intervened in human history by choosing a young virgin girl to be the mother of the Son of God. God sent the angel Gabriel to the Galilean village of Nazareth where a pure, unmarried Jewish girl was living. The angel's first words to Mary were that God was very pleased with her, an obvious cause for rejoicing; but Mary was startled and wondered what this greeting meant. Gabriel immediately told her she had nothing to fear for she had found favor with God.

The angel then gave her an amazing message. She would conceive and give birth to a son whom she would name Jesus. He would be great and be called the Son of the Most High with an eternal kingdom. Mary responded by asking how she could become pregnant when, even though she was engaged, she had never had sexual relations with a man. Gabriel told her that the Holy Spirit would empower her to conceive without a man and this child would be the Son of God. Mary immediately declared she was willing to accept God's plan for her life (Luke 1:26-38).

The narrative of the virgin birth need not stagger us. Surely the One who made the first woman with the wonderful ability to produce children could cause a woman to have a child without a human father. In some mysterious way, beyond the grasp of human intelligence, God miraculously transferred the life of His Son from Heaven to the womb of the virgin Mary. In fulfillment of Isaiah's prophecy (7:14), the Son of God became man by His birth to Mary. Jesus had no human father. Christians honor Joseph as the guardian, protector, and foster father of Jesus.

The abundance of historical evidence in favor of the virgin birth should lead to its acceptance. All the manuscripts in all the ancient versions contain the record of it. All the traditions of the early churches recognized it. *The Apostles' Creed*, written in the fourth century; *the Nicene Creed*, adopted at the Council of Nicea in A.D. 325 ; *the Athanasian Creed*, written about A.D. 450; the *Chalcedon Definition*, adopted at the Council of Chalcedon in A.D. 45 ; and *The Small Catechism of Martin Luther* of 1529 are only a few of the historic creeds that recognize the authenticity of the virgin birth. Only in modern times have Bible critics begun to cast doubt on a doctrinal truth that Christians have long since historically endorsed. To deny the virgin birth is to assail Mary's reputation and life. Jesus was of "*the seed of the woman*," not of the man (Luke 1:34).

THE VIRGIN BIRTH IN THE OLD TESTAMENT

The earliest intimation of the virgin birth is in Genesis 3:15, when the coming of the future deliverer was first announced. It was said that this deliverer would proceed from the "seed of the woman." While it is true that no explicit mention is made of the virgin birth in this promise, it is significant that a male parent is not mentioned and that the one to come is called merely the woman's offspring. The seed of the woman was understood as referring to the Savior.

The clearest prophecy in the Old Testament occurs in Isaiah 7:14, in which the prophet speaks of a virgin (*almah*) conceiving and bearing a son. In commenting on the controversial Hebrew word *almah*, R. Dick Wilson states: "We have a right to assume that . . . the *almah* of Isaiah 7:14 and all other *almahs* [in the OT], meant *virgin*." Furthermore, Matthew understood this prophecy as referring not only to a virgin, but specifically to the virgin birth of Jesus Christ (Matt. 1:22, 23). Thus, he endorses the virgin birth interpretation. Matthew used a Greek term that can only mean "virgin," one who has never had sexual intercourse with a man.

THE VIRGIN BIRTH IN THE FOUR GOSPELS

Matthew 1:18, 22-25 and Luke 1:26-38 teach that the birth of Jesus resulted from a miraculous conception. He was conceived in the womb of Mary by the power of the Holy Spirit without any human male's seed.

If one accepts the possibility of miracles, the virgin birth presents no great difficulty. For a Bible believer, the fact that this doctrine is taught in God's Word settles such questions.

The hypothesis put forth by some scholars that the virgin birth is a story invented by the early church to buttress its emphasis on the deity of Christ, withers when confronted with an unbiased view of the facts. In the birth narratives of Matthew and Luke, Jesus is described as the Old Testament Messiah, the son of David, the fulfillment of prophecy, the one who will rescue God's people through mighty deeds, exalting the humble and crushing the proud (Luke 1:46-55). The writers draw no inference from the virgin birth concerning Jesus' deity; rather, they simply record the event as a historical fact and (for Matthew) as a fulfillment of Isaiah 7:14.

The third gospel was written by Luke, Paul's associate and fellow traveler (Col. 4:14). He also wrote the Acts of the Apostles (2 Tim. 4:11; compare the *we* passages in Acts, such as 27:1ff; Luke 1:1-4; Acts 1:1-5). Luke was a careful historian who claims to have made a diligent study of the historical data, and that claim has been repeatedly vindicated. Furthermore, he had access to some of those who knew Jesus Christ in the flesh (Luke 1:1-4). His vocations of historian and physician would have prevented him from gullibly swallowing the reports of a virgin birth.

THE VIRGIN BIRTH IN THE REST OF THE NEW TESTAMENT

It has been thought significant that other writers of the New Testament do not mention the virgin birth. However, this silence is not to be explained by ignorance or denial of the virgin birth on the part of other New Testament writers. The New Testament deals chiefly with (1) Jesus' preaching, life, death, resurrection; (2) the preaching and missionary work in the early church; (3) teaching concerning the theological and practical problems of the church (Acts, epistles); (4) and assurances of the triumph of God's purposes and visions of the end times

(Revelation and other NT books).

The main function of the virgin birth was to prove the fulfillment of prophecy and to describe the events surrounding Jesus' birth.

Even though Mark, John, and Paul say nothing about the virgin birth, their silence does not establish the insignificance of the doctrine. For John says, "*The Word became flesh*" (John 1:14); and Paul speaks of God appearing in a human body (1 Tim. 3:16). Furthermore, Mark passes over thirty years of our Lord's life in silence. In no way could this be construed to mean that those 30 years are non-essential. John speaks often of the deity of Christ, and this supports rather than contradicts the doctrine of the virgin birth.

Some contend that the passages where Jesus is described as the son of Joseph demonstrate that Jesus did not have a miraculous birth (John 1:45; 6:42; Luke 2:27, 33, 41, 48; Matt. 13:55). Clearly, these references refer to Joseph as the legal father of Jesus without reference to the question of biological fatherhood. Moreover, it was those who were opposed to Jesus and what He stood for who spoke some of these words.

THE VIRGIN BIRTH IN POST-BIBLICAL LITERATURE

Belief in the virgin birth is widely attested in literature from the second century. Ignatius defended the doctrine strongly against the Docetists, who held that Jesus only "appeared" to have become a man. The Docetists and the Ebionites (who held Jesus to be a mere human prophet) were alone in denying the virgin birth in the early history of the church.

The silence of some church fathers, like the silence of Scripture, has been cited as evidence of the mythology of this doctrine; but the argument from silence can easily be countered, as we have seen.

DOCTRINAL IMPORTANCE

The consistency of this doctrine with other Christian truths is important to its usefulness and, indeed, to its credibility. For one thing, it pictures the supernatural birth that one must experience to become a child of God. Salvation is by God's act, not our human effort. We were born again, "*not of blood*," meaning salvation does not run through the blood stream. It is not produced by the natural power of our own will; rather, it is "*of God*" (John 1:12, 13). It is a birth of the Holy Spirit resulting in a new creation (2 Cor. 5:17).

The doctrine is fully consistent with the whole range of biblical doctrine. The virgin birth is important because the credibility of the Bible is at stake. If Scripture errs here, why should we trust its claims about other supernatural events?

The deity of Christ is supported by this doctrine. While it might be possible for God to enter the world through means other than a virgin birth, it would be vastly more difficult to prove Christ's deity without that event. In addition, it would be difficult to conceive how Jesus could have been exempted from the guilt of Adam's sin if he had been born of two human parents. Yet the sinlessness of Jesus as the new head of the human race and as the atoning lamb of God is absolutely vital to our salvation (2 Cor. 5:21; 1 Pet. 2:22-24; Heb. 4:15; 7:26; Rom. 5:18-19).

The doctrine of the virgin birth must be distinguished from the Catholic teaching concerning Mary's *immaculate conception*. According to Catholic tradition, Mary herself was, from the first moment of her conception, preserved, immune from all stain of original sin. This central teaching of the Catholic Church (made official by Pius IX on December 8, 1854) is rejected by most non-Catholics, and has nothing to do with the virgin birth of Christ.

CHAPTER 13

HOW DO WE KNOW
THAT JESUS CHRIST IS GOD?

When we come to the study of the person and work of Christ, we arrive at the very heart of Christian theology. Because Christians are, by definition, believers in and followers of Jesus Christ, their understanding of who He is and what He does is crucial. Nothing is more important than what a person thinks of Jesus Christ.

We have already taken note of the humanity of Christ. Not too many deny that a person by the name of Jesus lived in the Middle East in the first century. However, a good number of skeptics deny that He *came* from God, that He was *equal* with God, or that He was *fully* God.

One of the most controversial Bible topics is *the person of Christ*. At the same time, it is central to the validity of our faith. If Jesus was no more than a mere human being, our faith is vain, for our faith rests on Jesus' actually being God in human flesh. Admitting that He was simply a great religious leader, an extraordinary human being, the most unique person who ever lived, or even a lesser god, as the Jehovah's Witnesses do, does not satisfy the Biblical descriptions of His person.

Jesus was more than a mere human being. He was God in human flesh. He had two natures while He was here on this earth: divine and human. He was the God-man. He was not part God and part human. He was fully God and fully man. It is important to note that the incarnation involved the Son of God taking on

Himself a human nature, not the man Jesus acquiring divinity. In Jesus, these two natures were merged into one person.

WHAT JESUS SAID ABOUT HIMSELF

While Jesus did not say in so many words, "I am God," He made claims that would be inappropriate if made by someone who is less than God.

His claims to forgive sins resulted in a charge of blasphemy against Him (Matt. 9:1-8). When Jesus said to the paralyzed man that his sins were forgiven, some of the scribes who were present accused Him of blasphemy and indignantly declared that only God can forgive sins (Mark 2:5-7). Their reaction shows that they interpreted Jesus' comment as a prerogative belonging to God alone—the power to forgive sins.

Jesus claimed that He would judge the world, a power that could only be exercised by God Himself (Matt. 25:31-46).

When the Pharisees objected to Jesus and His disciples picking heads of grain on the Sabbath, Jesus asserted that He was "*Lord even of the Sabbath*" (Mark 2:27-29). He was claiming that He had the right to redefine the status of the Sabbath, a privilege that belongs only to God. By so doing, He implied His equality with God.

Jesus claimed to be one with the Father, and that to see and know Him is to see and know the Father (John 10:30; 14:7-9).

There is a claim to His eternal existence when He uses the term "*I am*" in reference to Himself, a term ordinarily ascribed to God (John 8:58; cf. Exo. 3:14-15). After making this statement, the immediate reaction of the Jews who heard Him was to take up stones and attempt to kill Him, an indication that they thought Him guilty of blasphemy (John 8:59).

One of the strongest claims to deity is found in Jesus' reply to the high priest at His trial. The straightforward question was asked: "*Are you the Christ, the Son of God*" (Matt. 26:63)? Jesus replied by telling him that from now on he would see the Son of man seated at the right hand of power and coming on the clouds of heaven (Matt. 26:64). This is an obvious declaration of His deity.

When Jesus appeared the second time to His disciples after His resurrection, Thomas conceded that He was no longer dead, and he exclaimed, "*My Lord and my God*" (John 20:28). Rather than rebuke

Thomas for what some would consider blasphemous presumption, Jesus accepted his response.

THE TEACHING OF THE NEW TESTAMENT
The Gospel of John.

The Gospel of John is especially noted for it references to the deity of Jesus. Other than verses already alluded to in John, the very first verse of chapter one is explicit in expressing His deity (John 1:1). The *Word* (Jesus) is distinguished from God but at the same time identified with Him. The remainder of the Gospel of John supports this emphasis on the deity of Christ.

The Book of Hebrews.

In the opening chapter, the author speaks of the Son as the heir of all things, the one by whom God made the world and everything there is. The Son reflects the glory of His Father and is the exact representation of His nature. He sustains the universe by the power of His Word. After He died to cleanse us from sin and clear our record, He sat down at the right hand of the Majesty in Heaven (Heb. 1:1-3). The Son is called *God* in vs. 8. The argument in Hebrews is that the Son is superior to angels, Moses, and the Levitical priesthood. He is not merely a human or an angel, but someone higher, namely, God.

Other New Testament references to the Deity of Christ.

In Colossians 1, Paul writes that the Son is the visual expression of the invisible God (v. 15), the one who created all things (v. 16), and the one who holds all things together (v. 17). The latter reference denotes that Christ is the one who sustains the universe and controls the laws by which it functions in an orderly manner. No one but God could do this. Paul states in Colossians 2:9 that all the fullness of deity dwells in bodily form in Christ. Christ is spoken of as the one who is to be the final judge (2 Tim. 4:1; 2 Cor. 5:10). Philippians 2:5-11 is a clear assertion of the deity of Christ.

HISTORICAL DEPARTURES FROM THE DEITY OF CHRIST
Ebionites.

This was a sect of heretical Jewish Christians that flourished between the first and the fourth century. They insisted on the observance of the whole Jewish law, rejected Paul as a heretic, and used only the Gospel of Matthew. They repudiated both the virgin birth and the deity of Jesus, claiming that He was an ordinary man possessed of unusual but not superhuman or supernatural gifts.

Arianism.

The teaching of an Alexandrian named Arius (d. 336) became the first major threat to the Biblical teaching on the deity of Christ. Arius taught that God alone possesses the attributes of deity. Everything other than God has come into existence through an act of creation. He taught that Jesus is a created being, though the first and highest of the created beings. Although condemned by the church at the Council of Nicea in 325 and at subsequent councils, Arianism lingers on to our day in various forms. The largest and most aggressive variety of Arianism is the movement known as *Jehovah's Witnesses*.

CONCLUSION

The worship of Jesus Christ is not only appropriate, it is essential. He is not merely the highest of the creatures, He is God in the same sense and to the same degree as the Father. He is deserving of our praise, adoration, and obedience.

One day everyone will confess that Jesus Christ is Lord, to the glory of God the Father (Phil. 2:10, 11).

CHAPTER 14

HOW DO WE KNOW JESUS IS THE MESSIAH?

Little is said in the Gospels concerning Jesus' childhood and youth. We read of His circumcision and naming on the eighth day (Luke 2:21); His consecration to the Lord thirty-three days later (Luke 2:22-24); His parents escaping with Him to Egypt (Matt. 2:13-15); and their return to Nazareth, the hometown of Joseph and Mary (Matt. 2:19-23). The only other incident mentioned in the Gospels before His baptism by John was His journey to Jerusalem with Mary and Joseph to observe the Feast of the Passover (Luke 2:41-42). Jesus was twelve years old at the time. Luke writes of this period in Jesus' life as a time when He grew in wisdom and stature, and in favor with God and men (Luke 2:51-52).

JESUS' BAPTISM

John the Baptist was chosen by God to be the forerunner of the Messiah. His ministry was to call the Jewish people to repentance (Matt. 3:2; Mark 1:4). He also proclaimed that one more powerful than he would come after him who would baptize with the Holy Spirit and with fire (Matt. 3:11; Mark 1:7; Luke 3:16; John 1:15, 26, 30).

John explained that his practice of baptizing with water was so that the Messiah should be revealed to Israel (John 1:31).

One day, Jesus approached while John the Baptist was baptizing in the Jordan River. Upon seeing Him, John proclaimed to the assembled multitude that Jesus was the *"Lamb of God"* who takes away the sin of the world (John 1:29, 36).

Jesus submitted to John's baptism, expressing to him that He did so to *fulfill all righteousness* (Matt. 3:15). Jesus did not need to repent of sin as others whom John baptized, but He did need to identify with sinners for whom He would provide redemption through His sacrificial death on the cross. In one sense, His baptism by John constituted His initiation into His public ministry as the Messiah, since it resulted in His anointing by the Holy Spirit and His approval by God the Father (Matt. 3:16,17).

JESUS' MESSAGE AND MINISTRY

The purpose of John the Baptist's ministry was to prepare the Jewish people for their Messiah. Throughout the three years of His public ministry, Jesus boldly presented Himself to the Jewish people as their promised Messiah.

When He began His ministry, Jesus' message was much the same as John's—*"Repent for the kingdom of Heaven is at hand"* (Matt. 4:17; Mark 1:14-15). At the synagogue in Nazareth, Jesus read part of a messianic prophecy from Isaiah that applied to His earthly ministry; He then proclaimed that the prophecy was fulfilled that very day (Luke 4:16-21; cf. Isa. 61:1-2).

Toward the close of His ministry, Jesus made a triumphal entry into Jerusalem, and in doing so was presenting Himself to the Jewish people as their Messiah (Matt. 21:1-11; cf. Isa. 62:11; Zech. 9:9). Most of the Jews, however, rejected His Messianic claims (Mark 14:63-64). In fact, they condemned Him for blasphemy (Matt. 26:65-66). When Pilate asked Jesus if He was the King of the Jews, Jesus' response plainly suggested that indeed He was the King of the Jews (Luke 23:3; John 18:33-37).

JESUS' CLAIM TO BE MESSIAH
AUTHENTICATED BY MIRACLES

The Gospels record a total of thirty-five separate miracles that Jesus performed. The first was turning water into wine (John 2:1-10). All the miracles He performed identified Him as the Messiah prophesied in the Old Testament (Isa. 35:5-6; 61:1).

No miracle Jesus performed was for His own gratification. They were always for the benefit of others. In addition to feeding five thousand people with five loaves and two fish, stilling a storm, walking on water, and raising the dead, His miracles relieved physical suffering and hardship of various kinds (e.g., Matt. 8:2-4; 9:2-8; 12:9-13). Matthew wrote that Jesus healed many sick and diseased people (4:23-24).

Jesus severely rebuked the Jewish people for their failure to respond to His miracles and accept Him as their Messiah. He referred to the Old Testament prophets as examples of how God has used miracles or signs to aid people in their suffering and to demonstrate His power. When the people in the cities of Galilee failed to repent after Jesus preached to and performed signs among them, He reminded them that if the same miracles had been performed in Tyre, Sidon, and Sodom, the people would have repented long ago in sackcloth and ashes (Matt. 11:21-24).

JESUS' DEATH: A PART OF GOD'S ETERNAL PLAN

Jesus' death on the cross as the sinner's substitute was part of God's eternal plan to provide salvation for all who believe on Christ. In the book of Revelation He is called *"the lamb that was slain"* before the world began (13:8).

Some theologians erroneously teach that, at the beginning of His public ministry, Jesus believed He could win the people over to His cause, throw off the Roman yoke, and establish His kingdom. According to their theory, Jesus was totally unaware of His coming sacrificial death. However, this is not consistent with the numerous predictions He made concerning His death.

After driving the moneychangers from the temple, Jesus responded to the question of His critics—"By what authority do you do these things"—by proclaiming that if the temple were destroyed, He would raise it again in three days (John 2:18,19). John explained that the temple Jesus spoke of was His body (vs. 21). After His resurrection, the disciples recalled what He said and believed the Scripture and the words that Jesus had spoken (vs. 22).

Jesus told Nicodemus that, just as Moses lifted up the serpent in the wilderness, so the Son of Man must be lifted up; and all who believe in Him are granted the gift of eternal life (John 3:14,15). In these statements it is obvious that Jesus knew both the manner of His death and its significance.

Jesus plainly told His disciples that He must go to Jerusalem and suffer many things at the hands of the religious authorities, and that He would be killed and on the third day be raised to life (Matt. 16:21; Mark 8:31; Luke 9:22).

After Jesus' arrest, Peter took his sword and struck the servant of the high priest, cutting off his ear (Matt. 26:51). In response, Jesus told Peter that the Scriptures could not be fulfilled if it did not transpire in this fashion, implying that He had to die (Matt. 26:53-54). He spoke of the necessity of drinking the cup the Father gave Him (John 18:11), signifying not only His complete submission to the Father's will, but also that He knew of His impending death.

The death of Christ on the cross was unlike the death of any other person who has ever lived. Hundreds have died by crucifixion, and all of them suffered for crimes they may or may not have committed. In the eyes of the state, they were all guilty. However, the death Jesus died was not for sins He committed. It was a sacrificial death, meaning He was taking the place of others who deserved to die.

When Jesus cried out from the cross, *"It is finished,"* (John 19:30), He did not mean merely that His life was soon to end or that His hopes for setting up an earthly kingdom were dashed. Primarily He meant that all the types and prophecies of the Old Testament, which pointed to the sufferings of the Messiah, were accomplished and answered (Isa. 53). The one final, perfect sacrifice had now been made (Heb. 7:26-28; 9:11-10:12). The death of Christ marked the end of the Mosaic Covenant and the establishment of the New Covenant based on the finished work of Christ.

The death of Jesus, followed as it was by His resurrection, also marked Satan's defeat (Heb. 2:14; John 12:31; 1 John 3:8). Satan's influence has not yet been removed from this world, but he is a defeated foe; his final destiny is certain (Rev. 20:1-3, 7-10). Christians can enjoy victory over him and his evil cohorts (Eph. 6:10-17; 1 Pet. 5:8-9; 1 John 4:4).

CHAPTER 15

DID JESUS TRULY
RISE FROM THE DEAD?

Before Jesus' death, the disciples were so preoccupied with the restoration of the kingdom to Israel that they could not grasp the prediction and significance of His approaching death and resurrection (Mark 8:31-32; 9:31-32; Luke 9:21-22, 44-45). The two disciples to whom Jesus appeared on the road to Emmaus illustrate this state of mind. They were returning from Jerusalem where they had witnessed the crucifixion. Their disappointment with that event was made apparent by their sad countenance, for they had hoped that Jesus was the one who would redeem Israel (Luke 24:21). Even after His resurrection, when the disciples saw the resurrected Jesus for the first time, they asked if He purposed to restore the kingdom to Israel (Acts 1:6). The significance of His death and resurrection had not yet impacted their hearts.

Consider the following reasons for believing in the resurrection and ascension of Jesus Christ:

JESUS' RESURRECTED BODY

The Lord Jesus was the first person to experience resurrection and to occupy an immortal body. All those who had been restored to life during His ministry were not resurrected to immortality. They experienced death a second time.

The same body of Jesus that expired on the cross was resurrected to an immortal, imperishable existence. His resurrected body is the pattern of the resurrected bodies believers will receive when Christ returns for His own (1 Thess. 4:13-18; Rev. 20:4-6).

Paul explained to the Corinthians that the Christian's earthly body, which dies and decays, will be altogether different when it is resurrected. It is a body that will never die. It is weak now, but when it is raised, it will be powerful and eternal. It is a natural, human body now, subject to all the weaknesses of such bodies, but when it is raised, it will be a spiritual body. Our physical bodies are inherited from Adam, the man of the earth, but someday we will have bodies like Christ, the man from Heaven (1 Cor. 15:42-58).

At the same time, it is important to note that Jesus' resurrected body resembled in appearance His body prior to His resurrection. This is attested by His invitation to the disciples who were gathered on the evening of His resurrection to look at His hands and feet (Luke 24:39-40). His body still bore the nail holes of His crucifixion. When Jesus appeared the second time to His disciples, He asked "doubting" Thomas to put his hand into the wound in His side (John 20:27). Earlier, Jesus told His disciples to touch Him, that He was unlike a ghost that has no flesh and bones (Luke 24:39).

Another evidence of the physical reality of Jesus' resurrected body is the fact that He ate food (Luke 24:42-43; John 21:12-13). That His body was unlike a normal human body is seen in His ability to appear or disappear at will (John 20:19; Luke 24:31, 36). He also seems to have been able to conceal His identity. The disciples on the road to Emmaus were at first kept from recognizing Him (Luke 24:16, 31).

THE EMPTY TOMB

The fact of the empty tomb is one of the strongest evidences of Jesus' resurrection. The soldiers who guarded the tomb were bribed into confessing that Jesus' disciples stole His body while they slept (Matt. 28:11-15). This blatant falsehood spread quickly among the Jews and is still current today. But there is one very important consideration: If the disciples had stolen the body, as the guards insisted, why were they willing to suffer horrible persecution and even death for something they knew to be untrue?

Others have suggested that Mary Magdalene and the other women were confused about the location of the tomb and went to the wrong one. Furthermore, according to skeptics, they had hallucinations of seeing angels and Jesus. But Mark writes that these women saw where Jesus was laid, and knew exactly the location (Mark 15:47).

THE RESURRECTION APPEARANCES

Luke declares that Jesus appeared to His disciples over a period of forty days, giving them substantial proof that He was alive (Acts 1:3).

Contrary to what many modern skeptics contend, the disciples did not hallucinate about Jesus' resurrection merely because they had such an intense desire for Him to come back to life. As a matter of fact, the mood of the disciples was the exact opposite. Mark reports that a number of women brought spices after the Sabbath was over to anoint Jesus' body (Mark 16:1). They were apprehensive about who might roll away the stone from the entrance of the tomb (Mark 16:3; Luke 24:1). They were not anticipating a resurrection.

On the morning of the resurrection when Mary Magdalene went to the tomb and saw that the stone no longer covered the opening, she ran and told Peter and the other disciples that someone had stolen the body of Jesus (John 20:1-2). There is no convincing evidence that she believed Jesus had been resurrected. Upon returning to the tomb, she stood outside weeping. The angel from inside the tomb asked why she was crying. She replied that someone had stolen the body of Jesus and hid it (John 20:11-15). Then she told the supposed gardener that she would take the body away. At no time did she imply that Jesus had been resurrected. The two disciples on the road to Emmaus expressed the same attitude of sadness and disbelief (Luke 24:16-17, 22-24).

The skeptical disciples had to be convinced by many persuasive proofs that Jesus was alive (Acts 1:3). The word variously translated as "infallible proofs," or "convincing proofs," does not appear elsewhere in the New Testament. It denotes an infallible sign or argument by which a thing can be conclusively known. The evidence spoken of consisted in His eating with the disciples, conversing with them, meeting them at various times and places, and performing miracles (John 21:6, 7). This evidence was infallible because there were enough of them to avoid the possibility of deception.

The one confirmation that should put to silence the argument that the disciples were merely hallucinating about the resurrection is

Paul's claim that more than 500 people were witnesses of the resurrection, most of whom were still living in Paul's day (1 Cor. 15:6).

THE ASCENSION

Forty days after His resurrection, Jesus' ministry on earth was completed. Then, in the presence of His disciples, He ascended to Heaven to sit on the throne at the right hand of the God the Father, to remain there until His Second Advent (Acts 3:21). Luke describes this event in Luke 24:51 and in Acts 1:9.

According to the Gospel of John, our Lord referred on three occasions to His ascension to Heaven (John 3:13; 6:62; 20:17).

Paul speaks of Christ ascending far above all heavens in order to permeate the whole universe with His presence and power (Eph. 4:10). Such phrases as *"taken up to glory"* (1 Tim. 3:16), *"gone into heaven"* (1Pet. 3:22), and *"passed through the heavens"* (Heb. 4:14) refer to the same event. Paul urged the Colossian believers to seek the things that are above, where Christ is seated at the right hand of God (Col. 3:1).

With the ascension, our Lord's visits with His disciples in this world came to an end, and the heavens received Him from their sight. This made possible, as Christ promised, the Holy Spirit's ministry among believers. The disciples would no longer have the Lord's personal presence, but would have the Holy Spirit's presence and power for their witness as Christ's representatives (John 14:16-18, 26; 16:7-15; Acts 1:4-5, 7-8).

CHAPTER 16

WHY IS JESUS CALLED A PROPHET, A PRIEST, AND A KING?

In the Old Testament, the offices of prophet, priest, and king were unique, generally requiring a consecration service involving anointing (1 Kings 19:16; Exo. 30:30; 2 Sam. 5:3). According to prophecy, the coming Messiah (*Christ* or the *Anointed One*) was to fulfill all of these offices. As prophet, Christ proclaimed God's will to us. As priest, He represents us to God. As king, He wields God's gracious authority over His people.

JESUS CHRIST THE PROPHET

God revealed to Israel that He would raise up a prophet like Moses (Deut. 18:18). While preaching in the Temple area shortly after Pentecost, Peter quoted the passage from Deuteronomy, explaining that the prophet spoken of by Moses was none other than Jesus Christ (Acts 3:17-24). Some of Jesus' contemporaries recognized that He was the fulfillment of this prediction (John 6:14: 7:40).

Jesus referred to Himself as a *prophet* (Luke 13:33). He proclaimed with prophetic authority the principles of the kingdom of God (Matt. 5-7; 22:36-40). On numerous occasions He revealed future events (Matt. 24:1-51; Luke 19:41-44).

Peter affirmed that the Spirit of Christ was within the Old Testament prophets, and he revealed how Christ gave them prophecies about His sufferings and subsequent glory (1 Pet. 1:10-12).

JESUS CHRIST THE PRIEST

A divine oath firmly established the Messiah's priesthood (Ps. 110:4). Christ was not a descendant of Aaron. Like Melchizedek, His right to the priesthood came by divine appointment (Heb. 5:6, 10).

Christ's earthly priesthood.

Jesus qualified perfectly for the office of priest. He was truly man, and He was called by God and acted "in things pertaining to God" with the special task of offering *"gifts and sacrifices for sins"* (Heb. 5: 4, 10).

The priest was to reconcile the worshippers to God through sacrifice, which represented the provision of atonement for sin (Lev. 1:4; 4:29, 31, 35; 5:10; 16:6; 17:11). The continual sacrifices at the altar of burnt offering symbolized the availability of continual atonement.

The sacrifices were not sufficient. They could not make the one who offered them perfect. They could not take away sins or produce a clear conscience (Heb. 10:1-4; 9:9). They were merely a shadow of the good things to come (Heb. 10:1; cf. 9:9, 23, 24). The Old Testament said that the Messiah would take the place of these animal sacrifices (Ps. 40:6-8; Heb. 10:5-9).

These sacrifices, then, pointed to the vicarious sufferings and atoning death of Jesus Christ. As the Lamb of God, He became *sin* for us, a *curse* for us. His blood cleanses us from all sin (2 Cor. 5:21; Gal. 3:13; 1 John 1:7; cf. 1 Cor. 15:3).

During His earthly ministry, Christ was both priest and offering. After His sacrifice on the cross and His resurrection and ascension, Christ's priestly intercession in Heaven began.

Christ's heavenly priesthood.

What Jesus did for his followers when He was on earth, He continues to do for all believers while in the heavenly world with His Father. Presently our High Priest sits at the right hand of the throne of God, ministering in the heavenly sanctuary (Heb. 8:1-3; 9:24).

Christ's intercession offers encouragement to His people (Heb. 7:25). Paul asks rhetorically, *"Who will condemn or pronounce judgment on us?"* Implied in the question is the answer—no one; the reason being, that Christ, our Advocate, is at God's right hand interceding on our behalf (Rom. 8:34).

As our Intercessor Christ does not stand like an Old Testament priest with his hands uplifted before the throne of God. He is seated at the right hand of God. The symbolism is highly significant. Old Testament priests never sat down because their work was never finished. On the other hand, the one sacrifice of Christ was a never-to-be-repeated sacrifice. It is on the basis of this once-for-all sacrifice that He now intercedes for His people.

Jesus does not plead our cause with strong crying and tears in the presence of a reluctant God. As our heavenly High Priest, He asks what He will from His Father who always hears and grants His requests.

JESUS CHRIST THE KING

Isaiah predicts the birth of a Child on whose shoulder all government one day would rest (Isa. 9:6). When Jesus rode into Jerusalem on a donkey on the first Palm Sunday, Matthew (quoting Zechariah), implied that the king spoken of in that passage was none other than Jesus of Nazareth (Matt. 21:4, 5; cf. Zech. 9:9).

From the earliest accounts of Jesus' life, He was proclaimed a king. The wise men who came from the east to worship Him called Him *"the King of the Jews"* (Matt. 2:1, 2). When asked by Pilate, *"Are you the King of the Jews?"* Jesus answered that He was (Matt. 27:11). In the book of Revelation, He is designated, *"King of Kings and Lord of Lords"* (Rev. 19:13, 16).

Jesus stressed that the first phase of His Kingdom would commence during His earthly ministry. Hence, *"the Kingdom of heaven"* or *"the Kingdom of God"* are both a present reality and a future hope. Paul wrote that God has rescued us from the dominion of darkness and transferred us into the kingdom of His Son, Jesus Christ (Col. 1:13). This kingdom is not presently a material kingdom. It is not a kingdom of this world (John 18:36). It does not consist of external commodities such as food and drink, but righteousness, peace, and joy in the Holy Spirit (Rom. 14:17; cf. Matt. 6:31-33). In this present world, the members of Christ's kingdom are surrounded by a host of people that is hostile toward the gospel; however, Christians are expected to conduct themselves as Christ's faithful subjects despite all the unwholesome influences seeking to impede their spiritual progress (Titus 2:11-14).

The eternal kingdom

The material manifestation of Christ's kingdom on earth will begin after His return (Rev. 19:11-22:1-21). Cataclysmic events will transpire before Jesus Christ establishes His earthly, material kingdom, the throne of which will be set up in Jerusalem. The first stunning event will be when the church hears the trumpet blast and Jesus' war cry as He calls His people to be with Him in Heaven. Following that event, the Tribulation horrors will be experienced by all the inhabitants of the earth who are left behind (Matt. 24-25). Then Jesus will return in power and great glory with all His saints to bind Satan and reign as King for a thousand years ("the millenium" Rev. 20:4-6). When the thousand years has ended, the battle of Gog and Magog will begin, a war that will be quickly won by the King of Kings. Jesus Christ will be the supreme ruler throughout eternity. The angel Gabriel announced to Mary that Jesus was to reign over the house of Jacob forever and there would be no end to His Kingdom (Luke 1:30-33; cf. Isa. 9:7).

Only by accepting Jesus Christ as Savior and Lord may one become a citizen of His eternal kingdom (John 3:3).

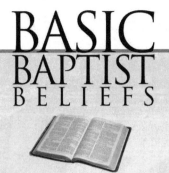

BASIC BAPTIST BELIEFS

THE TRUE GOD
THE HOLY SPIRIT

We believe that the Holy Spirit is a divine person, equal
with God the Father and God the Son and of the same
nature; that He was active in the creation; that in His
relation to the unbelieving world He restrains the Evil one
until God's purpose is fulfilled; that He convicts of sin,
of righteousness, and of judgment; that He bears witness to
the Truth of the Gospel in preaching and testimony; that
He is the agent in the New Birth; that He seals, endues,
guides, teaches, witnesses, sanctifies
and helps the believer.

CHAPTER 17

WHAT IS THE HOLY SPIRIT LIKE? IS HE GOD?

We have drawn attention in our study of theology to the Father's work in creation and providence, and how the Son, through His sacrificial death and resurrection, has guaranteed redemption to every sinner who believes on Him. We have seen how the Father and the Son are equally God. Now we will consider who the Holy Spirit is, how He relates to the Father and the Son, and how He applies the redemptive work of Christ to mankind, thus making salvation a reality.

THE IMPORTANCE OF THE DOCTRINE OF THE HOLY SPIRIT

There are several reasons why the study of the Holy Spirit is of special significance for Christians:

The Holy Spirit is fully God.

The Holy Spirit is the third person of the divine Trinity, equal in every respect with the Father and the Son. One of the best-known Biblical evidences of this equality is the baptismal formula given in the Great Commission (Matt. 28:19). The benediction of Paul in 2 Corinthians 13:14 is another evidence. Peter likewise, in the salutation of his first epistle, links the three together (1 Pet. 1:2).

The Holy Spirit makes the Trinity more personal.

Without the presence of the Holy Spirit in one's life, the tendency is to think of God as being far away in Heaven; so far, in fact, as to be indifferent to the plight of humans. In like manner, the Son lived on the earth 2,000 years ago and may seem to some a distant figure. But the Holy Spirit is resident within the life and body of each individual believer, encouraging, assuring, guiding, and consoling. Hence, the Holy Spirit is the one member of the Trinity through whom the entire Triune God works in and through us.

We live in what some have referred to as "the Age of the Holy Spirit."

The Father's work was the most prominent in the Old Testament era, as was the Son's in the period covered by the four Gospels. The ministry of the Holy Spirit has been in the forefront from the Day of Pentecost (Acts 2:1-4, 33) to the modern era.

The current culture stresses experience over dogmatic assertions.

Because it is primarily through the Holy Spirit that we *feel* God's presence within and experience the wonder of His various attributes, it is vital that we understand who the Holy Spirit is and what He does. In addition, living the Christian life and witnessing effectively for the Savior are made possible only through the Spirit's guidance and power (Acts 1:8).

THE NATURE OF THE HOLY SPIRIT

A number of Biblical references make it abundantly clear that the Holy Spirit is God in the same sense and to the same degree as the Father and the Son.

The terms *Holy Spirit* and *God* are sometimes used interchangeably.

In Acts 5, after selling a piece of property, Ananias brought the proceeds to Simon Peter and offered it as a donation to the Jerusalem church. However, he misrepresented the amount he received from the transaction. In rebuking him, Peter asked why he had lied to the Holy Spirit and kept back part of the proceeds from the sale (vs. 3). In the next verse, Peter accuses Ananias of lying to God, not to men. The inference is that lying to the Holy Spirit is the same as lying to God.

In 1 Corinthians, Paul maintains that to be indwelt by the Holy Spirit is to be indwelt by God. By equating the phrase *"the temple of*

God" (3:16) with *"the temple of the Holy Spirit"* (6:19), Paul establishes that the Holy Spirit is God.

The Holy Spirit possesses the same attributes as God.

He is declared to be all-knowing (*omniscient*) (1 Cor. 2:10-11). His *omnipotence* is spoken of numerous times in the New Testament (Luke 1:35; Rom. 15:19; John 3:5-8). He is referred to as *the eternal Spirit* (Heb. 9:14). Only God is eternal (Heb. 1:10-12). All of these descriptions are compelling reasons to believe the Holy Spirit is God.

The Holy Spirit performs works that are commonly attributed to God.

He was involved in creation (Gen. 1:2; Ps. 104:30). He is vitally active in the spiritual life of believers. Jesus spoke pointedly of the Spirit's role in regeneration (John 3:5-8). Paul declared the same truth in Titus 3:5. The Holy Spirit raised Christ from the dead and will one day give life to our mortal bodies (Rom. 8:11). The Spirit's role in giving the Scriptures is affirmed in 2 Peter 1:21.

THE PERSONALITY OF THE HOLY SPIRIT

Some see the Holy Spirit as the energy of God, an impersonal power or influence, not an actual person in the same sense God is. The historic position of the church, in contrast, is that there is one God, eternally existing in three persons, Father, Son, and Holy Spirit. Certain Scriptures present unmistakable evidence of the personality of the Spirit.

The masculine pronoun is used in representing Him.

When Jesus describes the Holy Spirit's ministry in John 16:13-14, He does not use the Greek word *pneuma*, which is neuter, but rather a masculine pronoun. The use of the masculine pronoun instead of the neuter conveys to us that Jesus is referring to a person, not an influence or thing.

His work in Scripture is described by Jesus in a manner similar to the work of someone else who is a person.

The Greek word *parakletos*, which is applied to the Holy Spirit in the New Testament, can be translated "counselor," "comforter," "consoler," "intercessor," or "advocate." It is used to refer to the ministry of the Holy Spirit in John 14:26; 15:26; 16:7. In each of these cases it is obvious that it is not some abstract influence that is intended, for Jesus is also spoken of as a *parakletos* in 1 John 2:1. In John 14:16, Jesus promises to send another *parakletos*, meaning one of the same kind as Himself. This demonstrates that the Spirit is meant to replace Jesus in this age and will carry on the same role, an unmistakable clue that He must be a person.

He possesses certain personal characteristics.

Among these characteristics are intelligence, will, and emotions, generally regarded as the three fundamental elements of the human personality. Jesus promised that the Spirit would *teach* (intelligence) and bring to the remembrance of His disciples all that He had taught them (John 14:26). In 1 Corinthians 12:11, Paul states that the Holy Spirit distributes the various spiritual gifts to individual recipients as He *wills*. In Ephesians 4:30, Paul warns against grieving the Spirit, a confirmation that the Spirit has *emotions*.

The sin of *blasphemy against the Holy Spirit* (Matt. 12:31; Mark 3:29) surely cannot be committed against what is impersonal.

In addition, the Holy Spirit engages in actions that can only be performed by a person. He teaches, speaks, intercedes, testifies, guides, commands, searches, and reveals.

LESSONS TO BE LEARNED

The Holy Spirit, being a person, is someone with whom we can have a personal relationship. He particularly assists us in understanding Scripture and in framing our prayers.

Considering that the Holy Spirit is God, hence not inferior to the other members of the Trinity, He is to be accorded the same honor and respect that we give to the Father and the Son.

In the Holy Spirit, the Triune God comes close, so close as to actually enter and take up His abode in each believer. God is even more intimate with us now than when Jesus walked the earth 2,000 years ago. Then, God was *with His disciples*. Now He is *in His disciples*.

CHAPTER 18

WHAT IS THE MISSION OF THE HOLY SPIRIT?

The evening before His death, Christ's words about His impending departure greatly troubled the disciples. He immediately assured them that they would not be left as orphans (John 14:18), but would receive the Holy Spirit as His personal representative. The Holy Spirit would be to them and do for them what Christ was to them and what He did for them while on earth.

The Holy Spirit has been active in the world since the dawn of creation (Gen. 1:2). Throughout the Old Testament His activity is frequently portrayed. When Jesus was here on the earth, the Spirit was present in great power. But it was at Pentecost that the principal work of the Holy Spirit was inaugurated.

THE HOLY SPIRIT'S MISSION TO THE WORLD

He exalts Christ.

The Lordship of Christ can only be acknowledged through the influence of the Holy Spirit. Paul affirmed that no one can say that Jesus is Lord except by the Holy Spirit (1 Cor. 12:3).

Jesus declared that the main thrust of the Spirit's mission was to glorify Him (John 16:13, 14). Some make the mistake of conceding more glory to the Holy Spirit than they do to Christ. This is a direct contradiction of what Jesus says in these verses.

He convicts.

Jesus taught that the Holy Spirit's mission is to convict the world of sin, righteousness, and judgment (John 16:8). First, the Holy Spirit brings to us a deep conviction of sin, especially the sin of failing to believe on Christ (16:9). Second, the Spirit urges all to accept the righteousness of Christ. Jesus lived a sinless life, but men said He had a demon. The Spirit contradicts those misguided men and witnesses to the righteousness of Christ and our need to have His righteousness imputed (credited) to us. Third, the Spirit warns us of a coming judgment, a powerful tool in stirring up sin-darkened minds to the need of repentance and conversion.

Having exalted Christ and convicted the sinner, the Spirit enables him/her to be born again (John 3:3-16). A new life results, for the believer has become the dwelling place of the Holy Spirit.

THE HOLY SPIRIT'S MISSION TO BELIEVERS

The majority of texts concerning the Holy Spirit pertain to His relationship with God's people. His sanctifying influence leads to obedience (1 Pet. 1:2). But no one continues to experience the full power available from the Holy Spirit without meeting certain conditions. Believers are warned about resisting, grieving, and quenching the Spirit (Acts 7:51; Eph. 4:30; 1 Thess. 5:19). Here are some of the noteworthy things the Holy Spirit does for believers:

He baptizes believers.

This important topic will be considered more fully in the next chapter, but suffice it to say that this remarkable event, referred to in Scripture as "*the baptism of the Holy Spirit*," transpires at the moment of conversion. It is not an after-conversion experience, as some claim. The Bible makes this clear in 1 Corinthians 12:13. Writing to the Christians at Corinth, Paul states, "*we are all baptized by one Spirit into one body.*" By his use of the word "*all*," Paul excluded no believer in that Corinthian church. To lend further proof to this assertion, Paul tells the Roman Christians that if any one does not have the Holy Spirit, he does not belong to Christ (Rom. 8:9). We conclude, then, that every true Christian—those who belong to Christ—have been baptized (*immersed*) with the Holy Spirit; and once that event transpires, the believer's body becomes the *"temple,"* or dwelling place, of the Spirit of God (1 Cor. 3:16, 17).

He assists believers.

When introducing the Holy Spirit, Christ called Him another *Parakletos* (John 14:16), a Greek word that can be translated "Helper," "Counselor," "Comforter," "Intercessor," "Mediator," or "Advocate." As we have noted, the only other *Parakletos* mentioned in Scripture is Christ Himself. He is our "Advocate" or "Intercessor" before the Father (1 John 2:1). As Intercessor, Mediator, and Helper, Christ presents us to God and reveals God to us. Similarly, the Spirit guides us to Christ and manifests Christ's grace to us. This explains why the Spirit is called the *"Spirit of Grace"* (Heb. 10:29).

He highlights the truth of Christ.

Jesus called the Holy Spirit the *"Spirit of truth"* (John 14:17; 15:26; 16:13). His functions include bringing to our remembrance what Jesus has said (John 14:26), and guiding believers into the truth (16:13). One of His major functions is to exalt Jesus Christ (John 15:26; 16:13,14).

He makes possible the presence of Christ.

Through the Holy Spirit, it is possible for Jesus to be anywhere in the world at any given moment (John 14:17,18). The Holy Spirit is Christ's representative.

He seals believers.

The three phases of salvation are given in Eph. 1:13, 14. First, one must hear the word of truth, the gospel. Second, one must believe the gospel. Third, at the point of conversion, the Holy Spirit *seals the believer.* In the ancient world the seal was a guarantee. Sealing was used to authenticate contracts, laws, invoices, military orders, etc. A seal indicates ownership. God owns the believer, having purchased him or her from the slave market of sin (Eph. 1:7; 1 Cor. 6:20). The Holy Spirit's seal is a guarantee of the believer's eternal security (Eph.4:30).

He guides the operation of the church.

Since the Holy Spirit brings the very presence of Christ, He is the true Vicar of Christ on earth, not the pope of Rome. As the center of authority in matters of faith and practice, the ways in which He leads the church accord fully with the Bible.

The Holy Spirit was intimately involved in administrating the apostolic churches. In selecting missionaries, the churches obtained His guidance through prayer and fasting (Acts 13:1-4). Paul reminded the church leaders at Ephesus that they had been placed in their position by the Holy Spirit (Acts 20:28).

The Holy Spirit played an important role in resolving serious difficulties that threatened the unity of the churches. Indeed, Scripture introduces the decisions of the first church council with an acknowledgment of the importance of the Holy Spirit in those deliberations (Acts 15:1-29).

He equips Christians with special gifts.

The Holy Spirit has bestowed special gifts on God's people. In Old Testament times the Spirit came upon certain individuals, giving them extraordinary powers to lead and deliver Israel (Judges 3:10; 6:34; 11:29; etc.). He gave the ability to prophesy (Num. 11:17, 25, 26; 2 Sam. 23:2).

In the early churches it was through the Holy Spirit that Christ bestowed His gifts on individual Christians. The Spirit distributed these spiritual gifts to believers as He saw fit, thus benefiting the whole church family.

The same is true today. The Holy Spirit bestows certain special gifts upon believers within the body of Christ. Three passages in the Bible figure most prominently in the discussion of what are commonly referred to as spiritual gifts (Rom.12:3-8, 1 Cor. 12:1-11; Eph. 4:7-16). Certain observations need to be made regarding these lists of gifts. While all of them have reference to the gifts of the Spirit, they differ in several distinct ways. Romans 12 records several basic functions which are performed in each congregation. Ephesians 4 lists various offices in each church, or leaders who are God's gifts to the church. 1 Corinthians 12 catalogues gifts given to certain individuals to help the church minister more effectively. These lists, then, are illustrative of the various gifts with which God has endowed the church.

Some of the more spectacular gifts have attracted particular attention and prompted considerable controversy in recent years, especially *glossolalia* or speaking in tongues. In the Scriptures, *"tongues"* always refer to the God-given ability to speak in a language that is unknown to the speaker. Without a doubt the tongues mentioned in Acts 2 were actual human languages, although they were unknown to those who spoke them. There is no reason to believe that the tongues in 1 Corinthians were any different.

The signs and miracles, including tongues, were given to confirm the truth of the Christian message, especially to Jewish people (1 Cor. 14:5, 21,22). Speaking in tongues is, therefore, a sign for unbelievers so they could understand what was being said (1 Cor. 14:19-25). The gift of healing is similar. In the New Testament it was used only for the benefit of unbelievers (especially among the Jews, who looked for signs) to reach their conscience, to confirm the Word that was preached, and to establish the new faith. We do not read about any healing of believers (see 1 Cor. 11:30; 1 Tim. 5:23; 2 Tim. 4:20; Gal. 4:13, 14; 2 Cor. 12:7).

Is the gift of tongues a part of God's program for Christians today? If it is, we would be wrong if we closed our minds to it. If it is not, we are wrong to insist upon the exercise of tongues-speaking. Among the Corinthians, speaking in tongues was prominent. Quarreling and division also defined the church, but the fruit of the Spirit—love—was missing. Paul said in 1 Cor. 13, that love would last, whereas tongues would cease. The Corinthians, like many today, put the emphasis on the least important of all the gifts—a gift that would cease with the completion of the canon of Scripture.

Our churches today do not need new revelations, new apostles, or new self-styled miracle workers. What each church needs is to return to the Word of God and proclaim the whole counsel of God in the power and love of the Holy Spirit.

CHAPTER 19

ARE THE BAPTISM AND THE FILLING OF THE HOLY SPIRIT THE SAME?

The baptism of (*in, with*) the Holy Spirit has caused considerable controversy in Christian circles in the last one hundred years. Christians in mainline Pentecostal churches commonly use the term to refer to an act subsequent to conversion and accompanied by speaking in tongues. A careful study of the New Testament leads to a different conclusion. The baptism of the Holy Spirit is not an exclusive experience reserved only for the "Christian elite;" it is a universal experience encompassing all true believers. Reference is made to the baptism in the Holy Spirit by only four persons: Jesus Christ, John the Baptist, Peter, and Paul.

The baptism of the Holy Spirit and the filling of the Holy Spirit are often thought of as the same experience, but they are separate divine works. Although several groups try to *equate* them, the biblical evidence *contrasts* them.

THE BAPTISM OF THE HOLY SPIRIT
John the Baptist was the first to make mention of it.

He predicted that the Messiah would baptize with the Holy Spirit (Matt. 3:11; Mark 1:8; Luke 3:16; John 1:33).

Jesus confirmed what John first enunciated.

However, Jesus did not mention the baptism of the Holy Spirit until just before His ascension into Heaven. He announced to the eleven apostles that they would be baptized with the Holy Spirit not many days hence (Acts 1:5). Ten days later on the Day of Pentecost the Holy Spirit filled the room where the Apostles had gathered. It was then that the Apostles were baptized in the Spirit (2:1-4).

Peter declared the necessity of the baptism of the Holy Spirit.

In recounting to the church in Jerusalem the conversion of Cornelius and his household, Peter said the experience of these Gentiles was like that of the apostles on the Day of Pentecost (Acts 11:1-17).

At the precise moment Cornelius and his household repented and believed, they were baptized in the Holy Spirit (10:43-44; cf. 11:18). It was not a subsequent experience, a prolonged time of waiting, praying, and agonizing. Since Cornelius and his household were the first Gentile converts, their experience is the normative standard for believers in this age, rather than that of the apostles who were baptized in the Spirit a few years after their conversion.

The apostles became believers before the death, resurrection, and ascension of Christ. The Spirit had not yet come because Christ had not yet ascended to Heaven. Hence, their baptism in the Spirit came after conversion and was not concurrent with it.

Paul was the first to precisely define the term.

The expression *baptize(d) with the Holy Spirit*, occurs six times in the Bible (Matt. 3:11; Mk. 1:8; Lk. 3:16; Jn. 1:33; Acts 1:5; 11:16). A careful examination of these references and of the whole New Testament idea of baptism yields the conclusion that *baptism in the Spirit* refers to an aspect of Christian initiation. It is one of several ways the New Testament describes the act of becoming a Christian: repentance and faith, justification, conversion, regeneration, ingrafting into Christ, adoption, and so on. Hence, at the moment of salvation every true believer in Christ has been baptized in the Spirit, just as they have been regenerated, adopted, and justified.

As we have noted previously, Paul emphatically claims that no one is truly converted who does not have the Holy Spirit living within them (Rom. 8:9-11). The baptism of the Holy Spirit is a work that Christ does for us. It is not an experience that one should seek after conversion. It is a routine part of spiritual regeneration.

Hence, to use the phrase *baptized in* (or *with*) *the Spirit* to describe a subsequent experience of the Spirit's power and blessing goes beyond the biblical usage and is misleading. Nowhere does the Bible suggest that one must seek the baptism of the Spirit or that only a select group of believers have been baptized in the Spirit.

The baptism in the Holy Spirit is not evidenced by speaking in tongues. Paul posed the question, *"Does every believer speak in tongues?"* (1 Cor. 12:30). The rhetorical question was intended to prompt a *no* answer. Thus speaking in tongues is not the initial evidence of the baptism in the Holy Spirit.

THE FILLING OF THE HOLY SPIRIT

The baptism of the Holy Spirit and the filling of the Holy Spirit are two separate divine works. Notice these *contrasts* between the baptism and the filling:

The baptism of the Holy Spirit is a once-for-all operation, whereas the filling of the Spirit is a continuous process.

When a person accepts Christ as Savior, the Holy Spirit comes into (indwells) his life *permanently*. But indwelling alone does not guarantee that Christ will be glorified by the believer's life. For this reason, Christians are urged to be *filled* with the Holy Spirit (Eph. 5:18). This command is in the present tense (*"keep on being filled"*), indicating an experience that can be repeated. It involves action on the believer's part. Certain conditions must be met. It is not automatic but the result of obedience. No command is given in Scripture for any believer to be baptized in the Holy Spirit, but the command in this verse plainly spells out the necessity for Christians to be filled with the Spirit.

The baptism of the Holy Spirit is something God does for us at the time of conversion. The filling of the Spirit is an experience to be desired and must be experienced if the believer is to reach spiritual maturity. The baptism of the Holy Spirit is universal among all Christians (1 Cor. 12:13). The command to be filled with the Spirit implies that some believers were not filled.

When a person believes in Christ for salvation, at that very moment he or she is baptized in the Holy Spirit. When a believer is separated from known personal sin and is totally yielded to the indwelling Spirit, he will be filled with the Spirit (Acts 4:8; 5:32; 13:9).

LESSONS TO BE LEARNED

We must evaluate our spiritual experiences by the clear teaching of the Word of God. We must not view our experiences as more authoritative than the Bible. Spiritual discernment must be exercised when people claim experiences that are not supported by Scripture.

We need to examine carefully the claims of those who say there can be no spiritual power unless a person has experienced the baptism of the Holy Spirit, an event which, in their view, comes after salvation and is evidenced by speaking in tongues. If this is true, we must ask, what about Jonathan Edwards, George Whitfield, Charles Spurgeon, G. Campbell Morgan, Billy Sunday, W. A. Criswell, Billy Graham, Charles Stanley, and the list could go on and on? These men and many non-Pentecostal believers like them, *did not* and *have not* spoken in tongues, nor *did they*—nor *do they*—believe in a post-conversion baptism in the Holy Spirit.

We must rejoice in all the spiritual blessings God has bestowed on us in Christ (Eph. 1:3). It is not necessary to seek a second or third post-conversion blessing, something beyond what the Bible teaches. Our position in Christ is complete.

When we continually allow the Holy Spirit to influence us, we will be obedient to God (1Peter 1:2). But no one experiences the full power available to us from the Holy Spirit without meeting certain conditions. Believers are warned about resisting, grieving, and quenching the Spirit (Acts 7:51; Eph. 4:30; 1 Thess. 5:19). We need to desire a continuous filling of the Spirit (Romans 15:13; Eph. 3:19; Col. 1:7-12).

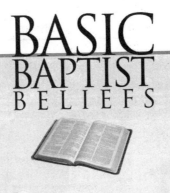

BASIC BAPTIST BELIEFS

THE DEVIL AND OTHER ANGELIC CREATURES

We believe that the Devil, also called Satan, was once a holy angel and enjoyed heavenly honors, but through pride and ambition to be as the Almighty, fell and drew after him a host of angels; that he is now the malignant prince of the power of the air, and the unholy god of this world. We hold him to be man's great tempter, the enemy of God and His Christ, the accuser of the saints, the author of false religions, the chief power back of the present apostasy; the lord of the Antichrist, and the author of all the powers of darkness; destined, however, to final defeat at the hands of God's Son, and to the judgment of an eternal justice in hell, a place prepared for him and his angels. Not only are there bad or fallen angels led by Satan, the Bible is replete with references to good angels who do God's bidding.

CHAPTER 20

HOW DID THE DEVIL ORIGINATE AND WHAT IS HIS MISSION?

When God created the world, He made everything *"very good"* (Gen. 1:31). Even the angelic world did not have evil angels or demons in it at the time. But sometime between the events of Gen. 1:31, when God saw that everything was good, and the appearance of the serpent (the Devil, also called Satan) in the Garden of Eden (Gen. 3:1), there must have been a rebellion in the angelic world with many angels turning against God and becoming evil. The Bible speaks of *"the angels who sinned"* (2 Pet. 2:4). Jude 6 describes certain angels who failed to keep the authority they were given by God, thereby abandoning their lofty position. The result is that God is keeping them in prisons of darkness awaiting the Day of Judgment.

Of the fallen angels, Satan alone is given particular mention in the Scriptures. It is possible that when Satan fell he drew after him a multitude of lesser angelic beings. Of these, some are confined until the judgment, as we have seen, while others are free and are the demons or devils to whom reference is constantly made throughout the New Testament. They are Satan's emissaries in all his undertakings and share his doom (Matt. 25:41). Since his dramatic fall, Satan has been the persistent foe of God and the greatest enemy of God's people. One must know the teaching of the Bible concerning this archenemy if one is to understand something of the conditions around him and how to cope with and be victorious over the adversary's attacks.

THE ORIGIN OF SATAN

Among the heavenly host, Satan's creation alone is mentioned in particular. This fact suggests the supreme place that Satan holds in relation to all the invisible creatures of God. In Ezekiel 28:11-18, there is a description of the King of Tyre, and while this may have had a secondary application to an earthly king by that name, it is evident that the primary application is to the supreme one among all the creatures of God. The description given could apply to none other than Satan as he existed before the sin that resulted in his fall.

The fall of Lucifer (another name for Satan) is described in Isaiah 14:12-15. Five times Lucifer uses the expression "*I will*" in verses 13 and 14. The cherub lifted up his heart in self-will against God and was punished for his rebellion (compare 1 Tim. 3:6).

THE VARIOUS DESIGNATIONS OF SATAN

He is "a liar and the father of lies" (John 8:44).

In contrast to Satan, Jesus speaks of Himself as "*the truth*" (14:6). To fail to acknowledge this is to give unmistakable evidence of spiritual descent from him whose very nature is falsehood, and whose entire object is to deceive the human heart—Satan himself. When Satan tells a lie, Jesus says in John 8:44, he is speaking his native language, for he is a liar and the father of lies.

He is "the god of this world" (2 Cor. 4:4), **"the prince of this world"** (Jn. 14:30), and **"the prince of the power of the air"** (Eph. 2:2).

He is so designated because of the special interest he has in this world, the homage that is paid to him by multitudes in the world, the great sway that, by divine permission, he wields in the world and in the hearts of his subjects.

The "Devil" (Matt. 4:1).

The most common Greek word for Satan in Scripture is *diabolos* (devil, adversary, accuser). How apt a description this is of our number one enemy. He does his utmost to malign and impugn God's children, just as he did to Job (Job 1:6-12).

The "dragon" and a "serpent" (Rev. 20:2).

This is no doubt a reference to Satan's capacity to menace, as well as to the subtle tactics he employed when tempting Adam and Eve in the Garden of Eden (Gen. 3:1ff).

All of the many names given to Satan in the Bible convey something of his character and activity.

THE CHARACTER OF SATAN

He is the enemy of God and man.

The word Satan means *adversary*. As the adversary, he is motivated by a disposition hostile to all attempts on the part of humans to worship and glorify God. The apostle Paul states that flesh and blood foes are merely Satan's tools. The real foe lurking behind them is Satan himself (Eph. 6:12). This passage also teaches that Satan has unseen assistants. The innumerable host of demons who do his bidding increases his power immeasurably. As Beelzebub, he is chief of the devils or demons (Luke 11:15). Unlike God, he is not omnipresent, but through the demonic hosts, he is in touch with the whole earth.

He is shrewd and cunning.

Paul warned of his treachery in 2 Corinthians 11:3. He is such a master of disguise that, though he is the *"prince of darkness,"* he is able to transform himself into an *"angel of light"* (2 Cor. 11:13-15). It should come as no great surprise that hypocrisy is so prevalent in the world, when we recall that Satan—the master hypocrite—is able to transform himself into almost any form and appear even as an angel of light in order to promote his kingdom of darkness.

He is extremely wicked.

He has sinned from the beginning, and still goes on sinning (1 John 3:8). He is the author and patron of sin, and has been a practitioner of it and an instigator to it even from the beginning of the world.

He is powerful.

Although not all-powerful (omnipotent) as God is, Satan's power is far beyond that of humans (Luke 4:5, 6).

THE WORKS OF SATAN

In His divine wisdom and providence, God sometimes allows Satan to do harmful things to humans.

He seeks to undermine and distort the Word of God (Mark 4:13-15; Gen. 3:4-5).

The Devil is determined that the Word will exert no influence in the lives of people who are exposed to it. He "snatches" the Word away before it can take root in a person's heart. If someone is exposed to the Word, the Devil is certain to distort its true meaning. He successfully used this ruse on Adam and Eve.

He blinds humans to their need of the Gospel of Christ (2 Cor. 4:3, 4).

Because Satan is the prince of darkness and the ruler of the darkness of this world, he deliberately and maliciously keeps people in the dark, blinding their minds with ignorance, superstition, prejudices, and error, so that they may not believe *"the glorious gospel of Christ."*

He is "the tempter" (1 Thess. 3:5).

As he tempted our Lord, so he levels his attack at the Lord's followers. Satan is a subtle enemy and uses many stratagems to deceive us. For that reason we should not be ignorant of his devices (2 Cor. 2:11).

He attempts to hinder and devour the children of God. (1 Thess. 2:18; 1 Pet. 5:8).

Satan is a constant enemy to the work of God and does all he can to obstruct it. He is no common adversary. He is more cruel and vigilant than the worst human antagonist. Like a *"roaring lion,"* he is hungry, restless, fierce, strong, and cruel, the determined and greedy pursuer of souls. His whole design is to devour and destroy the lives and reputations of those who align themselves with God.

He sometimes enters into humans and uses them as pawns in his schemes (John 13:27).

The Devil is in every wicked person that does his bidding (Eph. 2:2), yet sometimes he enters more powerfully than at other times, especially when he arouses them to accomplish some monstrous evil.

CHAPTER 21

HOW DOES ONE OVERCOME THE DEVIL AND WHAT WILL BE HIS FINAL END?

One of the chief reasons for the incarnation of Jesus Christ was to destroy the works of the Devil (1 John 3:8). The Devil has calculated and endeavored to ruin the work of God in this world. Hence, the Son of God has undertaken a holy war against him. Jesus came into our world, was manifested in our flesh, that he might conquer the Devil and dissolve his works. The writer of Hebrews affirms that through the death of Christ, the Devil who has the power of death will be destroyed (Heb. 2:14, 15). The Devil may be said to have the power of death, for he was the first sinner, the first tempter to sin, and sin is the underlying cause of death. In a very real sense, the Devil has already been defeated; but his ultimate demise is yet future.

HOW TO HAVE VICTORY OVER SATAN
Believe that the Devil is a real being, not some mythological character.

One of the strange ironies associated with the Devil is that he likes nothing better than for humans to deny his existence. A person is much more susceptible to Satan's wiles who questions his reality.

You must recognize that he is real, he is a creature of great power and deception, he is intent on causing you to fall, and he is the enemy of your soul. He is more aware of your weaknesses than you are, and whether it is pride, lust, or covetousness, he will always aim for the chink in your armor. It pays to know your enemy, to be aware of the tactics he uses to achieve your destruction.

Believe that victory is possible, although it cannot be achieved through human strength alone (2 Cor. 10:3-5).

The weapons of our warfare are powerful because we wage war, not by force of arms, not in our own strength, but in the power of Almighty God (Zech. 4:6). As the hymn writer states it:

The arm of flesh will fail you,
You dare not trust your own.

Whatever Satan uses as strongholds to oppose us or to thwart the advancement of the gospel, whether vain imaginations, fleshly reasoning, or proud conceits, these strongholds are pulled down by the power of God. No stronghold, not even Satan himself, is able to withstand the mighty force of a spiritual weapon wielded in the name of Jesus Christ.

Believe that God has made provision for your victory over the Devil.

He has supplied you with all the spiritual armor you need (Eph. 6:10-17). We have an enemy to fight against (*the Devil*), a captain to fight for (*the Lord Jesus Christ*), a banner to fight under (*the gospel*), and certain rules of warfare by which we are to govern ourselves (*the Word of God*).

In the battle in which we are engaged, no one can be victorious unless well armed. Paul admonishes us to "*put on the whole armor of God,*" and make use of all the proper weapons for repelling the temptations and stratagems of Satan (vs. 11). The *whole* armor must be put on, not leaving any part of the body exposed to the enemy. It is even more urgent, considering that our enemies are principalities, powers, rulers, and wicked spirits in high places.

It is the *armor of God.* We are not free to choose our own weapons. God has set limitations on the types of armor and weapons we are to employ. The purpose for putting on the armor is plainly stated: that we may be able to stand against the wiles of the Devil (vs. 11).

Paul specifies each piece of the armor that is to be put on. The order in which the pieces of armor are described is the order in which

a soldier in ancient times would put them on. First, the Christian soldier is to be *"girded with truth"* (v. 14). Before the armor can be put
on, the garments underneath must be bound together. God desires
truth in the inward parts. Truth is the Christian soldier's belt.
Girded with this, he is not susceptible to Satan's absurd and persistent lies.

The next weapon to put on is *"the breastplate of righteousness"* (vs.
14). Uprightness of character, loyalty to the Word of God, is the
thought here. To neglect what we know to be righteous action is to
leave a gaping hole in our armor.

The next piece of armor is proper footwear: *"the preparation of
the gospel of peace"* (vs. 15). It is the gospel that gives one firm foot-
ing in the ongoing conflict with the Devil.

Next comes *"the shield of faith"* (vs. 16), which covers all the rest
of the body. By faith, Paul means total reliance on God, which is the
essence of faith. This part of the soldier's weaponry, according to
Paul, is the most important of all. *"Above all,"* he says, *"take the
shield of faith."* The *flaming darts* the shield repels, signify people's
sharp tongues, impurity, selfishness, doubt, fear, disappointment, all
of which are planned by the Devil and his cohorts to burn and
destroy. Paul knew that only faith's reliance on God could quench
and deflect such destructive "darts."

The next weapon, *"the helmet of salvation"* (v. 17), refers not only to
God's gift of salvation from the penalty of sin, but even more of his saving help to protect from the power of sin. Without that hope to fortify, and the confidence of rescue from the bondage of the past, the
Christian may easily be wounded in the conflict (see Ps. 140:7). The
Devil would tempt us to despair, but the hope of present and future
deliverance keeps us trusting in God and rejoicing in Him.

The last, but certainly not least, part of the Christian's armor is *"the
sword of the Spirit"* (v. 17). At the time Paul wrote these words, a sword
was a very necessary and useful part of the soldier's weaponry. The
Word of God, like Goliath's sword, is unlike any other. Jesus resisted
Satan's temptations in the wilderness with a word from Scripture (*"It is
written,"* Matt. 4:1-11). May that be an incentive and example for us
to fortify ourselves with the knowledge and understanding of the Word
that we may be able to stand in the day of temptation. Scripture arguments are the most powerful arguments to repel temptation. About to

sin? Think Scripture.By faith, put on this armor every day without fail, but especially when facing some critical event in your life. A soldier preparing for battle does not forget to put on his armor and take up his weapons. His life depends on being properly equipped for the conflict. So it is in the experience of the believer. One must always be prepared, for every day offers its challenges and its temptations. The warfare in which we are engaged will not end until death snatches us away or until Christ comes to receive us to Himself.

When you resist the Devil, he will flee from you (James 4:7). It is when you give a foothold to the Devil that trouble looms (Eph. 4:27). You may also take comfort in the truth that God has given to all believers the gift of the Holy Spirit, who is said to be greater than any foe you might come up against in this world, and greater than the Devil himself (1 John 4:4).

THE DESTINY OF SATAN

The Bible makes clear that a serious and intense struggle is going on between Christ and His followers on the one side, and Satan and his forces on the other. Evidences of this intense confrontation include the temptation of Jesus (Matt. 4:1-11), and Jesus' numerous encounters with demons (Luke 22:31-34).

Satan's ultimate destruction was foretold in Gen. 3:15, in which God warned him that some day the seed of the woman, Christ (Gal. 3:16), would bruise his head.

In Revelation 20 we read that Satan will be bound for a thousand years (vss. 2, 3) and then released for a time before being cast into the lake of fire and brimstone (vs. 10). Jesus reveals that this will also be the fate of Satan's angels (Matt. 25:41). These events result in the utter destruction of the Devil's kingdom. No longer will he and his willing accomplices be free to roam at will, like roaring, ferocious lions, eagerly searching for someone to devour.

No matter how apparently powerful and indestructible Satan may appear to be, we may rest assured that his days are numbered. Scripture guarantees his impending doom. The happy day will come when he will be confined to the *lake of fire* forever.

CHAPTER 22

IF GOOD ANGELS EXIST, WHAT DO THEY DO?

Before leaving the subject of the Devil, the chief of the fallen angels, it will benefit us to consider whether good angels exist, and if so, the nature of their ministry. Some angels are fallen, as we have seen, but not all angels are fallen creatures, giving their allegiance to Satan. That good angels are actual spirit beings whose function is to glorify God and do His bidding is a fact the Bible clearly teaches.

Some years ago, many people in the intellectual and scientific communities scoffed at the existence of angels. They claimed they could not believe that such beings existed, or that even a supernatural realm existed. More recently, with the rise of New Age philosophy and the occult, people are re-examining the spiritual and supernatural world, including the study of angels. Scores of books on the subject of angels have been published in the last twenty years, not to mention the numerous television programs devoted to the subject. Sadly, many of these books and programs promote speculations about angels that are foreign to the Bible. They tend to be based largely on imaginary experiences and interactions with angels rather than grounded in Scripture. During the Middle Ages, there was an excessive interest in the subject of angels. While it is inappropriate to exaggerate the significance of angels, it is equally improper to neglect such a study. The consideration of angels is necessary because they are so often referenced in the Bible.

THE EXISTENCE OF ANGELS

While many today see angels as mystical characters belonging only in fables, the Bible makes it absolutely clear that these spirit beings do exist. Almost 300 times the word "*angel*" occurs in the Bible. Of course, any truth has to be stated only once in Scripture to acknowledge it as truth, but when it is mentioned as often as angels are, then it becomes impossible for a serious Bible student to ignore or deny it.

The existence of angels was a point of hot contention between the Pharisees and the Sadducees, as the latter did not believe in angels or spirits, or the resurrection of the dead (Acts 23:6-8).

Another important fact about angels is that the mention of them is not confined to one period of history or one part of Scripture. Angels are mentioned in at least 34 books of the Bible, from Genesis to Revelation.

In the Old Testament, angels are always represented as real beings, not as illusions or mythological creatures. They do specific things in character with their service as *messengers* (which is the meaning of both the Hebrew and Greek words for angels.) Many of the references in the Pentateuch and in Judges are to the Angel of the Lord who appears to be Deity. An angel executed judgment on Israel after David wrongly took a census of the people (2 Sam. 24:16). Isaiah refers to seraphim (6:1-3), and Ezekiel to cherubim (10:1-3). Daniel speaks of Gabriel and Michael (9:20-27; 10:13; 12:1). Zechariah mentions angels as agents of God (chap. 1) and interpreters of visions (chaps. 1-6). In the Psalms, angels are depicted as God's servants who worship Him and who deliver God's people from harm (34:7; 91:11; 103:20).

In the New Testament our Lord taught the existence of angels. He declared that the human state in the resurrection would be like the angels (non-procreative, Matt. 22:30). He said that angels will separate the righteous from the wicked at the end of the age (13:39), and will accompany Him at His second coming (25:31). In Matthew 18:10, He supports the idea of individual *guardian angels* for believers (see also Heb. 1:13-14 & Acts 12:15).

The writers of the New Testament affirmed the real existence of angels. They revealed that angels were connected with Christ's birth, temptation, life, resurrection, and ascension (Matt. 2:19; Mark 1:13;

Luke 2:13; John 20:12; Acts 1:10-11).   In the book of Acts angels were involved in helping God's servants, opening prison doors for the apostles (Acts 5:19; 12:5-11), directing Philip and Cornelius in ministry (8:26; 10:1-7), and encouraging Paul during the storm on his voyage to Rome (27:23-25).

THE NATURE OF ANGELS
They are created beings.
There was a time when they did not exist (Neh. 9:6; Col. 1:16). That they were created is clearly implied in Psalm 148:2, 5. Scripture describes them as being innumerable (Rev. 5:11; Heb. 12:22).

They are spirit beings.
They do not have physical or material bodies. Physical manifestations of angels recorded in Scripture must be regarded as appearances assumed for the occasion.

They are above the laws of nature.
Apparently angels are able to circumvent physical obstacles and travel over distant spaces in brief periods of time (Acts 12:7ff.)

They differ in rank and power.
The Bible speaks of archangels, angels, principalities, powers, dominions, thrones, might and authorities (Col. 1:16). They excel in power (Ps. 103:20; 2 Peter 2:11; 2 Kings 19:35; 2 Sam 24:15, 16; Matt. 28:2-4). One angel will some day bind the Devil and keep him imprisoned for a thousand years (Rev. 20:1-3).

THE MISSION OF ANGELS
In the affairs of mankind, God uses angels to help His children and to carry out specific divine missions (Luke 1:26-38).

They execute God's judgments and purposes.
Angels have been called *God's secret agents*, and indeed they are. An angel blocked Balaam's path (Num. 22:22). At the end of the age, the Son of Man will send His angels, who will remove everything that causes sin and all who do evil (Matt. 13:41). King Herod died as the result of a lethal stroke administered by an angel (Acts 12:23).

They guide believers.

An angel informed Joseph not to divorce Mary, that the child she was carrying was not illegitimate but was conceived by the Holy Spirit. He was told to name the child Jesus, for he would save his people from their sins (Matt. 1:18-21). When the Ethiopian eunuch desired to know the meaning of Scripture, an angel directed Philip to his chariot. Philip knew nothing of the man's need, but God did. An angel was sent on this important mission to guide Philip to the needy sinner. When Philip opened up the Scriptures to the Ethiopian, he believed on Christ and was saved (Acts 8:26). This event implies that at times angels assist us in winning people to Christ.

They assist, protect and strengthen God's people.

When Jezebel sought to kill Elijah, he was cared for and protected by an angel (1 Kings 19:5). Daniel was secure and unharmed in the den of lions because God sent His angel to pacify those otherwise ravenous beasts (Dan. 6:22). After Jesus had His confrontation with the Devil in the wilderness, angels came and ministered to Him (Matt. 4:11). At a time when Paul needed encouragement during a storm at sea, an angel came and assured him that all would be well (Acts 27:23-24).

They will be involved in the Second Advent.

Just as angels were present at other significant events of Jesus' life, when He comes in His glory all the holy angels will accompany Him (Matt. 25:31). Paul affirms that same truth in 2 Thessalonians 1:7, 8.

Whether angels continue to function in all these ways throughout the present age is uncertain. God has chosen to use angels at certain key times in the past, as we have seen verified in Scripture, and it is not beyond reason to assume that the same could be true today.

According to Paul, angels are observing our lives (1 Cor. 4:9); and because angels witness how we are walking through life, it should mightily influence the decisions we make and the life we live. The charge to live righteously and godly in this present world should sober us when we realize that the walk and warfare of Christians is the primary concern of Heaven and its angelic hosts (1 Tim. 5:21).

BASIC
BAPTIST
B E L I E F S

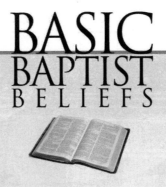

THE CREATION

We believe in the Genesis account of creation, and that it is to be accepted literally and not allegorically or figuratively; that man was created directly in God's own image and after his own likeness; that man's creation was not a matter of evolution or evolutionary change of species, or development through interminable periods of time from lower to higher forms; that all animal and vegetable life was made directly, and God's established law was they should bring forth only "after their kind."

CHAPTER 23

WAS THE UNIVERSE CREATED OR DID IT EVOLVE?

One of the most important and fundamental truths taught in the Bible is *creation*. The enemies of God and Holy Scripture know this; consequently, they have reserved their most vicious attacks for this foundational Bible truth. If faith in the Biblical account of creation can be destroyed, the rest is easy. There is no need of a Savior if humans were not created in the image and likeness of God, and, because of disobedience, are fallen, sinful creatures. The value of the Bible is marginal if the story of creation is merely the nonscientific assumptions of an unenlightened, primitive society.

When it comes to the origin of the universe, and specifically this planet we know of as earth, science may hazard its guesses but it can furnish no satisfactory reply. The Bible, however, is explicit, for it is by faith we understand that all things were created by the Word of God (Heb. 11:3). The very first words of the Bible spell out in no uncertain terms that God is the divine architect behind all of creation (Gen. 1:1). The word *Genesis* means "beginning." The book of Genesis is *a book of beginnings* (our world, humans, sin, salvation, etc.), and is foundational to the Biblical world-view.

GENESIS IS ACTUAL HISTORY, NOT MYTH

The first eleven chapters of Genesis, more than any other section of Scripture, have been rejected as true history. This is because no extra-biblical historical records exist for this period to confirm the

Genesis story, and because of supposed contradictions with science. Many scientists over the centuries have believed the Bible account of creation in Genesis is accurate. Many other scientists are willing to accept as reliable only the statements in Genesis 1 that express religious truths. They insist that to seek for even a kernel of historical fact in such cosmogonies is inconsistent with the scientific point of view which states that facts can only be proven through successful experimentation. Many historical facts have not gone through any rigorous scientific experiment. Nevertheless, with no experimental proof, many scientists tell us this passage must be stories that humans made up to help them cope with life. These scientists are not being scientific and following their own rules of conduct and logic. They have no successful experiments to prove the account given by God in Genesis is wrong. Understanding how God created the universe is still too big an idea for their current crude mode of experimentation.

The creation account in Genesis is real history, reporting on real persons and events in space and time.

Moses uses the same historical narrative style in chapters 1-11 as in the remaining chapters of Genesis.

The author does not change his style after chapter eleven or give any textual clue that he is moving from myth to history. Rather, the book is a unity, a record of historical events that sets the stage for the rest of the Bible. It makes references to actual places and people, and how long they lived. Myths have no interest in places and time, because they want to remove their characters from history.

The rest of the Biblical writers, and even Jesus Himself, regarded these early chapters of Genesis as real history.

The Psalmist praises God for creating the world as described in Genesis chapter one in the same way he praised God for delivering the Israelites from Egypt (Ps. 136; Exo. 6:1).

In answering the questions of the Pharisees about divorce, Jesus appeals to the verses in Genesis that speak of the creation of Adam and Eve and how they became one flesh in the marital union (Matt. 19:4-6). To say that Jesus was merely using language familiar to His audience and not meant to be taken literally is begging the question. If Jesus cannot be trusted here, where may He be trusted?

The biblical account of creation is fundamentally different from some of the ancient creation myths.

In fact, one of the main purposes of the Genesis account is to correct the erroneous creation myths of the ancient Near Eastern culture.

WHAT THE BIBLE TEACHES ABOUT CREATION
God is revealed through but distinct from His creation.

Just as we can learn something about an architect by studying his works, we can learn something about the Creator by studying His creation (Rom. 1:20). Even if the buildings designed by the architect burned up, the architect would remain. In the same way, God exists independently from His creation. God created the heavens and the earth (Gen. 1:1).

The Book of Genesis does not describe in great detail how God created the heavens and the earth, but it affirms emphatically that He did so. It says, *"In the beginning."* And it does not matter to a Christian how old the earth is.

We need not try to date the beginning. And there is no point in trying to answer the impossible question of where God was and how He spent His time before the beginning, since space and time are a part of the created world. We cannot even imagine before time or outside space. What matters is that the earth is the Lord's, that He created it (Ps. 24:1). He did it by the power of His Word (Ps. 33:6-9). And He did it as a triune God: Father, Son, Holy Spirit (Gen. 1:2; John 1:1-4).

The earth is not eternal.

What science has discovered about the origin of the universe and life on earth is not inconsistent with one very important fact about creation that is spelled out in Genesis 1:1. It had a beginning. For centuries, many scientists held that the universe was eternal, but now we know this is not the case. Many scientists now accept what is referred to as the "Big Bang" theory. Although scientists would insist that this theory does not validate the Biblical account, nor do Christians agree that creation took place in this manner, the theory nevertheless implies that the universe had a beginning.

The Bible explains what science could never explain, and that is, at the beginning point of creation, God *spoke* and the world appeared (Ps. 33:9). Robert Jastrow, in his book, *God and the Astronomers,* wrote:

> The details differ, but the essential elements in the astronomical and biblical accounts of Genesis are the same . . . We scientists did not expect to find evidence for an abrupt beginning because we have had, until fairly recently, such extraordinary success in tracing the chain of cause and effect backward in time. For the scientist who has lived by his faith in the power of reason, the story ends like a bad dream. He has scaled the mountains of ignorance; he is about to conquer the highest peak; as he pulls himself over the final rock, he is greeted by a band of theologians who have been sitting there for centuries.

The Bible teaches that God created the universe without using preexisting materials—*ex nihilo*, "out of nothing" (Heb. 11:3). In bringing the whole world of reality into being, God created merely by His Word. Everything we know is the shaping of some given material. A carpenter makes a chair out of wood; a sculptor makes a figure out of stone. Creation from nothing is completely beyond all of our experience. To say that God made all things and that He did it out of nothing is to say that there is no eternal reality alongside or apart from Him.

God did not create evil. Humans have pondered the problem of evil since the beginning. If God did not create evil, why would He, being holy, permit it? Though no explanation is entirely satisfactory, we can say that God in His infinite wisdom allowed the possibility of situations which would permit sin to be a reality in the human experience. But by the death of His Son for our sins, along with His overruling providence, they together assure us of the final triumph of righteousness.

CONCLUSION

The overriding issue in all of this is the authority of God's Word versus man's opinions. By "man's opinions" we are referring to the majority or "establishment" view of earth (and human) history, as taught and believed in the scientific community and in most educational institutions today.

Lee Strobel in his book, *The Case for Faith*, quotes prominent evolutionist William Provine of Cornell University as conceding that if Darwinism is true, *"there are five inescapable implications: there is no evidence for God; there is no life after death; there is no absolute foundation for right and wrong; there is no ultimate meaning for life; and people do not really have free will."* No God, no life after death, no right and wrong, no meaning for life, no free will is what Darwinism gives a human. Where are the scientific experiments that prove there is no God, no right and wrong, no meaning for life, no free will? No scientist can put God in a bottle and measure Him or on a scale and weigh Him or look at Him on His throne through a space probe. *The earthly scientist does not have the expertise to evaluate God.* The wise human accepts what God has revealed about His creative work in the Bible.

The Apostle Peter exhorts us to always be ready to give an answer for the hope that is in us (1 Pet. 3:15). This is another way of saying that we must always be prepared to defend as well as extend the faith, and one very important component of our faith is the account of creation. To shirk that responsibility is to give ground to the enemy. The area of greatest attack is creation. According to Scripture, the universe is not an accident; it is the result of deliberate design. The distinction between species is not a missing link, it is divine intention (Gen. 1:24). Nor is man the end result of millions of years of evolution—he is the zenith of God's creation, intended for fellowship with his Creator (Gen. 1:27).

CHAPTER 24

ARE HUMANS THE PRODUCT OF EVOLUTIONARY FORCES?

Professor John Gerstner tells a story about Arthur Schopenhauer, the nineteenth-century German pessimistic philosopher, who was seated on a park bench in Berlin. A policeman, taking him to be a bum because of the way he was dressed, asked him who he thought he was. He answered him, "I would to God I knew." All who deny the reality of God as Creator, the One who gives and sustains life, have a problem with their *identity*. They are ignorant of who they are and what life is all about. If the question, "Where did I come from?" is answered without any reference to God, life is totally without meaning or purpose. The way the question is answered depends on one's world-view, which in turn leads to conclusions of a momentous nature.

Those who hold atheistic, naturalistic, evolutionary presuppositions propagate a school of thought about the origin of humans that is a widely accepted view in the modern world. Those in this camp eagerly accept the evolutionary hypothesis while insisting that God had nothing at all to do with the origin of life or the universe. Notice the word, hypothesis, which can be defined as a possibility with not enough evidence to be declared a scientific fact. All who support this view see humans primarily as members of the animal kingdom, derived from some of its higher forms. They have come into being through the same sort of process as have all other animals, and will have a similar end. The only difference between human beings and animals is one of degree. Still another group accepts evolution as the best explanation for man's origin, but insist that God initiated the process in the beginning. This is called *theistic evolution.*

By contrast, the Biblical view is altogether different. Humans are not the product of blind chance or the fortuitous concurrence of atoms. They are creatures of God, fashioned in His image. This is sometimes referred to as the theistic or creationist view. Because humans are the product of a divine Creator and not blind chance, there is a reason for our existence, a reason which lies in the intention of the Creator.

GOD CREATED HUMANS

God formed man from the dust of the ground (Gen. 1:26, 27; 2:7). He did not cause human beings to evolve gradually from other forms of life, such as marine or land animals. The unproven but commonly accepted view of many today is that human beings originated from the lower forms of animal life and are the result of natural processes that took billions of years. Such an idea cannot be harmonized with the Biblical record.

The Biblical account in Genesis affirms that God fashioned man in His own image, a being like Himself, except inferior in intelligence and strength. In our spiritual and mental faculties we possess a certain resemblance to God. It is a great honor that of all creatures on this earth, only humans are created in the image of God. All other creatures, except angels, are inferior to humans (Gen. 1:28).

Because humans are created in the image of God, it means the sacredness of human life is an extremely important principle in God's scheme of things. Abortion, euthanasia, and murder are all opposed to this divine principle.

Adam was the first of the human species; from him all future life was to spring. Some argue that the Hebrew word for Adam is a generic term meaning only "man," and that the name Adam did not refer to a specific person. That Adam was an actual human being is confirmed by the genealogical table given by Luke (3:23ff.), in which he traces the descendants of Jesus straight back to Adam, whom he designates as *"the son of God."*

The Apostle Paul builds his theology of redemption in Romans around the first and second Adam (Rom. 5:12-21; see also 1 Cor.

15:20-22, 45-49). The first Adam was the inhabitant of the Garden of Eden, our first ancestor through whom sin with all its dreadful consequences originated. And it was the first man's sin that made necessary the second Adam's sacrifice on the cross of Calvary. To argue that the first Adam was a mythical figure while holding that the second Adam was a genuine historical person turns Scripture on its head.

God made the first two humans innocent, but they were given a free will and could choose to obey or disobey God (Gen. 2:16, 17). The first human pair was told to be fruitful, multiply, fill the earth and subdue it (Gen. 1:28). Thus all human beings who ever lived or who ever will live are related to one another (Acts 17:26).

GOD'S PURPOSE IN CREATING HUMANS

Evolution teaches that humans are here on this planet by accident. Our existence is due to a chance of fate. However, the Bible presents an entirely different picture. The God of order and design who fashioned us has a purpose for our existence. There are at least five reasons why God brought His creation into being.

He did it for His own pleasure (Rev. 4:11).

Something in God's nature inspired Him to create. It was for His pleasure that we received the gift of life. It was not that we might have a good time in our own way and do as we please. We are happiest when we are living to please our Creator. We are least happy when we are doing our own thing, indulging in pleasure for the mere sake of pleasure (Luke 12:16-21; 1 Tim. 5:6).

He did it for His own glory.

The original creation sang its Creator's praise (Job 38). The Almighty declared that He created humans for His glory (Isa. 43:7). To those inclined to say that God would be a selfish, egotistical being who would expect His creatures to forever extol Him, we would answer in the words of Paul: *"What human being has the right to criticize God? Does the clay have the right to ask the potter why he shaped it the way he did? The potter can make anything he wants to make"* (Rom. 9:20-21, paraphrase). These verses imply that the Creator has the right to expect from His creatures whatever He wishes.

He did it for fellowship with humans.

God delights in fellowship with His creatures. Since man was created in the moral image of God, he was given the opportunity to demonstrate his love and loyalty to his Creator. Like God, he had the power of choice—the freedom to think and act according to moral imperatives. Thus he was free to love and obey or to distrust and disobey. The entrance of sin into the world broke this fellowship between God and man, and so precipitated the Bible drama of redemption.

He did it so humans could interact with each other.

God said it was not good for the man to be alone, so He made him a helper, someone perfectly suitable for him. What Adam lacked, Eve supplied (Gen. 2:18). Just as three members of the Trinity are united in a loving relationship, so we were created for the fellowship and interaction found in marriage and friendship with other humans. In these relationships we have the opportunity to live for others. God intended for humans to be relationship oriented in units we call the family, our church family, etc.

He created us to be stewards of the earth's environment (Gen. 1:26).

It was as God's representative that man was placed over the lower created orders (see also Ps. 8:5-8). The animal kingdom cannot understand the sovereignty of God, but many animals are capable of loving and serving mankind. Man's responsibility is to rule graciously over the world, reflecting God's beneficent rule over the universe. We are not the victims of circumstances, dominated by environmental forces. Rather, God has commissioned us to make a positive contribution by shaping the environment. We are not to selfishly squander the earth's natural resources or to indiscriminately pollute the air and water, which will lead to an increasing deterioration of the quality of life. We are to be good stewards of the environment and the lower order of beings over which we have dominion.

CONCLUSION

How can anyone have an awareness of significance who believes we are the product of chance evolutionary forces? On the other hand, how can we possibly remain long in an attitude of despondency or hopelessness when we consider that the Creator God has given us the gift of life, has redeemed us by the blood of His Son, and has assured us of a glorious future in His very presence?

Well-known British atheist Antony Flew, who for more than fifty years argued against the existence of God, publishing such books as "Atheistic Humanism" and "Darwinian Evolution," recently shelved his atheism (December, 2004) in favor of a belief in God and a theistic view of the universe. The former professor at Oxford, Aberdeen, and Reading universities in Britain, influenced by arguments from the "intelligent design" movement, admitted that he was forced to go where the evidence leads. In his case, it led him away from Darwinism and atheism to a belief in God.

The view derived from the Bible that behind all of creation is an intelligent Designer, a divine being who created the entire universe, who made man out of the dust of the ground and fashioned him in the moral and spiritual image of Himself, answers the question, "Where did life originate?" This explanation alone endows life with a genuine purpose.

BASIC
BAPTIST
B E L I E F S

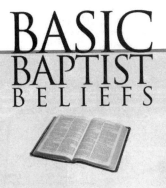

THE FALL

We believe that man was created in innocence under the
law of his Maker, but by voluntary transgression fell from
his sinless and happy state, in consequence of which, all
mankind are now sinners, not by constraint, but
of choice; and therefore under just condemnation
without defense or excuse.

CHAPTER 25

HOW DID SIN ORIGINATE?

Though created in God's image and placed in a perfect environment—the Garden of Eden—Adam and Eve disobeyed the explicit command of God, ate the forbidden fruit, and plunged themselves and their posterity into a fallen, sinful state. After the passing of many centuries, and in spite of remarkable scientific and technological progress in many areas of life, sin remains a stubborn, hideous reality. Furthermore, the world has never been totally free of wars, rumors of wars, disease, crimes of violence, and death. What human, however good he or she may appear to be, can rightfully claim to be totally free from envy, pride, lust, deceit, greed, malice, or hate? But how did such a radical and terrible transformation come about? How did our first parents, in such an idyllic setting, agree among themselves to violate the clear command of their Creator? Moreover, if God created a perfect world, how could sin develop?

GOD AND THE ORIGIN OF SIN

Is it possible that God is the author of sin? This is a question that has perplexed humans since time immemorial. The Scriptures make it abundantly clear, however, that by nature God is holy (Isa. 6:3). There is no unrighteousness in Him (Deut. 32:4). Scripture states that God cannot do wickedness nor commit iniquity (Job 34:10).

Furthermore, God cannot be tempted by evil, nor does He Himself tempt anyone (James 1:13). The psalmist affirms that God hates sin (Ps. 5:4; 11:5).

God's original Creation was *very good* (Gen. 1:31). Far from being the author of sin, He is the author of salvation to all who obey Him (Heb. 5:9).

THE BEGINNING OF SIN

God could have prevented sin by creating a universe of robots that would do only what they were programmed to do. But God's love demanded that He create beings who could respond freely to His love, and such a response is possible only from beings who have the power of choice.

Providing His creation with this kind of freedom, however, meant that God must take the risk that some created beings would turn from Him.

Angels, beings of a higher order than humans, were created to enjoy intimate fellowship with God (Rev. 1:1; 3:5; 5:11). Of superior strength and obedient to God's Word (Ps. 103:20), they function as servants or "*ministering spirits*" (Heb. 1:14). Though generally invisible to the human eye, at times they appear in human form (Gen. 18, 19; Heb. 13:2). It was through one of these angelic beings that sin was introduced to the universe.

Although sin's rise is mysterious and unjustifiable, its roots can be traced to Lucifer. As a high-ranking being in the angelic world, he became defiantly proud (Eze. 28:17; cf. 1 Tim. 3:6). Dissatisfied with the exalted position the Creator had given him, he selfishly began to covet God's own place of authority (Isa. 14:12-14; cf. Jude 6). Lucifer's rebellion against God's government was the first step in his transformation into Satan, *the adversary*.

In an attempt to take control of the universe, this fallen angel sowed seeds of discontent among his fellow angels, and won the allegiance of many. The resulting conflict ended when Lucifer, now known as Satan, or the Devil (the adversary), and his angels were expelled from Heaven (Rev. 12:4, 7-9).

THE ORIGIN OF SIN IN THE HUMAN RACE

Undeterred by his expulsion from Heaven, Satan determined to entice others to join his rebellion against God's government. His attention was drawn to the newly created human race. How could he lead Adam and Eve to rebel? They lived in a perfect world, with all their needs provided for by their Creator. How could they ever become discontented and distrust the One who was the source of their happiness? The account of the first sin gives the answer.

When God created Adam and Eve and placed them in the Garden of Eden, He only imposed one prohibition on them. The tree in the middle of the garden, "*the tree of the knowledge of good and evil,*" was off limits. To eat of this tree would be an act of deliberate disobedience and would result in estrangement from God as well as death (Gen. 2:16-17).

In his assault on the first human beings, Satan decided to catch them off guard. Approaching Eve when she was near the tree of the knowledge of good and evil, Satan, in the guise of a serpent—the most subtle of all the creatures God had made—questioned her about God's prohibition against eating fruit from the tree (Gen. 3:1-2).

When Eve replied that God said they would die by eating the fruit of the tree, Satan challenged the divine prohibition, insisting that she would not die as God had warned. He aroused her curiosity by suggesting that God was trying to keep her from a wonderful new experience: that of being like God (3:4, 5).

Immediately, doubt about God's Word took root. Eve became infatuated with the grand possibilities the fruit was said to offer. The temptation began to play havoc with her mind. Belief in God's Word now changed to belief in Satan's Word. Suddenly she imagined that the tree was not something to be shunned, but that its fruit was nourishing, it was pleasant to look upon, and it would make her much wiser than before (3:6a).

Dissatisfied with her position, Eve yielded to the temptation of becoming like God. She took the fruit and ate it. Adam is said to have been with Eve at the time of the temptation and should have been her protector. Instead, he foolishly allowed her to eat without expressing his disapproval, and then ate the fruit himself (3:6b).

CONCLUSION

In trusting their senses rather than God's Word, Adam and Eve severed their dependence upon God, fell from their high position, and plunged into sin. The fall of the human race, therefore, first and foremost was characterized by a breakdown in faith—faith in God and His Word. This unbelief led to disobedience, which in turn, resulted in a broken relationship and finally a separation between God and man.

Though the term is not used in Scripture, the word *fall* is appropriate, because it echoes the language and teaching of Scripture. The New Testament consistently treats sin as a fall, a descent.

The fall of Adam and Eve has affected the whole human race; but little falls occur every time a believer sins. Hence, Paul warns against overconfidence. Those who think they would never commit such and such a sin, must be vigilant lest they fall (1 Cor. 10:12). The Bible cautions against a haughty spirit; such a careless attitude often results in a fall (Prov. 16:18). There is nothing Satan relishes more than to reenact, insofar as it is possible, the fall of our original parents. As Paul warns, we should constantly be on our guard against his efforts to make us fall.

CHAPTER 26

WHAT ARE THE EXTENT AND EFFECTS OF SIN?

The Scriptures clearly teach that Adam and Eve fell from their first estate by disobeying God's command to forego eating from the tree of knowledge of good and evil, a tree positioned in the middle of the Garden of Eden. The freedom of Adam and Eve in Eden was limitless, except for the one prohibition God placed on that particular tree. When Adam and Eve deliberately chose to disregard God's prohibition, immediate and long-term consequences were imposed on them because of their sin. The dire repercussions that resulted reveal the seriousness of their transgression.

THE IMMEDIATE CONSEQUENCES OF SIN
Sin brought about a change in human nature.

This affected interpersonal relationships, as well as their relationship with God. The initial exhilarating, eye- opening experience in due course brought Adam and Eve only feelings of shame (Gen. 3:7). Instead of becoming God's equals, as Satan had promised, they became afraid of God and attempted to hide from Him (3:8-10).

When God interrogated Adam and Eve about their sin, instead of admitting their fault, they tried to pass the blame along. Adam faulted Eve (3:12). His words imply that both Eve and, indirectly God, were responsible for his sin, clearly showing how sin had broken his relationship with his wife and his Creator. Eve, in turn, sought to absolve herself from blame by pointing the finger at the serpent (3:13).

A curse was placed on Satan's instrument, the serpent.

Condemned to move on its belly, the serpent would be a perpetual reminder of the fall (3:14). The serpent had been the most cunning of animals (3:1); now it was the most cursed. It is possible the serpent had legs up until the moment of the curse.

The woman's pain would be greatly increased in childbirth.

And though her desire would be for her husband, he would be her master (3:16). The marriage relationship would be adversely affected as the two struggled to help each other.

The earth was cursed to increase the anxiety and toil of Adam's labors (3:17-19).

No longer would Adam and Eve live in an unspoiled paradise, but on an earth that is cursed. The good fruits and vegetables it produces must now be extorted from it by the ingenuity and industry of humans. This is merely a sample of the actual effects on the creation. Paul states that all of creation has been affected by the entrance of sin into the world, and is now in bondage to change and decay (Rom. 8:20-22).

They were expelled from Eden and became subject to death.

In reaffirming the unchangeableness of His law that such a transgression would lead to certain death, God reminded Adam that he was made from the dust of the ground and to dust he would return (3:19). God executed this verdict by expelling the disobedient pair from their home in Eden, severing their direct communication with Him (3:23-24). In addition, God prevented them from reentering the Garden to eat of the tree of life, the source of eternal life. Thus Adam and Eve became subject to death (3:22).

THE LONG TERM CONSEQUENCES OF SIN

Many Scripture passages, particularly the account of the Fall in Genesis, make it abundantly clear that sin is a moral evil, the result of a free moral agent's choosing to violate the revealed will of God (Gen. 3:1-6; Rom. 1:18-22).

Biblical definitions of sin include the following: it is breaking the law of God (1 John 3:4); it is neglecting to do good when one knows to do good and fails to do it (James 4:17); it is any act that does not spring from faith (Rom 14:23). Sin may also be defined as any deviation from the known will of God, either neglecting to do what He has specifically commanded or of doing what he has specifically forbidden.

Sin knows no neutrality. Jesus said that anyone who was not with Him was against Him (Matt. 12:30). Failure to believe in Him is sin (John 16:9). Any sin, great or small, results in the verdict, "guilty." The Bible makes it clear that though a person keeps the whole law, yet fails in only one point, he is still guilty of breaking all of it (James 2:10).

Sin involves thoughts as well as actions. Frequently sin is spoken of only in terms of actual acts of lawbreaking. But Christ said that lustful desires transgress the command not to commit adultery (Matt. 5:28; cf. Ex. 20:14). Sin, therefore, involves not only overt disobedience in actions but also thoughts and desires.

Sin darkens man's reason.

Although naturally attainable, the knowledge of God was obscured by sin (Rom. 1:18-23). Darkened reason led to irrational urges that flared up in numerous ways, but notably in lusts of the flesh (Rom. 1:24-27). Nothing is sacred to the person who wallows in sexual indulgence. No law is too binding not to be broken (or breakable) by one who is enslaved by the flesh (Rom. 1:28-32).

Sin produces guilt.

From the Biblical perspective, guilt implies that the one who has committed sin is liable to punishment. And because all are sinners, the whole world is guilty before God (Rom. 3:19). If not attended to properly, guilt devastates the physical, mental, and spiritual faculties. And ultimately, it produces death, for the wages of sin is death (Rom. 6:23).

Sin affects all of humanity.

Some may feel that the sentence of death was too severe a penalty for eating the forbidden fruit. But we can only gauge the seriousness of the transgression in light of the effect of Adam's sin on the human race. Adam and Eve's first son committed murder. Their descendants soon violated the sacred marriage union by engaging in polygamy, and it was not long before wickedness and violence filled the earth (Gen. 4:8, 23; 6:1-5, 11-13). God's appeals for repentance and reformation went unheeded, and only eight persons were saved from the Flood that destroyed the unrepentant in Noah's day. The history of the race after the Flood is, with few exceptions, a sad account of the culmination of the sinfulness of human nature.

The Bible teaches, and history verifies, that Adam's descendants share the sinfulness of his nature (Ps. 143:2; cf. 14:3; 1 Kings 8:46; Prov. 20:9; Eccl. 7:20; Rom. 3:23; 1 John 1:8). Paul said, "*In Adam all die*" (1 Cor. 15:22). He reaffirms this when he declares that sin entered the world through Adam, resulting in death; and then death spread to all mankind, because all have sinned (Rom 5:12).

THE CONTROL CENTER OF SIN

The seat of sin is in what the Bible calls the heart—what we know as the mind and emotions of a person. Accordingly, the Bible cautions to guard the heart, for the good or bad decisions we make proceed from that source (Prov. 4:23). Jesus reveals that it is the person's thoughts that defile (Matt. 15:19). It is by the heart that the entire person—the intellect, will, affections, emotions, and body—is influenced. Because the heart is deceitful and desperately wicked (Jer. 17:9), human nature can be described as corrupt, depraved, and thoroughly sinful.

THE REMEDY FOR SIN

Fellowship with God is restored only through the *new creation*. For humans, the new creation means the restoration of that which we lost in Eden. In our fallen condition we stand in desperate need of a new creation. Only God can rectify the situation. To bring fallen humanity back into fellowship with Himself, He sent His only Son to be their Savior. Those who respond to this gracious message, God creates anew (2 Cor. 5:17; Eph. 2:10). His regenerating grace brings forth a new world within the soul. All things are new. As Matthew Henry says, "the renewed person acts according to new principles, by new rules, with new purposes, and in new company."

For the universe, the *new creation* means "*a new heaven and a new earth.*" Since Adam and Eve by transgression fell, the whole creation has staggered under the load of sin. But one day God will once more act in creative power. He will create new heavens and a new earth (Isa. 65:17; 2 Peter 3:10, 13). This creation will endure forever.

BASIC BAPTIST BELIEFS

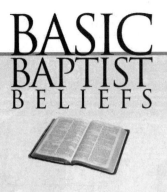

THE ATONEMENT FOR SIN

We believe that the salvation of sinners is wholly of grace; through the mediatorial offices of the Son of God, who by the appointment of the Father, freely took upon Him our nature, yet without sin, honored the divine law by His personal obedience, and by His death made a full and vicarious atonement for our sins; that His atonement consisted not in setting us an example by His death as a martyr, but was the voluntary substitution of Himself in the sinner's place, the Just dying for the unjust, Christ, the Lord, bearing our sins in His own body on the tree, that, having risen from the dead, He is now enthroned in Heaven and uniting in His wonderful person the tenderest sympathies with divine perfection, He is every way qualified to be a suitable, a compassionate and an all-sufficient Savior.

CHAPTER 27

WHY DID JESUS HAVE TO DIE?

The question, "What must I do to be saved, to experience God's favor and be assured of a home in Heaven?" has both perplexed and fascinated humans since the days of Adam and Eve. Those who remain perplexed about the matter are the ones who are reluctant to submit to the authority of God's Word. A correct answer to the question can only be discovered in Holy Scripture. For the next several chapters we will consider the all-important topic of *salvation*.

The question, "Why did Jesus have to die?" relates to what the Bible calls the *atonement*. This first in a series of chapters on salvation stresses the *atonement*. When we say that the atonement is the *crucial* doctrine of Christianity, we are not only propounding a theory that is generally accepted among Christian groups, we are also, perhaps unwittingly, illustrating our belief with the use of a choice word—*crucial*. *Crucial* is from the Latin *crux*, meaning "a cross." So, whenever we say, "this the *crucial* point" or "the *crux* of the matter is this," our language means, "just as the *cross* is central to Christianity, so the point I am making is central to the present discussion." The centrality of the cross to the Christian faith has shaped the language we use.

Right at the heart of Christianity is a cross, and on that cross the Son of God wrought man's salvation. Put simply, the atonement means that Jesus Christ in His death dealt completely with the problem that man's sin had brought about. Whatever had to be done He did it, and now those who come to Him in faith may enter into the blessing of salvation. The Apostle Paul believed the doctrine of the atonement is essential, and includes it in his classic definition of the gospel in the first four verses of 1 Corinthians 15. "Gospel" means "good news" and this was the best news humans ever received.

THE MEANING OF CHRIST'S ATONEMENT

Three principles underlie the atonement. These are closely related to, and associated with, the fact of sin.

The principle of "covering."

The safety of the Israelites on that first Passover night in Egypt depended solely on the shedding and application of the lamb's blood and their position beneath the covering (Exo. 12:1-13; 1 Cor. 5:7). The parallel is obvious. The blood of Jesus Christ that was shed on the cross of Calvary covers the believer's sins. To be *under the blood* is to be in a place of complete safety.

The principle of "reconciliation through payment of the penalty."

The one time the word *atonement* is used in the New Testament, it means *reconciliation* (Rom 5:11). Sinners are alienated from their Creator (Eph. 4:18). The death of God's only Son, Jesus Christ, is the one act which could produce reconciliation between sinful man and a holy God.

The principle of "substitution."

Christ did not die as a martyr for some worthy cause. He died *"for our sins."* The concept of *substitution* is found many times in the New Testament. We see it in the saying of Jesus when He declared that He came to give His life a ransom for many (Mark 10:45). Paul expresses a similar thought when he states that God made Jesus, who knew no sin, to be sin for us (2 Cor. 5:21). This identifies Christ in His death with sinners. When Paul wrote that Christ redeemed us from the curse pronounced by the law, taking upon Himself our curse (Gal. 3:13), he meant that Christ bore the curse that we should have borne. And this is *substitution*. He died in our place. He died the death we deserved (Isa. 53:5).

In my place condemned He stood;
Sealed my pardon with His blood.

THE DIFFERENCE BETWEEN CHRIST'S ATONEMENT AND THE OLD TESTAMENT PROTOTYPE

A *prototype* is an original or model after which anything is copied or patterned. Though there are similarities between the Day of Atonement in the Old Testament and the atonement of Christ in the New Testament, there are also significant differences. The Old Testament priest shed the blood of an animal; Christ shed His own blood. The Hebrew priest made atonement first for his own sins and then for the sin of the nation. The sinless Christ needed no personal atonement, but offered His own blood for the sins of the human race. Christ has received a ministry far superior to that of the ancient priesthood (Heb. 8:6)

THE ADEQUACY OF CHRIST'S ATONEMENT

The Hebrew priest entered into the Holy of Holies once every year. The sacrifice on the Day of Atonement was an annual celebration. Christ offered Himself only once. His one offering was adequate to atone for sin forever (Heb. 9:26).

The final sacrifice has been made.

When our Lord cried out on the cross, *"It is finished,"* He was not admitting that His death would put an end to what He was trying to accomplish. Rather, the ultimate and final sacrifice for sin was now completed.

There is no need to search for or substitute other "plans of salvation."

Any effort to substitute another medium of salvation is a denial of the revelation of Holy Scripture and a defiance of God's eternal purpose in Christ Jesus (Rev. 1:5).

Calvary, the Christian's "Day of Atonement," does not need to be repeated.

Any repetition of Calvary, as for instance in the Catholic Mass, is a refusal to accept Christ's atonement as being forever complete.

THE EXTENT OF THE ATONEMENT

That the death of Christ was designed to include all mankind is the historic view of the church, being held by the vast majority of theologians, reformers, evangelists, and fathers from the beginning of the church until the present day. Even John Calvin, who is appealed to by those who believe in limited atonement or particular redemption, had this to say regarding Mark 14:24 (*"This is my blood . . . which is shed for many"*): "By the word 'many' he means not a part of the world only, but the whole human race."

When the Bible says, *Christ died for all*, it means just that. The word should be taken in its normal sense unless some compelling reason exists to take it otherwise. Isaiah 53:6; John 3:16; 2 Cor. 5:15; 1 Timothy 2:1-6; 4:10; 1 John 2:2; and Hebrews 2:4 make no sense if not taken in the normal way. No one denies that Christ died for the elect. But it is wrong to claim that he died *only* for the elect.

APPROPRIATING THE BENEFIT OF CHRIST'S ATONEMENT

At Calvary God stooped in infinite mercy to the needs of a sinful race (Eph. 2:4-7). The question arises, "How may I be sure that Christ's offering for sin was for me?" Understanding a general principle is one thing; making it personal and practical is another. Food on the table may be appealing, but the sight of food, or even the knowledge of what food can do for you, will not satisfy hunger. Food must be eaten before it can be useful for your body.

The wonderful truth of the Atonement, that someone has taken our place, suffered what we deserved, is appealing. But, unless and until we acknowledge our sinful condition, open our heart to Jesus Christ, submit to Him as the Son of God whose blood atones for our sin, accept Him by faith as our Lord and Savior, we will not receive the benefits of His atonement (John 1:12; 4:24; Eph. 2:8).

CONCLUSION

Implicit in the doctrine of the atonement is the inference that Jesus is the *only* Savior. Jesus said of Himself that He was *"the way, the truth, and the life,"* and that no human being can enjoy a saving relationship with God unless they come through Him (John 14:6). He is not one way among other ways or one truth among other truths. Christianity stands or falls on the answer the church and its people give to a single question. The question has been unavoidable for almost two thousand years. It is the question Jesus Himself posed to His disciples at Caesarea Philippi: "Who do you say that I am?" (Matt. 16:15).

BASIC
BAPTIST
B E L I E F S

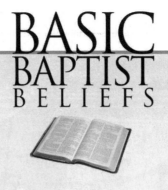

REGENERATION,
OR THE NEW BIRTH

We believe that in order to be saved, sinners must be born
again; that the new birth is a new creation in Christ Jesus;
that it is instantaneous and not a process; that in the new
birth the one dead in trespasses and in sins is made a
partaker of the divine nature and receives eternal life, the
free gift of God; that the new creation is brought about in a
manner above our comprehension, not by culture, not by
character, nor by the will of man, but wholly and solely by
the power of the Holy Spirit in connection with divine
truth, so as to secure our voluntary obedience to the gospel;
that its proper evidence appears in the holy fruits
of repentance and faith and newness of life.

CHAPTER 28

WHAT DOES IT MEAN TO BE "BORN AGAIN?"

The *new birth* (also referred in the Bible as "*regeneration*") is an act of God by which He imparts spiritual life to the believer in Jesus Christ. It is the divine side of that change of heart, which, viewed from the human side, we call conversion. As such it is simultaneous with the other aspects of this religious experience, such as justification, redemption, adoption, and sanctification.

It is of the utmost importance that we have a clear understanding of this vital doctrine. By *regeneration* we are admitted into the Kingdom of God (John 3:3-7). There is no other way of becoming a Christian but by being "*born again.*" It is the door of entrance into the family of God. Those who do not enter here do not enter at all.

THE NATURE OF REGENERATION
Regeneration is not baptism.

When the Ethiopian requested baptism, Phillip pointed out that he must first believe with all his heart (Acts 8:35-37). It was the act of believing, not the act of baptism, that saved the Ethiopian. Paul assured the Philippian jailer that if he believed on the Lord Jesus Christ he would be saved (Acts 16:31). If baptism and regeneration were identical, why should the Apostle Paul seem to make so little of the rite (compare 1 Cor. 4:15 with 1 Cor. 1:14).

Jesus told Nicodemus that he must be born again if he expected to be admitted into the kingdom of God (John 3:3). Nicodemus posed the question as to how a man could be born when he is old? Would it be possible for him to re-enter his mother's womb and be born a second time? (3:4). Perhaps he was being facetious. Even so, Jesus seized the opportunity to introduce the contrast between physical and spiritual birth and the necessity of experiencing both to enter the kingdom. He said, "*Unless a man is born of water* (physical birth) *and the Spirit* (spiritual birth), *he cannot enter the kingdom of God*" (3:5). It is obvious that one must first be born physically before one can be born spiritually. But why does the word "*water*" in this instance refer to physical birth and not baptism? For the first nine months of an unborn baby's life, it lives in a sack of *water* (or amniotic fluid) in its mother's womb (Nicodemus had just talked about re-entering his mother's womb). Physical or "*water*" birth comes first, as Jesus makes clear; however, physical birth alone does not equip one to be a child of God (John 1:13). Jesus said if one were only born of the flesh, one would always remain flesh. But if one is born of the Spirit, one becomes spirit (3:6). Only then can one have a personal relationship with God *who is Spirit*. This transformation can only become a reality by experiencing a spiritual birth.

Some believe that being "*born of water*" is a reference to the Word of God. Ephesians 5:26 and Titus 3:5 are verses used to buttress this viewpoint. Metaphorically, being regenerated is pictured in these verses as being cleansed by water.

Regeneration is not reformation.

To reform one's life is to go through a step-by-step process of improving one's behavior. Regeneration, on the other hand, is a supernatural act of God (James 1:18). *It is a spiritual crisis, a divine intervention. It marks the beginning of one's eternal life.* No one could justly condemn a person for wanting to improve his or her life, but our very best efforts, unaided by divine initiative, will not produce within us that change which alone is acceptable to God (Titus 3:5).

Regeneration is a spiritual quickening, a new birth.

By nature, humans are physically "alive," but spiritually "dead" in trespasses and sins (Eph. 2:1). The new birth imparts a new spiritual life, the life of God, so that henceforth the re-born person is as someone who has come forth from the dead—someone who has passed from spiritual death to spiritual life (John 5:24).

When speaking to Nicodemus about the new birth, as we have noted, Jesus compared the experience of being born again to physical or natural birth (John 3:3-8). At birth a child enters a new sphere of existence. The child must accommodate himself or herself to new conditions. Likewise, the one who is *born again* enters a new realm of life. The sins one previously relished are now distasteful. There is a new set of values, a fresh hope and confidence, and an altered mind-set (2 Cor. 5:17).

Regeneration is the impartation of a new nature.
This new nature is really God's nature (2 Pet. 1:4; Eph. 4:24; Col. 3:10). Christ now lives in the believer, a truth of great mystery but of immense comfort as well (Gal. 2:20). As physical birth enables us to have the life (nature) of our parents within us, so spiritual birth enables us to share in the life of God. We could not live in Heaven just as we are, with merely our human life. To live in Heaven it is necessary to have the life of God within us.

THE NECESSITY OF REGENERATION
The sinful condition of humans demands it.
All humans by nature (physical birth) are born into the wrong family. Our Lord denounced His enemies by declaring that their father was the Devil, and they enjoyed doing the evil things their father did. "Like father, like son" (John 8:44).

This sobering truth implies that no one who rejects Jesus Christ can rightly claim God as Father. A popular teaching today is that everyone is a child of God. Admittedly, God is the Creator of all, and in that sense He is the *father* of all, but only through regeneration does one become a true child of God.

Being spiritually dead, the unsaved exist in a state of alienation from God (Eph. 4:18). They are spiritually lost (Luke 19:10). And if they should die in such a condition they will perish (1 Cor. 1:18; John 3:16). Hence, humans must be *born again* to enter the family of God.

God's holiness requires a new birth.
If "*without* [holiness] *no one shall see the Lord*" (Heb. 12:14); and

if holiness is not to be attained by natural development or sustained by self-effort, then *regeneration* is absolutely necessary. The change which enables one to be holy, takes place only when one is *born again*. To have the *life of God*, one must have the *nature of God*.

THE MEANS OF REGENERATION

If one is to be born again, one must give assent to a message. He must "*believe on the Lord Jesus Christ.*" In his unsaved condition the sinner cannot impart spiritual life to himself or admit himself to God's Kingdom. But by His atoning death for the sins of the world (1 John 2:2), Jesus paved the way for God to forgive those who repent and believe the gospel, to impart to them eternal life, which is required for His Kingdom (John 3:16).

Personal faith in Christ as Redeemer is the condition of *regeneration* (John 1:12, 13). This is the message of the Word of God, and only by subscribing to this Word, does one have hope of being "*born again*" (1 Pet. 1:23).

Jesus announced that the Holy Spirit acts as the agent in *regeneration* (John 3:5, 6). It is the Spirit that brings conviction and opens the heart to receive the message of salvation. The Spirit imparts spiritual life in place of spiritual death, and turns humans from sin to God.

CONCLUSION

Some Christians know the precise time of their new birth. The resultant change was dramatic because it came when they were older and perhaps after a prolonged life of sin. Those who were brought up in a Christian home and professed faith in Christ at an early age may not remember the exact time or place of their salvation experience. The details are somewhat vague. In whichever one of these groups you may be, if you are trusting solely in Christ as Lord and Savior, you may rejoice in the inner witness of the Spirit, and know that you are a *born again* child of God (Rom. 8:16).

BASIC BAPTIST BELIEFS

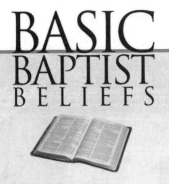

SALVATION IS A FREE GIFT

We believe in God's electing grace; that the blessings
of salvation are made free to all by the gospel; that it is the
immediate duty of all to accept them by a cordial, penitent
and obedient faith;
and that nothing prevents the salvation of the greatest sinner
on earth but his own inherent depravity
and voluntary rejection
of the gospel, which rejection involves him in
an aggravated condemnation.

CHAPTER 29

IN WHAT SENSE IS SALVATION FREE?

According to a recent Associated Press news report, a wealthy farmer in Italy left over a million dollars to the Roman Catholic Church. When asked, before he died, why he was planning to make such a generous contribution, he replied, "to atone for my sins." Like many well-meaning people today, the farmer thought of salvation as a commodity to be purchased.

In proclaiming God's universal call to salvation, the prophet Isaiah makes it abundantly clear that the only requirement necessary is a consciousness of need (thirst). Furthermore, Isaiah insists in picturesque language that God's offer of salvation does not come with a price tag (55:1). In the closing words of the Bible a similar emphasis is given. When the Spirit and bride give an invitation to those who are thirsty (a metaphor describing the spiritual condition of those without Christ), the appeal is universal in its scope, and again the offer has no invoice attached (Rev. 22:17).

THE OFFER OF SALVATION

On the last day of the Feast of Tabernacles in Jerusalem, Jesus cried out, *"If anyone is thirsty, let him come to me and drink"* (John 7:37). Jesus did not single out good people only, or even bad people only. He said, *"If **anyone** thirsts."* *"Anyone"* refers to rich or poor, religious or non-religious, Jew or Gentile. It is a universal call, because everyone in the world is spiritually thirsty. And again, no cost is attached to the invitation.

Paul echoed Isaiah's strong statement about God's universal offer of salvation when he affirmed that there was no distinction between Jew and Greek. The same Lord, who is over all, will generously give to all who call on Him. Indeed, anyone who calls on Him will be saved (Rom. 10:12, 13). The cross of Christ is broad enough and deep enough to cover all the sins of everyone who will come to Him.

Even though the offer of this great gift from God is genuine and available to all, many do not receive it. They refuse to believe in Jesus Christ. Jesus offered Himself to His own people, the Jews, during His earthly ministry; but His own people, by and large, rejected Him (John 1:11). However, the next verse points out that anyone who receives Him will be granted the *"right"* to become *"children of God"* (1:12).

When the Jewish leaders sought to kill Jesus, He got to the heart of their problem. He said they were not willing to come to Him that they might have life (John 5:40). The universal call of the gospel becomes effective only when it is joined with faith in the finished work of Jesus Christ (1 John 5:10).

THE CONVICTING WORK OF THE HOLY SPIRIT

The convicting work of the Holy Spirit is another facet of the truth of salvation (John 16:7-11). The one who brings about *conviction* when the gospel is presented is the Holy Spirit. Jesus said the Holy Spirit is our *Helper*, a word translated from the Greek, *parakletos*, "one called alongside to help." Jesus Christ is also our *parakletos*, our "advocate," the one who pleads our cause before God the Father in response to Satan's accusations against us. Also called *"the Spirit of truth"* (John 14:16-17; 15:26), the Holy Spirit is the other *parakletos*, the one called alongside to help sinners comprehend the true nature of sin and convince them that Christ is the answer to their dilemma.

The Greek word *elengkho* in John 8:46, usually translated as "convince" or "convict," basically means "to bring to light, to expose," that is, to demonstrate something clearly beyond the fear of successful contradiction. Jesus used the word in response to the Pharisees who challenged His claims about Himself. He charged the Pharisees to demonstrate beyond refutation that He was a sinner.

Hence, when the Holy Spirit convicts sinners, He is making the case stick, so to speak. The person being convicted in this way will know the truth of the matter in his or her heart. If they refuse the truth, it is because they allow Satan to blind their eyes to the truth. Salvation is free for the asking, but the asking part is essential.

The Holy Spirit convicts of *sin*, not just *sins*. We may help an alcoholic get over his drinking problem, thus sparing him some physical and social problems, but he will be no closer to Heaven by making such a choice. We may help a drug addict get over his addiction, or a liar to stop lying. But reformation alone is of no more value in one's spiritual quest than tying a plastic apple on an apple tree and pretending it is the real thing.

An unsaved person's real need is *not* to just get rid of certain sins. The Spirit of God never convicts the sinner of *sins* only. Instead, He chiefly convicts sinners of the sin of not believing on the Lord Jesus Christ. Getting people to put away their sins will not bring them to Christ. They need to be reborn spiritually. Only then will they receive a new nature—God's nature—which gives them new desires, a new outlook, and the power to gain victory over the sins that have enslaved them.

You can spend a lot of time picking leaves off a tree, but if you wait until the sap stops flowing, the leaves will fall off by themselves. Some trees are different. Oak trees often retain many of their leaves all through the blustery winter months. Not until the new sap comes up through the branches and twigs will the old leaves drop off. Instead of trying to force people to give up their sins, we need to confront them with the number one sin that plagues them—the sin of unbelief. Consequently, when they come to Christ, the new life surging through them causes the old, debilitating habits to drop off. The Holy Spirit's presence and power prompts all of this.

THE FIERCE OPPONENT OF SALVATION

The fact that the Holy Spirit is making a case for Jesus Christ through the truth spoken by believers to sinners does not mean the Devil has folded his hands and backed off. In fact, if anything, the battle has intensified. Satan and his minions desire to hide and distort the truth. Jesus reminded the Pharisees that the Devil was *"a liar and the father of lies"* (John 8:44).

The apostle Paul spoke of the Devil's insidious tactics. He presents a tantalizing commercial that seems perfectly suited to bring happiness to the sinner, but it is the way of death (2 Cor. 4:3-4). In Jesus' parable of the sower, He spoke of birds that devour the seed that is sown (Luke 8:5), and then explained that this pictures Satan's work (8:12).

In light of Satan's craftiness—remember the Garden of Eden—we need to be certain when conveying the gospel message that we are providing content that the Holy Spirit can use in defeating Satan and lifting the veil that blinds unbelievers.

We must never lose sight of the fundamental truth that the Gospel means *good news*, not *bad news*. When we give people the gospel in all its clarity and simplicity, we become instruments through whom God focuses His light on darkened human hearts.

One tool Satan has used perhaps more effectively than any other is that salvation is somehow to be merited and is not free. Something must be done to win God's favor. Thus, many try to bargain their way into favor with God. Others try to perform good deeds to win approval, while some strive to keep the Commandments or the Golden Rule or some religious ritual, hoping that will suffice.

CONCLUSION

Two things Scripture makes abundantly clear: first, salvation is freely offered to all who will receive it (Rom. 10:13; John 3:16); and second, salvation can never be merited or earned. The grace of God is the source of salvation, and faith is the channel through which God's grace flows. But it must be faith in the Lord Jesus Christ—nothing more, nothing less (Eph. 2:8, 9).

BASIC
BAPTIST
B E L I E F S

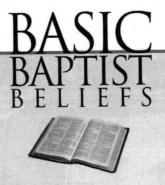

JUSTIFICATION

We believe that great gospel blessing which Christ secures
to such as believe in Him is Justification; that Justification
includes the pardon of sin and the gift of eternal life on
principles of
righteousness; that it is bestowed, not in consideration
of any works of righteousness which we have done,
but solely through faith in the Redeemer's blood.
His righteousness is imputed unto us.

CHAPTER 30

IS JUSTIFICATION BY FAITH OR FAITH PLUS WORKS?

Justification by faith is one of the most significant doctrines in the Word of God. It constituted a major part of Paul's teaching on salvation, but in the course of time the doctrine became greatly perverted and almost totally neglected. We are indebted to Martin Luther and other reformers in the 16th century for restoring this doctrine to its rightful place. Indeed, Luther declared that justification by faith is *"the article upon which the church stands or falls."* A proper understanding of this truth is essential to a comprehensive knowledge of salvation's meaning.

THE DEFINITION OF JUSTIFICATION

Justification may be defined as that act of God by which He declares a penitent sinner righteous, or regards him as righteous. The basis for this justification is not our obedience, goodness, or noble deeds, but the perfect righteousness of Jesus Christ (Rom 5:18, 19). The supreme need of unjust persons is righteousness. It is this lack of righteousness that is supplied by Christ on behalf of the repentant sinner.

By nature humans are not only children of the Devil; they are transgressors of God's law (Col. 1:21; Titus 3:3). On his own merit, the sinner stands before his holy Judge as a condemned criminal, guilty of sin and worthy of death. God's holiness requires Him to condemn and to punish the sinner. By His infinite love and mercy,

God provided that His sinless and perfect Son, Jesus Christ, would become the sinner's substitute.

As the sinner's substitute, Christ perfectly satisfied all the requirements of the law. He obeyed the law's precepts and suffered the law's penalty. He did this, not for Himself, but for guilty sinners (2 Cor. 5:21). The believer's sin is *charged* to Christ, and Christ's righteousness is *imputed* (*credited*) to the believer (Rom. 4:3).

When repentant sinners receive Jesus as their Substitute, they become vitally united to Him. They enter *into* Christ, and Christ enters *into* them. In consequence of this vital relationship, God can justly treat the sinner as if he himself had done those things which his Substitute did for him.

In view of the sinner's relation to his Substitute, God imputes Christ's righteousness to the sinner. On the basis of this imputed righteousness, which the sinner receives through faith, God as Judge declares that the sinner is righteous in relation to the law. He is justified; he is without condemnation. He has been restored to God's favor. He is not yet righteous in himself, but he is righteous in the forensic sense; that is, from the legal standpoint. It is a matter of declaring the person righteous, as a judge does in acquitting the accused.

It is not a matter of making the person righteous or altering his or her actual spiritual condition. The key word here is *declare*. Justification is a *declarative* act; it is not something wrought in man, but a *declaration* by God of the believer's new standing with his Creator.

THE MEANS OF JUSTIFICATION

Since sin first entered into the human family, the question has been pondered, *How can a person be just with God?* Justification is not a doctrine peculiar to the New Testament. Paul reminds us that Abraham was justified by faith (Rom. 4:1-5, 9-12). David also rejoiced in the fact of an imputed (or credited) righteousness (Rom. 4:6-8).

It is not by the works of the law.

Works performed by the sinner cannot be a basis for justification (Rom. 3:20; Gal. 2:16). The Bible clearly teaches, especially in the epistles of Paul, that salvation cannot be earned. One's natural goodness is without merit in God's sight (Isa. 64:6). The law was given to define and reveal sin and to compel the convicted sinner to submit to Christ (Gal. 3:24).

It is by the grace of God (Rom. 3:24; Titus 3:7).

Seeing that *grace* (*unmerited favor*) is the source of our justification, we are compelled to admit that salvation originated with God, not in our own good intentions.

It is by the blood of Christ (Rom. 5:9a).

As grace is the *source*, the blood of Christ is the *ground* of our justification. Because Christ has borne the punishment of our sins in His own body, God is able to remit the penalty and restore us to His favor.

It is by faith.

Roman Catholicism virtually makes the church's sacraments, especially baptism and penance, the basis for a person's acceptance by God. The Roman Catholic view affirms that justification is by faith, but denies that it is by faith alone, adding good works as a necessary condition.

The Scriptures plainly declare that justification is "*by faith*" (Rom 3:22, 27; 4:16, etc.) As we have seen, faith is the channel or instrument by which Christ is received and by which we are united to Him. We might compare faith to an electric cord or wire through which the current passes to provide light to a lamp. The wire does not provide the power. It is only the conduit through which the power flows. A person's faith is not sufficient in and of itself to save. It is merely the channel through which God's grace flows to the believing sinner.

If it is true, as numerous Scriptures attest, that faith in Christ alone results in justification, it means quite literally that all works are excluded (Rom. 3:28; Eph. 2:8,9).

WHEN A PERSON IS JUSTIFIED

Justification is an act, not a process.

There are no degrees of justification. A person who has been saved for fifty years is no more justified than a person who has been saved for fifty minutes.

Justification occurs at conversion.

The believer is declared justified by the Judge of the universe the moment he receives the Lord Jesus Christ. It is something that occurs all at once, unlike the believer's transformation, which is gradual, progressive, and continues throughout life (Acts 13:39; Rom. 8:30).

THE RESULTS OF JUSTIFICATION

Peace with God (Rom. 5:1).

All enmity between creature and Creator is gone. When Adam sinned in the Garden of Eden, his first response was to hide from God. Enmity between Creator and creature, unknown before the Fall, became a tragic reality. However, the act of justification, which results from a person's faith response to an invitation to receive the Lord Jesus Christ as personal Savior, eliminates the enmity and restores peace.

An Heir of God (Titus 3:7).

God henceforth will treat us as children. As His heirs, we shall be partakers of that inheritance which He confers on His people. That inheritance is His favor here and eternal life hereafter.

Freedom from condemnation (Rom. 8:33, 34).

No one will be able to condemn or bring a charge against us, seeing it is God who has justified us. All accusers are reduced to silence, now and in the future when we are summoned to stand before the Judgment Seat of Christ.

Good works.

James warned about a misunderstanding of justification by faith, that one can be justified by faith without manifesting corresponding good works. He showed that genuine faith cannot exist apart from works. Faith and works are inextricably linked. The works performed do not save but they display to the world the legitimacy of our faith (James 2:17-26). Neither works nor a dead faith lead to justification. It can be realized only by a genuine faith that after salvation leads one to do works by love (Gal. 5:6).

Assurance of salvation (Rom. 5:9).

Assurance of salvation means the authority of the Christian to echo the words of Paul, "I *know* the One in whom I have put my trust, and I have no doubt at all that he is able to safeguard what I have entrusted to Him and what He has entrusted to me until the day of His return" (2 Tim. 1:12, paraphrase). The justified person is assured that he will be saved from the wrath to come.

Assurance of glorification (Rom. 8:30).

Paul's use of the past tense ("*glorified*") indicates the certainty of our future glory. It is spoken of as a thing already done. Our hope of glory, but more, our certainty of Heaven, depends on our *justification*.

BASIC BAPTIST BELIEFS

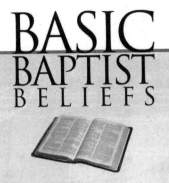

REPENTANCE AND FAITH

We believe that Repentance and Faith
are solemn obligations,
and also inseparable graces, wrought in our souls by the
quickening Spirit of God;
thereby, being deeply convicted of our guilt, danger, and
helplessness, and of the way of salvation by Christ, we turn
to God with unfeigned contrition, confession
and supplication for mercy; at the same time heartily
receiving the Lord Jesus Christ and openly confessing Him
as our only and all-sufficient Savior.

CHAPTER 31

WHAT IS TRUE REPENTANCE?

Sermons stressing the necessity of repentance are not heard too often these days. The reason for this is that *the concept of sin* has been minimized. Where there is no awareness of sin, there will be no disposition to repent. Nevertheless, this Bible truth is as essential today as it has always been. Human beings are still sinners who need a radical change in order to be brought into fellowship with their Creator. This change of attitude is spoken of in the Scriptures as *repentance*. It is the first condition of forgiveness (Acts 5:31).

THE MEANING OF REPENTANCE

The Greek verb repent (*metanoeo*) and the noun repentance (*metanoia*) are used many times in the New Testament. The common meaning is *a change of mind*. Repentance is a change of mind and attitude toward God and the things of which the gospel speaks (cp. Matt. 21:28, 29). The sinner normally is rebellious toward God, is hostile or indifferent toward the things of God, and often exalts himself above God (Rom. 3:11-12, 18; 1 Cor. 2:14).

Also, the sinner seeks to justify his wrongdoing or makes excuses for it. When he repents, he humbles himself before God and repudiates his sins. A keen awareness of the holiness of God and the enormity of his sins causes the sinner sorrow of heart, from which true repentance arises (2 Cor. 7:10). This change of mind and attitude was initiated by God Himself (Acts 11:18; 2 Tim. 2:25). Without true repentance there is no salvation (Luke 13:3).

Repentance involves confession of sin to God.

It involves confession to God and sometimes to fellow humans if the circumstances require it. The publican implied that he had broken God's law (Luke 18:13). The prodigal son confessed that he had sinned against God as well as his own father (Luke 15:11-21).

Priests, ministers, or other Christians do not have the right or the power to forgive sins, yet under certain conditions confession to them may be helpful. Any Christian has the authority to declare to a repentant sinner that his sins are forgiven for Jesus' sake.

Repentance involves forsaking sin (John 8:11; Prov. 28:13; Isa. 55:7).

The publican Zacchaeus in Luke 19, immediately after trusting in Jesus declared his willingness to make restitution for his practice of embezzlement, implying also that he was giving up his former dishonest habit.

Repentance involves turning to God.

No human is able to do what God has promised He would do for the repentant sinner. God alone can offer pardon and give peace. The apostle Paul stresses this point. The goal of his preaching was to turn unbelieving, skeptical, lost men and women from darkness to light, and from the power of Satan to God, that they might receive the forgiveness of sins and an everlasting inheritance among the saints (Acts 26:18).

Some Christians weaken the concept of repentance by emphasizing that it is only a change of mind, not necessarily of conduct. However, if changing one's mind does not alter one's life, what does it do? There is an inviolable principle that our actions are nothing more than the flowering of our deepest thoughts.

Jesus told Peter that the things which proceed out of our mouths spring from the heart, such things as evil thoughts, murder, sexual immorality, theft, lying, and slander (Matt. 15:18-20). The words must have had their desired effect on Peter, because after his powerful message on the day of Pentecost, his audience was convicted in their hearts (Acts 2:37). The heart is the seat of our deepest reflections and thus the source of all of our actions. So the Jews asked, "*What shall we do?*" They urgently wanted to do something to rectify their previous actions. Their change of mind about Christ and their sins demanded a change of action.

THE IMPORTANCE OF REPENTANCE

The Old Testament in no uncertain terms repeatedly stresses the truth of repentance. A representative and very specific statement to that effect is found in 2 Chronicles 7:14, where God says to His people that if they will humble themselves, pray, seek His face, and turn from their wicked ways, He will hear from Heaven, forgive their sin, and heal their land.

No portion of the New Testament neglects repentance. The Gospels, the Acts of the Apostles, and the Epistles all stress it. On the opening pages of the New Testament, John the Baptist startled his hearers with a strong message on repentance (Matt. 3:1, 2). Our Lord began His public ministry with the same emphasis (Matt. 4:17). When the disciples were first sent out to preach, Jesus commanded them to preach repentance (Mark 6:12). His final mandate to them was merely a repetition of His first command: they were to preach repentance among all nations, beginning at Jerusalem (Luke 24:47).

After Christ's ascension the apostles faithfully proclaimed the message of repentance (Acts 2:38; 17:30). The letters that were written by the apostles to the churches echoed the same refrain (Rom. 2:4; 2 Cor. 7:9-10).

CONCLUSION

Our world is faced with a desperate need to repent. Politicians, teachers, scientists, clergymen, economists, and sociologists predict that the future outlook is gloomy for the human race. Decaying cultures, declining standards of morality, Islamic terrorism, and increasing lawlessness all portend that unless we have a resurgence of spiritual values, a worldwide conflagration could be in the offing.

Although national sins must be confessed and forsaken, a nation is made up of individuals. National repentance begins with individual repentance. It must originate in the minds and hearts of God's people, spread to unbelievers, and finally become a mighty, national stirring of collective repentance. The individual is the key to the problem.

The burden of the heart of God, and His one command to all humans everywhere, is that they should repent (2 Pet. 3:9). Indeed, failure to heed God's call to repentance means that the unrepentant shall surely perish (Luke 13:3).

CHAPTER 32

WHAT ROLE DOES FAITH PLAY IN SALVATION?

Almost everyone cherishes the prospect of entering Heaven some day, but they often attempt to travel there using their own made-up road maps. The vast majority of people think performing good works qualifies them for Heaven. They are to be commended for endeavoring to keep the law and be good citizens. Others believe that character qualities are determinative, consequently they attempt to develop this area of their life. Again, they are to be applauded for their good morals and upstanding character, but they are wrong, foolishly and tragically wrong.

The Bible contradicts every effort on the part of humans to earn or merit salvation. Nothing short of true repentance (a complete turning to God), and faith in the Lord Jesus Christ will satisfy God's requirements (Acts 20:21). The Bible repeatedly stresses that faith, not works, will save the sinner (Eph. 2:8, 9; Heb. 11:6). God accepts no other righteousness than that of His Son, Jesus Christ. The effort to be saved by one's own righteousness always ends in miserable failure (Titus 3:5).

When a group of inquisitive Jews asked Jesus what they might do to perform the works of God, He surprised them by replying that the work of God was that they might believe on Him whom God had sent, meaning Himself (John 6:28, 29). They expected to hear a list of things to do. It was their firm conviction that a person living a good life could earn the favor of God. But Jesus enlightened them with a provocative truth: God's work was to believe on Him as their Messiah and Savior. Underlying what Jesus told these Jews is the urgent message that faith is the essential ingredient in doing the work of God.

THE IMPORTANCE OF FAITH

What gas is to your car's engine, faith is to Christianity. You cannot understand what Christianity is unless you understand what faith is. If there is one passage that makes this crystal clear it is Romans 3:21-30.

Faith is essential to Christianity. Not only can you not understand Christianity if you do not understand what faith is, you cannot be a Christian unless you have faith. So important is faith that we are told in Romans 3:28 that there is no justification apart from faith. It is only possible to enter into God's presence and not be condemned for our sins if we are justified by faith.

WHAT FAITH IS NOT

Faith is not feelings.

Some refuse to believe that Jesus is the Son of God, that He died as their substitute and rose again from the dead; nevertheless, they are convinced they will be welcomed into Heaven when they die, if there is a Heaven. When asked to express the basis for their hope, they reply that they *feel* they have lived a good life. Their faith is simply a subjective *feeling* that they have a right relationship with God.

Faith is not credulity.

Faith does not foolishly and gullibly believe everything that someone says about religion. There would not be such profit to be had from fraud and swindlers unless there were plenty of naive people in the world. John warns us not to believe everyone who comes to us in the guise of religion. Their message must be tested to see if it squares with God's Word (1 John 4:1, 2). Then he adds a further warning: there are many false prophets in the world (1 John 4:3). Jesus echoed the same warning in Matthew 7:15-20.

Faith is not based on sight.

Almost everything we do in life is based on our sense mechanisms —what we can see, what we can touch, what we have experienced, in other words, what our five senses tell us is true. But faith is not sight. Faith operates in an entirely different realm.

We see this illustrated in the life of Abraham. If Abraham is the pattern for God's people, faith is not sight. Abraham left the familiar surroundings of home and friends that he knew so well. He did not know where he was going (Heb. 11:8). He had never seen the land to which God was directing him. He was entering into the kind of life that was not based on what he could actually see with his eyes. Abraham was told when he was 75 years old and childless that he would be the father of a great nation. His response to that seemingly impossible challenge enabled him to be called, "The father of the faithful" (Rom 4:13-25).

The world says, "*Seeing is believing.*" But in the realm of faith this maxim is reversed, for in the spiritual world *believing is seeing.*

Faith is not ignoring reality.

Many people believe that Christianity, in the words of Karl Marx, is simply "the opiate of the people." It is a crutch. It is for people who cannot face the harsh realities of life; who invent a world in which there is a God, in which there is a future afterlife, in which there are rewards or punishments.

But according to the Bible, faith is not running from reality. It is not refusing to face the facts. We are told in Romans 4:19 that Abraham faced the reality that his body was as good as dead—since he was about a hundred years old—and that Sarah's womb was also dead. Faith is not pretending that things are going well when they are not going well.

WHAT FAITH IS

Simply stated, *faith is taking God at His Word.* It is a believing response to what God has revealed in Scripture. According to Hebrews 11: 1, faith gives substance to our hopes and is proof of things we cannot see with our physical eyes.

In this chapter, we are particularly interested in the roll faith plays in our salvation experience. There are *three elements of true faith*:

Knowledge.

No person can be saved without knowing something. As we have seen, faith is not closing one's eyes to the facts. Faith is never afraid to look truth squarely in the face. A person is not saved by knowledge, but he cannot be saved without it. It is the Word of God that brings right knowledge (Rom 10:17). If one is not exposed to the gospel message about Christ, one cannot be saved. To be saved, one must know that Christ, the Son of God, died to pay the penalty for each human's sins, was buried, and was raised again for the sinner's justification (1 Cor. 15:1-4; Rom. 4:25). But the bare knowledge of the historical fact will not save a soul. Two steps must follow.

Acceptance of the fact.

Acceptance must follow knowledge. A person must give rational assent to the facts of the gospel, that Jesus has paid the sin debt. Many people have long been exposed to the truth of the gospel, but they have not accepted it. To know the truth is not sufficient. Acceptance, or mental assent, is the next step.

Personal appropriation.

Knowledge is not enough, nor is mental assent. A decision must be made. This implies action—a movement toward an object. Jesus Christ is to be the object of one's faith if salvation is to be experienced.

The Scriptures affirm that Christ, not the church, not religious rituals, is to be the sole object of our faith. In the final analysis, ***whether or not we believe in Him will determine our eternal destiny.***

The Bible teaches that faith is essential for the following reasons:
- We are saved by faith (Rom 3:28; Eph. 2:8)
- We live by faith (Gal. 2:20)
- We are kept by faith (1 Pet. 1:5)
- We resist the Devil and overcome him by faith (1 Pet. 5:8, 9)
- We walk by faith (2 Cor. 5:7)

CONCLUSION

God has joined together repentance and faith in the act of salvation; and what God has joined together, humans must not separate. It is useless to argue which comes first, repentance or faith. What we do know is that we cannot have one without the other. Wherever there is true faith, there will be repentance; and wherever there is true repentance, there will be faith.

In order to please God, one must exercise faith. In no other way, or by no other means or method, is it possible to please God (Heb. 11:6).

D. L. Moody once commented that in his earlier days as a Christian, he often prayed for more faith, but faith did not come. One day he read in the Bible that faith comes by hearing the Word of God. At once he saw the light: faith is increased in proportion to our knowledge, understanding, and acceptance of the Word of God.

BASIC BAPTIST BELIEFS

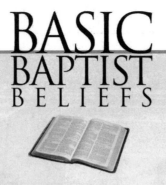

SANCTIFICATION

We believe that Sanctification begins at the moment a person is born again, when, by the will of God, we are made partakers of His holiness; that it is a progressive work; that it is carried on in the hearts of believers by the presence and power of the Holy Spirit, the Sealer and Comforter, in the continual use of the appointed means-- especially the Word of God, self-examination, self-denial, watchfulness, and prayer; that it will not be completed until we are changed into the likeness of Christ in the heavenly world.

CHAPTER 33

ARE ALL CHRISTIANS SANCTIFIED?

When a person is regenerated ("*born again*"), he immediately becomes a *child of God*, although many changes will later emerge in his life. He is a "baby" in Christ. However, we do not say of infants that they are not yet human because they are unable to do the things adults do, such as walking, talking, reading, reasoning and working. A new Christian, like a new baby, must go through a maturing process. At the outset of one's Christian experience, a believer may be unable to do what more mature Christians do; nevertheless, they are as much saved as they will always be. One can never be "more" saved than when first converted, anymore than a baby can ever be more human or more alive than when first born.

A new Christian, in one sense, is already sanctified, having received that gift at conversion; but the growth process leading to spiritual maturity is also called sanctification, a progression that will take many years and will not be entirely completed in this life.

The word "*sanctification*" is a translation of the Greek *hagiasmos* (from *hagiazo*), meaning "to make holy," "to consecrate," "to set apart." The Hebrew equivalent is *qadash*, "to separate from common use." Justification is what God does *for* us, while sanctification is what God does *in* us. Neither justification nor sanctification is the result of meritorious works. Both are solely due to Christ's grace and righteousness.

THE THREE PHASES OF SANCTIFICATION

First, sanctification is an accomplished act in the believer's *past.*

As to the believer's past, at the moment of conversion the believer is sanctified (*set apart*) because of what the Lord Jesus and the Spirit of God did for him (1 Cor. 6:11). He or she becomes a "*saint*." At that point the new believer belongs fully to God (6:19-20).

As a result of God's call, believers are identified as "*saints*" (Rom 1:7; 1 Cor. 1:2). They are such, not because they have achieved a state of sinless perfection, or because a College of Cardinals elevated them to that position, but because they are "*in Christ*" (Phil. 1:1; see also John 15:1-7). According to Paul, God's mercy has saved us (Titus 3:5), setting us apart and consecrating us to a holy purpose and walk with Christ.

Second, sanctification is a process in the believer's *present* experience.

There are two objectives in view with regard to sanctification: first, to put off the old way of life, that is, to eliminate the destructive behavior associated with our past; and second, to put on the new, to grow in grace and in the knowledge of our Lord and Savior Jesus Christ until we are conformed to His image.

"*Putting off the old.*" The Bible often refers to putting to death the old person, meaning that the believer is to remove the sins which characterized his life before being re-created in Christ Jesus. Indeed Paul says we are to consider ourselves dead to sin but alive to the things of God. Sin is not to control our lives in the manner it once did (Rom. 6:11, 12). Writing to the church at Colosse, Paul states that a Christian is to put to death the sinful, earthly things that may harm us, such as sexual immorality, anger, malicious behavior, slander, and filthy language (Col. 3:1-8; see also Gal. 5:19-21). Sanctification demands the elimination of those repulsive activities of the old nature that keep a Christian from being at his spiritual best for Jesus Christ.

"*Putting on the new.*" Some consider Christianity a negative faith. Unfortunately many seem to think that the test of sanctification is the commonly heard assertion: "I don't go to the movies, I don't dance, I don't smoke," etc. Yes, Christians must be warned to refrain from certain activities and pleasures which may be hazardous to their health or hurtful to their testimony.

On the other hand, we must not forget to stress the positive aspects of Christianity, which Paul is careful to do. Those harmful things that are to be removed must be replaced with *positive virtues* (Phil. 4:8). Since God chose us to be a set-apart, holy people, Paul appealed to believers to live a life dedicated to ethical values and moral purity (1 Thess. 4:7).

As new creations, believers have new responsibilities (Rom. 6:19; Gal. 5:25). Spirit-filled believers are controlled, not by their old, sinful nature, but by the Spirit of God (Rom. 8:3-9). The highest goal of the Spirit-filled life is *"to please God"* (1 Thess. 4:1). Sanctification is God's will for every believer (1 Thess. 4:3-7).

Third, sanctification is the final result the believer experiences in the *future* at Christ's return.

All of our very best, most determined efforts in this life fall far short of producing absolute perfection in our character. Even the greatest saints readily admit that the more intimate they become with the Lord, the more aware they are of their own flaws and failures. More times than we would like to admit, we feel compelled to echo Paul's words, *"Oh wretched man that I am"* (Rom. 7:24). When Isaiah caught a glimpse of the Lord seated on a throne, high and lifted up, it was as if he looked in the mirror and saw his own true self for the first time. The perfections of God, His holiness, justice, purity, and splendor, dazzled and humbled the prophet, and made him acutely aware of his own imperfections. No longer did he rationalize, "I'm as good as other men are and better than most." He admitted his utter weakness, wickedness, impurity, and deeply ingrained sinfulness (Isa. 6:1-5).

However, the day is coming when all the "former things" will pass away. When Christ returns, our weaknesses will vanish, our imperfections will be a distant memory, and our earthly, perishable bodies will be transformed into heavenly bodies that will never taste of death (1 Cor. 15:51-57). On that day of days, we shall experience a dramatic change that we have awkwardly and somewhat imperfectly attempted to accomplish during our earthly sojourn—we shall at last be "like Christ" (1 John 3:2; cf. Rom. 8:16, 17, 29; 2 Cor. 3:18). And if we are like Him, we will share in His perfections. Sanctification will have reached its final state.

THE EVIDENCE OF SANCTIFICATION

The sanctified life is the result of the power of the Holy Spirit working in the life of the believer, and manifests itself outwardly in the *"fruit of the Spirit"* (Gal. 5:22-24). Nowhere in this list of spiritual qualities are we told that we would always be happy, that we would be exempt from temptation, trials, difficulties or hardships.

The *"fruit of the Spirit"* relates to all the interactions of humans with others. *"Love,"* *"joy,"* and *"peace"* relate to the inner person. They cannot be demonstrated in life and action unless they first exist internally. *"Patience,"* *"kindness"* and *"goodness"* relate to one's fellow men. Sanctification sets one right with oneself and with others. *"Faith,"* *"gentleness"* and *"self-control"* relate to one's God. The balanced, sanctified life thus produces universally right relationships— to self, to others and to God.

The harvest of fruit the Spirit brings is completely opposite from the *"works of the flesh"* detailed in Galatians 5:19-21. Paul reminds us that when we live according to our new life in the Holy Spirit we will not fulfill the desires of the flesh (5:16).

AIDS TO SANCTIFICATION

God has not left His people to their own devices in their quest for spiritual maturity. He has provided means to assist us. These means are at our disposal but useless unless we intelligently and persistently avail ourselves of them.

The Holy Spirit is our helper.

The Holy Spirit lives within us to assist us on the journey to spiritual maturity. Being holy, He is able to make us aware of what it means to live a holy life and the blessing that results from pursuing such a life. To enable them to experience sanctification, believers are given the Holy Spirit, a gift bestowed by the Father and the Son (Acts 2:32, 33; Romans 8:1-39; Eph. 3:14-17).

The Word of God is our guide.

Just as the body needs food for physical growth and strength, so the soul needs food for spiritual growth and strength. Jesus prayed to the Father that He would *"sanctify"* Christians through the truth— *His* truth. Jesus added the all-important concept that the Bible is "*truth*" (John 17:17). Furthermore, as the body must be often cleansed with water, so the inner person needs the constant cleansing of the Word (John 15:3).

CONCLUSION

Sanctification has a beginning, a growth process, and a final result. It began the moment the believer was saved, it continues as the believer grows more like Jesus, and it will be complete when the believer is transformed at the return of Christ.

BASIC
BAPTIST
B E L I E F S

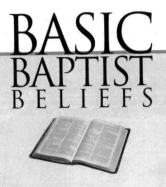

ETERNAL SECURITY

We believe that such only are real believers as endure unto the end, that their persevering attachment to Christ is the grand mark which distinguishes them from superficial professors; that a special Providence watches over their welfare; and that they are kept by the power of God through faith unto eternal salvation.

CHAPTER 34

CAN A SAVED PERSON
EVER BE LOST AGAIN?

Can those who have been truly born again cease to be saved; that is, revert to their former lost condition? Is it presumption to claim that a saved person is eternally secure? Contrary to what many Christian groups claim, it *is* possible for Christians to be certain of salvation and to know they will never cease to be children of God. They can sing with confidence:

> Blessed Assurance, Jesus is mine!
> O what a foretaste of glory divine!
> Heir of salvation, purchase of God,
> Born of His Spirit, washed in His blood.

Just as a good, responsible father assures his children they are loved, provided for, and protected, so our heavenly Father inspires confidence in His children in similar ways, namely through the promises of security in His Word. He does not want His children to feel unloved, fearful, or neglected. He is a caring, compassionate Father who never shirks his parental responsibilities. He not only begets us into His exclusive family circle, He safeguards His offspring. Consequently, the true believer knows he is promised eternal life (1 John 5:13). Doubt is minimized and he is able to walk with certainty because he knows, as Paul knew, that God is faithful and will keep him secure (2 Tim. 1:12). Paul deposited his soul in the safe-keeping of his Lord and Savior, and he was sure that He would faithfully guard that deposit.

It should be noted that there is a difference between assurance and security; yet they are inextricably connected. To have assurance is to be confident that Christ is your Savior, God is your heavenly Father, and the Holy Spirit is your ever present guide. A person may have assurance who does not accept as true the security of the believer; however, it is much more likely that one will experience assurance if one believes in the security of the believer. Security implies that even though a Christian may sometimes backslide and be disobedient, nonetheless, if he has been truly converted, he is secure even if there are lapses along the way.

THE SOURCE OF ASSURANCE AND SECURITY

It is a well-known and unfortunate fact that not every believer enjoys assurance of salvation. Because assurance is related to faith, and because every believer does not have strong faith, we can rightly expect that not every believer will enjoy the *"full assurance of faith"* (Heb. 10:22).

Assurance springs from faith, a faith that all believers can and should possess. On one occasion when our Lord had spoken some particularly difficult truths, His disciples pleaded with Him to increase their faith (Luke 17:5). This is a plea we often feel compelled to voice. So much of what we do or think or say is related to faith.

It is been said, *"faith is taking God at His Word."* Hence, we may conclude that if we are willing simply to believe what God has said— and He is not silent about the assurance that accompanies salvation—we will come into possession of that *"full assurance"* which is the rightful inheritance of every believer, not merely an elite few.

THE BASIS OF ASSURANCE AND SECURITY

Far too many make the common mistake of determining the status of their salvation on the basis of how they feel, their emotions, or their intuition. Human emotions fluctuate to such a degree that one would be unwise indeed to make those the basis of assurance. There are more reliable reasons that spring from the revealed truth of God. In other words, this comforting truth is not a matter of unfounded speculation, but of revelation. Consider the following fundamental reasons for assurance and security:

The unconditional promises of Almighty God (John 6:37).

God always clarifies whether or not His promises are conditional or unconditional. When conditional He uses the word *"if"* or its equivalent; when unconditional, He leaves out the *"if."* In John 6:37, there is no *"if."* Those who come to Him in faith, He will never cast out or drive away. In John 10 when Jesus said concerning His sheep (His true followers) that He had given them eternal life and they would never perish, He gave an unconditional promise (vss. 27, 28). He did not add, *"If they hold out,"* *"If they keep the commandments,"* or *"If they never commit another sin."* Either His promise is reliable or it is not.

God's ability to keep us.

It is one thing to *want* to keep us, it is quite another *to be able* to do so. The same God who sustains the world and protects it from disintegrating, is able to keep us (Jude 24, 25). Paul was convinced that the One who began the work of salvation in us would finish the job, or bring it to completion (Phil. 1:6). Had it been left to humans to achieve this, Paul would have expressed no such conviction. Just as we were woefully lacking in the ability or power to save ourselves, likewise we are noticeably deficient when it comes to keeping ourselves saved. If God is unable to keep us, what does this say about His power or attentiveness to our needs, not to mention His many promises to protect and keep us?

Peter, perhaps remembering his own weakness, asserted that we are *"kept by the power of God"* (1 Pet. 1:5). The word rendered *kept* in this verse means *to keep as with a military watch*. The idea is that there is a faithful guardianship exercised over us to protect us from danger, as a military post is watched to guard it against the approach of an enemy. The only reason that any Christian has to suppose he will ever reach Heaven, is the fact that God keeps him by His own power (2 Tim. 4:18; Rom. 8:31-39).

Christ's intercession for us (Rom. 8:34).

Christ's present ministry of intercession avails to keep us saved as much as His past work availed to save us in the first place (Rom. 5:8-10). If His death could accomplish so much in reconciling us to God, how much more may we expect that He will be able to keep us now that He is a living, exalted, triumphant Redeemer, who always lives to intercede for us (Heb. 7:25).

The promise of Jesus that He and the Father are pledged to keep us.

In the verses we considered previously (John 10:27-28), Jesus promised that none of His sheep would ever perish. To *"perish"* here means to be destroyed, or to be punished in Hell. The declaration of the Savior is that His followers, His true disciples, will never be lost again. That is His personal guarantee. He further affirms that both He *and* the Father are pledged to keep us so that we will never face the prospect of ending up lost.

Jesus goes so far as to declare that the saved person will *never* be condemned (John 5:24). The believer has been lifted out of the reach of condemnation and been given the gift of eternal life. If salvation can be forfeited, this statement of Jesus is meaningless.

The New Birth.

Scripture tells us that the believer has been regenerated—*"born again"*—and that in regeneration he becomes a new creation and receives a new life (2 Cor. 5:17). This new life is further described as *"eternal life"* (John 3:14-16).

Regeneration is a radical and supernatural change of the inner nature by which the person is made spiritually alive, and the new life of God implanted in the believer is immortal. Peter says the One who has called us by His divine power has given us everything necessary to live a godly life, including His very great and precious promises; and through them we have become partakers of the *divine nature* (2 Pet. 1:3, 4).

The born again person can no more forfeit one's relationship with the Heavenly Father than an earthly son or daughter can forfeit their relationship with an earthly father. But some might ask, "What if an earthly father disowns a child for some legitimate reason?" Does not that child cease to be his? Not at all. Indeed, nothing can change the fact that a father's genes and DNA are an integral part of that child's makeup. A father will never cease to be the father. Nothing can alter that reality. Though earthly parents may, for some reason, forsake their children, our heavenly Father plainly tells us that He will never leave us nor forsake us (Heb. 13:5). How implausible it would be for a person, once a child of God, to end up in Hell, bearing in his body His heavenly Father's DNA.

Furthermore, the Bible has nothing to say about being born again, and again, and again. The book of Hebrews makes clear that if a person *could* for some reason forfeit salvation, it would be impossible to be saved a second time (Heb. 6:4-6). The important phrase to consider in these verses is, *"if they fall away."* The writer does not say they *could* fall away, but *"if they fall away."* He is describing a hypothetical situation and demonstrating that salvation cannot be forfeited. If it were possible to lose one's salvation, there would be no hope of repeating the process and being *"re-saved"* (6:6). This goes counter to the practice of most Christian groups that affirm the possibility of losing one's salvation. Those who have gone back into sin and supposedly lost their salvation are often welcomed back into the fold after proper confession.

The writer of Hebrews adds in verse 9 that he is confident that no such apostasy would or could be committed by those reading his letter.

CONCLUSION

In faulting this belief, some have argued that if they believed in the security of the believer, they would get saved and then live as they please. This criticism, however, overlooks the power of change that occurs when one is born again. Paul says that those who are truly "in Christ" are "new creations." They are not the same as before, for the old life is gone and the new life has begun (2 Cor. 5:17).

The teaching of assurance and security is applicable only to those who have had a vital experience of salvation—the genuine elect of God. It does not apply to those who make a *"profession"* but who do not truly know Jesus Christ personally. Many who *profess* salvation do not *possess* salvation. Jesus warned about some on the Day of Judgment, who, though they had prophesied in the name of Christ, cast out demons, and done many mighty works, nevertheless would *not* be granted entrance into Heaven (Matt. 7:21, 22). Is it because they had somehow lost their salvation through disobedience? No, for Jesus will say to them, *"I **never** knew you"* (7:23). He did not say, "I *once* knew you but you sinned and lost everything."

This is not to say that a true Christian will never backslide, never fall into sin, or never be an embarrassment to the cause of Christ. Those who backslide can be assured of two things: first, their ever-watchful and loving Heavenly Father will be sure to discipline them (Heb. 12:5-11); and second, He will never abandon them (Heb. 13:5, 6). Furthermore, He will not leave unfinished the work He began in them the moment they first believed (Phil. 1:6).

BASIC BAPTIST BELIEFS

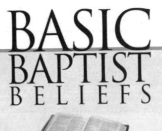

THE CHURCH

We believe that a church of Jesus Christ is a congregation of baptized believers associated by a covenant of faith and fellowship of the Gospel; observing the ordinances of Christ; governed by His laws; and exercising the gifts, rights and privileges invested in them by His Word; that its officers of ordination are pastors or elders and deacons, whose qualifications, claims and duties are clearly defined in the Scriptures. We believe the true mission of a church is found in the Great Commission; First, to make individual disciples; Second, to build up the church; Third, to teach and instruct as He has commanded. We do not believe in the reversal of this order; we hold that the local church has the absolute right of self government, free from the interference of any hierarchy of individuals or organizations; and that the one and only superintendent is Christ through the Holy Spirit; that it is scriptural for true churches to co-operate with each other in contending for the faith and for the furtherance of the Gospel; that every church is the sole and only judge of the measure and method of its co-operation; on all matters of membership, of polity, of government, of discipline, of benevolence, the will of the local church is final.

CHAPTER 35

WHO INSTITUTED THE CHURCH?

The all-important subject of *salvation* has been the theme in recent chapters. The crucial questions now arise: What are new believers to do once they have experienced conversion? Where do they go for spiritual nourishment and fellowship? Where can they find people like themselves? This is where *the local church* plays a vitally important role. New believers are not left to their own resources or to grope in the dark; nor are they to be an island to themselves.

The church is to become the focal point of the Christian's spiritual life, providing inspiration, fellowship, instruction, opportunity for corporate worship, and a means whereby they can put to use their spiritual gifts. Committed participation in a local congregation is essential to becoming what God wants us to be (Heb. 10:24, 25). For these reasons, it is essential that we know something of the church's founding and its true head.

IT WAS FOUNDED BY CHRIST

In the Scriptures the word "church" is a translation of the Greek *ekklesia* which means "a called out assembly." The Septuagint, the Greek version of the Hebrew Old Testament popular in Jesus' time, used *ekklesia* to translate the Hebrew *qahal*, which stood for "gathering," "assembly," or "congregation" (Deut. 9:10; 18:16; 1 Sam. 17:47; 1 Kings 8:14; 1 Chron. 13:2). Among the Greeks an *ekklesia* was an assembly of free citizens *called out* from their homes and places of business to give consideration to matters of public interest (Acts 19:32, 39, 41).

As the word is used in the New Testament, it denotes the institution founded by our Lord Jesus Christ. According to the New Hampshire Confession of Faith, a church is *"a congregation of baptized believers, associated by covenant in the faith and fellowship of the Gospel; observing the ordinances of Christ; governed by His laws; and exercising the gifts, rights, and privileges invested in them by His Word."*

The word *church* or *churches* is found in the New Testament over 100 times, and always it retains its primary and simple meaning—a public assembly or congregation. The majority of times the word *church* is used, its reference is unmistakably to a local congregation or assembly, in keeping with the primary and simple meaning of the term. The remaining instances refer to churches in general (Matt. 16:18; Eph. 1:22; 3:10, 21; 5:23,24, 25, 27, 29, 32; Col. 1:18, 24; Heb. 12:23). For example, if a pastor announces that he will begin a series of messages on "The Home," he is not referring to a particular home but to all homes in general. When Paul announced that *"Christ loved the church and gave himself for it,"* (Eph. 5:25), he meant not only the church at Ephesus, but all true, Bible-based churches that have ever existed or would ever exist.

IT IS A DIVINE INSTITUTION

It was born in the heart of God, not in the mind of man (2 Cor. 1:1; 1 Tim. 3:15). Scripture writers refer to *"the churches of God"* or the *"churches of Christ"* (1 Thess. 2:14; Rom. 16:16). Such expressions denote not only the divine origin of the church, but that every Bible-based church looks to God as its source of authority.

The church is first mentioned by our Lord in Matthew 16:18. In response to Peter's confession that Christ was *"the Son of the living God,"* Jesus stated that it would be on *"this rock"* He would build His church. This revelation had been hidden from previous generations, but was now made known to Peter and the rest of the disciples.

The statement was *not* meant to imply that Peter would be the rock on which the church would be built, as Roman Catholic's contend. When Jesus addressed Peter, He used the Greek word *Petros* for Peter's name. It means a specific stone or rock. When Jesus added,

"*On this* **rock** *I will build my church*," He used another Greek word for rock—*petra*, which mean a rocky crag or bedrock. Jesus did not say, "On you, Peter (*Petros*), and on your successors, I will build my church." Instead, it would be built "on *this* rock (*petra*)"—the divine revelation given to Peter, his confession that Jesus Christ was "*the Son of the living God*" (16:16). In other words, every Bible-based church would be built on Jesus Christ, not on any human being. The apostle Paul declared that no one can ever lay any other *foundation* than the one already laid, which is Jesus Christ" (1 Cor. 3:11).

IT IS THE BODY OF CHRIST

Being the body of Christ, each local church is the tangible representation of Jesus' life on earth (1 Cor. 12:21). The body analogy expresses Paul's belief that Christ is present on earth in tangible form—in His churches. To be "in Christ" means we cannot stand at a distance from this body. A body part detached from other parts is clearly useless. Life in Christ is a corporate affair; hence, the importance of participation in the ordinances and ministry of a local, Bible-believing church.

Because Christ founded the church, it follows that He should be the accepted Head of that institution. Paul affirms this when he pictures the church as a human body with only one head, Jesus Christ (Col. 1:17-18). As the Head of the body—the source of the body's life—Jesus Christ directs and guides. Jesus is the "Chief shepherd" of the church (1 Peter 5:4); the human leader is the "under-shepherd." A recognition of Christ as the Head of the church by both pastor and flock will manifest itself in a healthy congregation.

IT IS THE BRIDE OF CHRIST

In the New Testament, Christ is represented as the bridegroom and the church as His bride. All true churches make up the bride of Christ.

The bride is purchased by Christ.

The beautiful intimacy of Christ and His church is revealed by Paul in Ephesians 5:25. Paul holds up the conduct of Christ towards the church as the model for a husband to imitate. The love of Christ for His bride was so selfless and strong that He was willing to give up His very life on her behalf. This was the strongest love that has ever been demonstrated in this world. The purpose of this relationship between Christ and His bride is to produce fruit (Rom 7:4).

The bride is cleansed by the Word.

Not only did Jesus die for His bride, He provided the means whereby the bride can maintain her virtue (Eph. 5:26).

A similar thought is presented by Paul in 2 Corinthians 11:2. The allusion here is to the custom among Greeks of having an older person of rank and reputation, whose business it was to educate and form young women preparing for marriage (especially those from well-to-do homes), and then to present them to those who were to be their husbands. If this tutor, through negligence, permitted them to be corrupted between the engagement and the consummation of the marriage, great blame would result. Paul was anxious for the purity of the church which was to constitute *"the bride, the Lamb's wife"* (Rev. 21:9).

This purity is maintained by devotion to *"the Word."* By this means the church is *"sanctified"* and *"cleansed"* (John 15:3). Christ purifies the members of the church—taking away their filthy garment and clothing them in the robe of His perfect righteousness—through the sanctifying influence of the truth of God's Word (17:17).

The bride's glorious destiny.

Not only does Christ's love nourish His bride, the church, He will one day present it to Himself in all its splendor, not having a spot, a wrinkle, or any such thing. It will be holy and without blemish (Eph. 5:27). Here is a magnificent description of the final glory of the church. There will be no more imperfections, no more church fights or splits, no more lukewarmness, no more false doctrine.

It cannot be denied that here, even in the best of churches, there is much that is imperfect and impure. But in that future world, where the church shall be presented to Christ, clothed in the robes of righteousness, there shall not be one unholy member, one deceiver or hypocrite, one covetous or pride-filled person, one that shall grieve the friends of purity by an immoral life. That will truly be *"a day of rejoicing."*

CHAPTER 36

HOW IS A CHURCH
TO BE GOVERNED?

The local church was brought into existence to meet the needs of those who have become followers of Jesus Christ. It is to a believer what a home is to a family. A home is not a house; that is, it is not the physical materials out of which that edifice is constructed. Rather, a home is usually composed of a husband and wife, and oftentimes children, who come together at what is called the "house" for the purposes of nurture, intimacy, protection, sustenance, rest, and companionship.

Likewise, a church is not the building; it is the *ekklesia*, the "*called out*" group of individuals who come together at a certain location for a stated purpose. Our Lord takes into account the need of humans for corporate worship and fellowship. The church is designed to aid us in tangible and substantive ways. But the church exists for reasons other than providing a suitable atmosphere for worship and fellowship. It is to be a training center where men and women, boys and girls, are taught not only how to know God better, but how to make Him known to others. A smooth running, effective church with a strong teaching and evangelistic outreach reflects its leadership. How a church is governed is of such strategic importance that it will often spell the difference between the success and failure of that local congregation.

THE GOVERNMENT OF THE CHURCH

Baptists believe that the government of a church is congregational, that is, it is to be governed by the whole membership. The membership or constituency of each church is entrusted with the duty and responsibility of carrying out the law and will of Christ as it is expressed in the New Testament. This is to be done under the leadership of the Holy Spirit. A study of the life and practice of the church at Jerusalem, the mother of all New Testament churches, as well as other churches mentioned by the apostles, amply demonstrates this principle:

The equality of believers and deep sense of brotherhood characterized the early churches (Matt. 23:8-12; Acts 1:14; 2:33-47).

The New Testament churches could discipline and exclude their own members as well as receive them into fellowship (1 Cor. 5:4-5, 13).

Each church received and was responsible for the observance and protection of the ordinances (1 Cor. 11:2).

It is apparent that the churches cited in the New Testament regarded Christ as the Head, the Holy Spirit as the Administrator, and the Word of God as the only law.

Each Baptist church is *autonomous* (self-governing). No hierarchical body can dictate to any local church as to how its business is to be conducted. Each church selects its own pastor and staff. The church owns its own building—the denomination cannot seize the property—and should a church close its doors, the members dispose of the property as they see fit. The will of the local church is final. At the same time, a congregation manifests its unity by joining with other Baptist churches in fellowships, associations, conventions, networks, etc., for the purposes of fellowship, mutual assistance, and the support of common educational, evangelistic, and missionary goals.

The Officers of the Church

The New Testament speaks of two church offices: *pastors* and *deacons*. The importance of these offices is underscored by the high moral and spiritual requirements set for those who would fill them.

Pastors.

Three terms are used interchangeably in the New Testament to denote the person who is to give leadership to each church: "*pastor,*" "*elder*," and "*bishop*." This was and is the most important officer of the church.

The word "*pastor*" (Greek, *poimen*) means "*shepherd*" (Eph. 4:11). As a shepherd tends, feeds, protects, and leads his sheep, so the pastor performs a similar function for his congregation. "*Bishop*" (Greek, *episkopos*) means "*overseer*," one who superintends or looks after the church, being vigilant to protect it from scandal or false doctrine. The term "*elder*" means "*older one*," implying dignity and respect. The pastor's position is similar to that of the one who had supervision of the synagogue. Paul used these terms interchangeably, equating them with each other (Acts 20:17, 28; Titus 1:5-9). Those who held this position administered the newly formed churches.

The qualifications for the pastor are spelled out in ample detail in 1 Timothy 3:1-7. It is the responsibility of the pastor to lead his people well and set a godly example before them (1 Pet. 5:1-4). He is to model the Christian lifestyle, and set examples of liberality (Heb. 13:7; Acts 20:35). While both men and women are gifted for service in the church, the office of pastor is limited to men as qualified by Scripture (1 Tim. 3:2).

To a large extent, effective church leadership depends on the faithfulness of the pastor and the loyalty of the membership. Paul encourages believers to respect their leaders and to have a high regard for them because of the work they perform (1 Thess. 5:12, 13). It is the duty of the people to cooperate with the pastor and submit to his leadership (Heb. 13:7, 17). When members make it difficult for the leader to perform his God-assigned responsibilities, both will experience grief and the church will suffer.

This office, of course, is subordinate to the Head of the church, Jesus Christ. No man should seek to usurp His place and prerogatives. No Christian should aid or abet the schemes of any individual or group that seeks to deprive the Lord of His headship.

Deacons.

The word "*deacon*" comes from the Greek *diakonos*, meaning "servant," or "helper." The office of deacon was instituted to enable the apostles to give themselves fully to prayer and the ministry of the Word (Acts 6:3). While all Christians are to serve, certain ones were officially recognized in the New Testament as servants of the church.

The chief function of deacons is to look after the temporal affairs of the church, not only ministering to the poor and needy, but also assisting the pastor in the management of the church's properties and funds, and in the observance of the ordinances (Acts 6:1-7). Deacons are not to usurp the authority of the pastor, who is the rightful "overseer" of the church.

THE DISCIPLINE OF THE CHURCH

Christ gave the church the authority to discipline its members and provided the proper principles for doing so. He expects the church to implement these principles whenever necessary to maintain its lofty calling of being a "*holy priesthood*" and a "*holy nation*" (cf. Matt. 18:15-18; 1 Pet. 2:5, 9).

Two extremes usually prevail when it comes to church discipline. Either the church is too strict, developing stringent rules that go beyond Scripture, making it impossible except for a select few to measure up; or they are too lenient. Those in the latter category have too low expectations of their members.

The church must be careful to maintain high standards, being certain they are Biblical standards, while at the same time impressing upon erring members the need for amending their ways. Christ commends the church of Ephesus because it could not bear those who were evil (Rev. 2:2), but He rebukes the churches of Pergamum and Thyatira for tolerating heresies and immorality (Rev. 2:14, 15, 20).

For a church to impress the world, its members must live lives that are above reproach. Such conduct will silence the ignorant talk of those who foolishly oppose the Christian message (1 Pet. 2:15).

BECOMING A MEMBER OF THE CHURCH

The concept of *a regenerated church* membership or *a believer's church* is one of the chief distinctives of Baptists and one for which they were persecuted in times past. No one is knowingly admitted into a Baptist church who is unconverted. A Baptist church receives members in three different ways:

By baptism.

The next chapter offers a full discussion of baptism, how that ritual always follows true repentance, is a symbolic act, not part of the salvation decision, and is the door of admission into the church.

By letter.

This means the prospective member is a baptized believer and is coming from a sister church whose beliefs correspond with the one being joined.

By statement of faith.

This implies that the prospective member has been previously converted and properly baptized, but the previous church where the person was a member no longer exists or the address is unknown. Other special factors may be considered, depending on the policy of each local congregation.

BASIC
BAPTIST
B E L I E F S

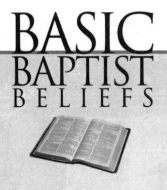

BAPTISM AND
THE LORD'S SUPPER

We believe that Christian baptism is the immersion in water of a believer in Jesus Christ in the name of the Father, of the Son, and of the Holy Spirit, with the authority of the local church, to show forth in a solemn and beautiful emblem our faith in the crucified, buried and risen Savior, with its effect in our death to sin and resurrection to a new life; that it is pre-requisite to the privileges of church membership and to the Lord's Supper; in which the members of the church, by the sacred use of bread and the fruit of the vine are to commemorate together the dying love of Christ; preceded always by solemn self-examination.

CHAPTER 37

WHY IS BAPTISM
A REQUIREMENT?

Only *two symbolic rites* are to be carried out by the church: *baptism* and *the Lord's Supper*, both of which were especially ordained by Jesus Christ Himself, thus called *ordinances*. An ordinance is a decree or command. Although the word "ordinance" is never used in the Bible in specific reference to baptism and the Lord's Supper, it best expresses the truth about these two rites (the Greek *paradosis* in 1 Cor. 11:2 can be translated "ordinance," "precept," or "tradition," and may indirectly refer to baptism and the Lord's Supper). Both baptism and the Lord's Supper are rites Jesus commanded believers to observe (Matt. 28:19; Luke 22:19; 1 Cor. 11:23-26). Each richly illustrates the saving work of Christ and the new spiritual relationship between Him and His people.

In the New Testament an inseparable link exists between salvation and baptism; yet they are not to be confused as being one and the same. Salvation or conversion is a new birth imparted from above. Baptism is an outward *picture* or *symbol* of salvation; it does not save or even contribute to the salvation experience (1 Pet. 3:21; 1 Cor. 1:17). Nevertheless, when there is a conversion in the New Testament, baptism soon follows (Acts 8:36-38). Baptism was considered a matter of extreme importance in the early churches. It symbolized a clean break with the past, which involved giving up the habits of the old life, and often family and friends as well.

Our Lord never gave an arbitrary command; thus while baptism is not essential to salvation, it is very clearly required by the Lord Jesus Christ, and believers are therefore bound to seek baptism in obedience to Him.

THE ORIGIN OF BAPTISM

The rite did not start with Jesus. Gentile converts to Judaism were required to submit to baptism as a sign of cleansing. When John the Baptist appeared on the scene he gave a new significance to baptism. Repentance and confession of sin were required of those who sought baptism at his hands (Matt. 3:6, 11). Jesus declared that the baptism of John was divinely authorized (Matt. 21:25). Some have denied that John's baptism was Christian baptism. Paul, however, maintained that John told the people that believing on Jesus Christ was a requirement for baptism (Acts 19:4). The converts at Ephesus were rebaptized, not because they had only experienced John's baptism, but because they failed to understand the full significance of John's baptism. When it became necessary to fill the vacancy in the apostleship left by Judas, one of the requirements was that the person had to have been baptized by John the Baptist like all the other apostles (Acts 1:22). If John's baptism was not Christian baptism, why was rebaptism not required of all the apostles?

THE IMPORTANCE OF BAPTISM

What makes baptism so important, considering it is not essential to the salvation of the one who has already believed on Jesus Christ?

It inspires churches.

It gives a clear declaration to that local church and to the world around that this new believer is ready to obey and serve his Lord and Master. If baptism is neglected, the Lord's command is disregarded and obstructed by the very people who should be His loyal followers.

It helps believers to solidify and express their own testimony.

It impresses their conversion experience upon their minds in such a way that their gratitude increases and their assurance is strengthened. Furthermore, they realize that whereas their conversion has been an inward, unseen transaction between themselves and the Lord, it must now be expressed and lived out before the eyes of the world and fellow believers.

It reminds believers of the importance of conversion.

Just as the Lord's Supper keeps the crucifixion in view, the act of baptism reminds us of the great importance of conversion, that we are a *"royal priesthood"* whose chief objective is to declare to the world the praises of Him who has called us out of darkness into His marvelous light (1 Pet. 2:9). Every baptismal experience profoundly moves the people of God, lifts their morale, and encourages them to become involved in the great task of reaching others with the gospel. Baptism places the necessity and glory of evangelism at the forefront of the life of the church.

It presents a powerful message to unbelievers.

When unbelievers are confronted by the visible testimony of those who pass through the waters of baptism, their complacency is often shattered in a new and dramatic way. They see that they must respond to the Word, and that nothing short of the new birth is genuine Christianity. The testimony of baptism often speaks powerfully to an unbeliever. Baptism says that to become a member of the family of God, a member of the church, an experience of conversion is essential.

WHAT BAPTISM SIGNIFIES
It is a picture of the death, burial, and resurrection of Christ (Rom. 6:3-5).

It is the believer's way of affirming his trust in the cornerstone of our faith: the *gospel*, which encompasses the *death* (under water), *burial* (covered by the water), and *resurrection of Christ* (brought out of the water alive by the strength of another, Acts 2:22-24). The Bible establishes that it is by believing the gospel that we are saved (1 Cor. 15:1-4). The sinner deserves death because of his sin, but Jesus died in the sinner's place.

It is a picture of new life (2 Cor. 5:17).

Baptism by immersion vividly illustrates this new life because it depicts the processes of burial and rising again. Paul echoes the same thought in Colossians 2:12. Baptism pictures a believer's death to his sinful past and former life-style. At the same time it speaks of how he was raised up (through the new birth) to live a new life.

It is a picture of obedience.

The message of Scripture is clear: *"Repent, and be baptized"* (Acts 2:38). The call to repent is obeyed in the privacy of one's heart, but the command to be baptized is obeyed in an outward, visible way as a public display of one's obedience to God. Obedience is a true test of one's conversion experience. Although baptism may be a humbling and sometimes frightening experience, obedience to the act is proof that one's conversion is authentic. Jesus declared that if we truly love Him, we *will* keep His commandments (John 14:15).

It is a picture of forgiveness.

It speaks to both believers and unbelievers, proclaiming that the washing away of sin is the vital heart of salvation. When believers are baptized, they figuratively say, *"I have been washed entirely clean in the blood of the Lamb of God, Jesus Christ."* Baptism is an eloquent declaration that the washing away of all guilt is necessary for real conversion to God. Naturally, only the complete submersion of the body in water gives an adequate picture of total forgiveness.

It is a picture of identification with Christ.

True believers now belong to Christ. They identify with Him, stand with Him, represent Him, love Him, live for Him, and they will be faithful to Him. In being baptized, believers follow the Lord's example, doing exactly what He did (Matt. 3:13-15). Jesus had no sin and did not need to be baptized as a sign of His own repentance. He did it to *"fulfill all righteousness."* Whatever the full implications of that statement might be, the important point is that, by submitting to baptism, Jesus saw fit to identify himself with the penitent people of God in order to fulfill his mission. Baptism, then, is a wonderful expression of our unity with Christ and with all His interests. At the same time, it is our way of identifying with the rest of God's people who have taken the same path. Jesus' baptism forever gave this ordinance divine sanction.

CONCLUSION

Often the symbolism of baptism is compared to *a wedding ring*. A ring on the third finger of the left hand usually represents the marital status of the person wearing the ring. The ring does not make the person married; it is merely a symbol identifying the person as being married. Nor does the ring reveal what kind of husband or wife the person may be. In like manner, baptism does not make the person a Christian; nevertheless, it identifies the person as a Christian, though it may not reveal what kind of Christian the person is or may become.

Can any born-again believer refuse baptism or question its importance, when our Lord set the example by walking almost 60 miles to be baptized by John the Baptist in the Jordan River? In baptism we say to the congregation we are joining and to unbelievers, "I am now a follower of the Son of God, the Lord Jesus Christ. From henceforth I will be obedient to Him who loved me and gave Himself for me."

Let us never forget that Christ *commanded* baptism for all His people. He does not merely suggest that we be baptized. Neither does He advise or recommend it. The same Lord who set the example for us by submitting to the rite of baptism; the one who suffered, bled, and died that we might participate with Him in the blessings of the heavenly world, commands that we follow Him and obediently submit to this act.

CHAPTER 38

WHY MUST BAPTISM BE BY IMMERSION?

Some claim the mode of baptism is immaterial. They say it is foolish to disagree over how much water is used. However, if baptism is a symbol designed by our Lord, the way it is carried out is obviously of great importance. He designed baptism as a picture of His own death, burial and resurrection. When Christ's body was buried, it was out of sight, completely submerged under the earth. Because baptism is intended to picture Christ's death, burial and resurrection, as well as our own death to sin and resurrection to a new life, much water is needed to convey the proper symbolism. The entire body must be buried beneath the water, and raised up out of the water by the power of another.

THE BIBLICAL MODE OF BAPTISM
It is by immersion.

The word *baptize* is an English spelling of the Greek *baptizo*, which means to dip in or under water; to immerse. Few will dispute the basic dictionary definition of the term. Why then was the Greek word *baptizo* not translated but merely anglicized? No doubt it was to avoid embarrassment on the part of the translators whose church tradition required sprinkling or pouring rather than immersion.

A large quantity of water seems to have been important to John, for it is reported that he was baptizing in Aenon near Salim because there was plenty of water there (John 3:23). Only immersion would require a large quantity of water. When Philip baptized the Ethiopian governmental official, they both went down into the water and both came up out of the water (Acts 8:38, 39). Going down into the water to baptize is a totally superfluous activity if sprinkling or pouring satisfies the meaning of the word *"baptize."*

John Calvin, the celebrated Reformation leader, was not an immersionist; nevertheless, he admitted that the words in these last two references refer to immersion. He wrote, *"From these words it may be inferred that baptism was administered by John . . . by plunging the whole body under water . . . Here we perceive how baptism was administered* [in New Testament times] *. . . for they immersed the whole body in water."*

WHY BAPTISTS DO NOT BAPTIZE INFANTS

The reason Baptists do not baptize infants is that the only baptism described in the New Testament is believer's baptism. Believer's baptism presupposes that the person being baptized has personally and consciously believed on the Lord Jesus Christ for salvation. This is made clear from the wording of the Great Commission in Matthew 28:18-20. Jesus commanded His disciples to "go" and *"teach"* all nations, then baptize them. The Greek word translated *"teach"* literally means "make disciples." First, the person becomes a disciple, that is, a believer in Jesus Christ (this cancels out baptismal regeneration), and then baptism follows. You cannot make a disciple of someone (for instance, an infant) who is incapable of understanding what a disciple is.

Peter's sermon on the Day of Pentecost ended with this appeal: *"Repent, and be baptized every one of you"* (Acts 2:38). Here, baptism follows repentance (which obviously refers to someone old enough to repent).

There is no record of infants being baptized in the Bible.

In writing to the churches of Galatia, Paul declared that they were children of God as a result of their faith in Jesus Christ (Gal. 3:26). In those days Paul could assume that every converted person had been baptized, and every baptized person had been converted. There is no recorded instance in the Bible where infants were baptized.

All the people named in the New Testament in connection with baptism were adult believers. Then where does the idea of infant baptism originate? It is simply an assumption. It has to be read into the text.

It is often assumed by those who believe in infant baptism (pedobaptists), that when the jail keeper at Philippi was baptized, his infant children were baptized along with him (Acts 16:33). But did he have infant children? The argument is solved for us by consulting the previous verse. There it declares that Paul and Silas spoke the word of the Lord to all that were in his house (16:32). In other words, they were old enough to understand the message and to personally respond to it. Furthermore, in verse 37 we are told that the jailer was rejoicing along with all his family members. Needless to say, infants are not old enough to rejoice in a salvation experience.

The point that baptism is for believers only is further reinforced in Acts 2:41, where it states that those who *"gladly received his word"* (i.e., the gospel, or the Word of God that Peter had preached) were baptized. Infants do not have the capacity to receive the Word, much less to receive it *"gladly."*

There is no proof that babies were included in "household baptisms."

Four times in the New Testament reference is made to *"household baptisms"* (1 Cor. 1:16; Acts 10:48; Acts 16:15; Acts 16:33). In the case of the household of Cornelius (Acts 10:48), the people who gathered to hear Peter were Cornelius' relatives and close friends (10:24). No infants are mentioned. Nothing is said about Lydia having a family in Acts 16. In fact, no mention is made of her being married. In all probability her household consisted of adult servants, old enough to have the capacity to believe. In the case of the household of Stephanus (1 Cor. 1:16), Paul says in the same letter that the members of this family had committed themselves to the service of the saints (16:15). The family was devoted to assisting the poor and needy in the church, which proves that it was a family of adults and older children. Only four passages mention *"household baptism,"* and no proof can be given that any of them involved infants.

CONCLUSION

We are confident that the apostles and pastors of the early

churches baptized only believers, and always by immersion. The New Testament offers no evidence that sprinkling was ever an apostolic practice; indeed, the evidence all points to it being a late introduction.

Infant baptism is first mentioned in a treatise on baptism by Tertullian, written between A.D. 200 and 206, long after the New Testament was completed. Only brief mention is made of infant baptism in the treatise, and Tertullian clearly points out that he strongly opposed it. However, during the next two centuries, infant baptism became a widespread practice.

As we might expect, the original form of baptism (believer's baptism) did not completely die out. History records the existence of those who practiced believer's baptism from the first century after Christ. During those early centuries, and for centuries thereafter, many of those who insisted that believer's baptism alone satisfied the Biblical requirement were severely persecuted. During the reign of Mary Tudor (1553 to 1558) some of the almost 300 burned at the stake were those who refused to permit their infants to be baptized, believing rather that baptism was only for those old enough to personally trust in Christ.

Many Baptist churches frequently have special times of dedication for infants and their parents, but baptism is not part of this ceremony. It has nothing to do with the salvation of the child. The ceremony is merely recognition on the part of parents that *children are God's gift to them* (Ps. 127:3). They are pledging to bring up their child with that solemn thought in mind, hoping and praying that one day, when the age of accountability is reached, the child will receive Jesus Christ as Lord and Savior.

CHAPTER 39

WHAT IS THE PURPOSE OF THE LORD'S SUPPER?

Baptism is an ordinance of the church, approved and commanded by the Lord Jesus Christ, the prerequisite to the privileges of church membership, including participation in the Lord's Supper. The Lord's Supper is the only other ordinance committed to churches by Christ. As Jesus observed His last Passover with the disciples, He instituted this ordinance in place of the Passover to memorialize His great sacrifice. Taking the unleavened bread, He blessed it, broke it and gave it to the disciples, revealing to them that it was His body that was broken for them. He then admonished them to observe this ritual in remembrance of Him. Next, He took the cup and after giving thanks, gave it to them, reminding them to drink all of it, for it was His blood of the new covenant which would be shed for many for the remission of sins (Matt. 26:26-28; Mark 14:22-24; Luke 22:9-20). The Apostle Paul tells us that when we observe the Lord's Supper, we proclaim the Lord's death until He returns (1 Cor. 11:23-26).

Among non-Catholics the most common name for this rite is the *"Lord's Supper"* (1 Cor. 11:20). Other names are *"Communion"* (1 Cor. 10:16), *"the Lord's table,"* or *"the Table of the Lord"* (1 Cor. 10:21), and *"the Breaking of bread"* (Luke 24:35). Catholics generally refer to it as the *"Eucharist"* (from the Greek *eucharisto*, "I give thanks"), a reference to the thanksgiving and blessing aspect of the service (Matt. 26:26, 27; 1 Cor. 10:16; 11:24).

The Lord's Supper is to be a joyful season, not a time of sorrow.

Of course, the time preceding the Lord's Table should be a time of reflection and self-examination. Being assured that through the blood of Christ they are cleansed and forgiven, believers are ready to enter confidently into special communion with their Lord. They turn to His table with joy and thanksgiving, ready to celebrate the redemptive victory of Christ.

THE MEANING OF THE LORD'S SUPPER

The Lord's Supper replaces the Passover festival of the old covenant era. The Passover was fulfilled when Christ the *"Lamb of God"* gave His life. As we have seen, Jesus instituted the replacement on the night of the Passover. Hence, the roots of much of the symbolism of the Lord's Supper extend back into the Passover service.

It is a commemoration of the deliverance from sin.

As the Passover festival commemorated Israel's deliverance from bondage in Egypt, the Lord's Supper commemorates deliverance from the bondage of sin. The Passover lamb's blood applied to the lintel and doorposts of dwellings protected the inhabitants from death. The nourishment its flesh provided gave them the strength to escape from Egypt (Ex. 12:3-8). Even so, Christ's sacrifice brings liberation from spiritual death, or separation from God. The Lord's Supper proclaims that Christ's death on the cross made salvation available to all, provided forgiveness, and guaranteed eternal life.

It emphasizes the substitutionary dimension of Christ's atonement.

"This is my body," Jesus said, *"which is broken for you"* (1 Cor. 11:24; cf. Isa. 53:4-12). The expression *"for you"* is significant. At the cross the innocent was substituted for the guilty, the righteous for the unrighteous. The cross removed the repentant sinner's condemnation, providing him with the robe of Christ's righteousness, and assuring him of forgiveness, peace, and eternal life.

Jesus used many metaphors to teach different truths about Himself. He said, *"I am the door"* (John 10:7), *"I am the way"* (John 14:6), *"I am the true vine"* (John 15:1), and *"I am the bread of life"* (John 6:35). These expressions are not to be taken literally, for He was not an actual door, or vine, or bread. Instead, these metaphors illustrate deeper truths.

Roman Catholics teach that when Jesus commanded His followers to eat His flesh and drink His blood, He was speaking literally (see John 6:53, 54). To accommodate this untenable error, Catholics affirm that when the priest, in celebration of the Mass, consecrates the wafer and the wine, those elements are *"transubstantiated"* ("to change from one substance into another") into the actual body and blood of Jesus. This is one of the seven sacraments of the Catholic Church, participation in which is necessary for a person's salvation.

However, eating Christ's flesh and drinking His blood is symbolic language. By faith believers appropriate the benefits of Christ's atoning sacrifice when partaking of the unleavened bread and the fruit of the vine. We feed on Christ, the *"bread of life,"* through partaking of the Word of life—the Bible. With that Word comes the life-giving power of Jesus Christ. In short, the symbolism shows that we are as dependent on Christ for spiritual life as we are on food and drink for physical life.

It is an ordinance, not a sacrament.

By *ordinance* we mean the Lord's Supper was ordained by Christ Himself during His ministry on earth. As we have noted, there are only two symbolic ordinances commanded by Christ for each church to engage in: baptism and the Lord's Supper. We do not call these rites *sacraments* as liturgical churches do (such as Roman Catholics). A *sacrament* confers grace on the recipient. Catholics teach that both the Lord's Supper and baptism are considered essential elements in a person's salvation journey.

Baptists deny that grace is imparted through baptism or the Lord's Supper. These ordinances are purely symbolic, designed to remind God's people of great and foundational truths. Blessing does not come from the physical elements, but from personal understanding and appreciation of what these elements represent.

It safeguards sound doctrine in the church.

Churches are commanded to remember *the Lord's death*. The Supper and its symbolism must never be changed. Paul reminds us that each time we observe this ordinance we proclaim the Lord's death until He comes (1 Cor. 11:26). This Supper therefore reminds congregations that they must never repudiate the doctrine of the atonement. Christians must continually be reminded by the observance of this ordinance that Christ died as their substitute. Once this central doctrine is rejected, a church ceases to be a true, Bible-based church.

It emphasizes the duty of holiness.

The Lord's Supper is a time for honest appraisal before God (1 Cor. 11:27). Earlier in chapter eleven Paul rebuked the Corinthians for their careless living and attitude towards the Lord's Supper (11:17-22). They had forgotten their calling to live as members of God's holy family and to show love and compassion to one another. They had divided into exclusive cliques, and had lost all sense of mutual obligation. Above all, they had become indifferent to the price paid by Christ to redeem them and make them a holy people, an attitude that displayed its ugly self in their observance of the Lord's Supper.

Paul warns them of eating and drinking the Lord's Supper in an *unworthy* manner (1 Cor. 11:29). This refers to the cavalier manner in which they were observing the Supper. They were making it more of a "party time" than a time of remembering what Jesus did for their salvation.

Some Christians refrain from participating in the Lord's Supper because they consider themselves to be unworthy. This attitude results from a misreading of verses 27 and 29. In one sense, no Christian is worthy of participating in this ordinance. We are flawed, sinful creatures. But Paul did not imply that we had to be *worthy* to partake of the Supper, only that we should partake of it in a *worthy manner*. It is no light matter to approach the Lord's Table with a careless attitude. Before approaching this important event we are to examine our hearts and repent of our sins. To fail to do this could result in experiencing the Lord's discipline (11:30).

It is a reminder of Christ's Second Coming (1 Cor. 11:26b).

The Lord's Supper spans the interim between Calvary and the Second Advent. Each time we participate in this Supper, it is a reminder that Christ is coming back. The phrase, *"until He comes,"* is an integral part of the observance. Our memory needs to be continually refreshed so that we may recall that the day is coming when Christ shall appear and we shall be caught up together to be forever with Him. The Lord's Supper serves as that necessary reminder.

HOW OFTEN IT IS TO BE OBSERVED

Each local congregation is free to determine its own schedule for the observance of the Lord's Supper. No explicit command is given in Scripture detailing how often it is to be observed. Some churches observe it once a year at the Passover season, for at that festival Jesus instituted the rite. Others choose to observe it once a month or once a quarter, and some every Sunday.

Some interpret the words about breaking bread from house to house in Acts 2:46, as a reference to the daily observance of the Lord's Supper by the early Christians. The more plausible explanation is that the expression refers simply to regular meals they shared with fellow believers. The closest Scripture comes to setting a time is when Jesus said, *"As often as you eat this bread and drink this cup . . ."* (1 Cor. 11:25-26), an expression that leaves the door open for each local congregation to decide when to observe it.

QUALIFICATIONS FOR PARTICIPATION

Baptism is the gateway into the church, and the Lord's Supper benefits those who are members. Jesus administered His Supper only to His professed followers. The Communion service, therefore, is for baptized believers only.

As we have already noted, self-examination must precede participation in this ordinance. This examination is personal and is not to be conducted by other members of the church, for what human can read the heart or distinguish the wheat from the tares? Christ, our example, rejected exclusiveness at the Supper. Though open, unconfessed sin excludes persons from participating (1 Cor. 5:11), Jesus Himself shared the meal with Judas—outwardly a professed follower, inwardly a thief and a traitor. Judas was disciplined by God for participating in an unworthy manner.

What marks those who are qualified to participate in the Lord's table, then, is the condition of the heart—a full commitment to Christ, believer's baptism, and a desire to bring one's behavior into conformity with the Word of God.

BASIC BAPTIST BELIEFS

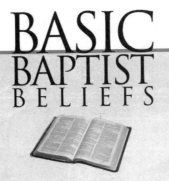

MISSIONS

The command to give the gospel to the world is clear and
unmistakable and this Great Commission
was given to the churches.

CHAPTER 40

WHAT IS THE MISSION OF THE CHURCH?

Jesus Christ gave the "Great Commission" to His disciples after His resurrection and immediately prior to His ascension to Heaven. It was a summary statement of the church's mission. The first believers in the Lord Jesus, the exploits of whom are recorded in the New Testament, not only linked themselves together for praise and worship, they voluntarily united together to carry out this solemn mandate. Just as all great businesses have a charter stating their purpose and scope, so the churches of Jesus Christ have a charter clearly stating their mission or function.

The Great Commission is recorded in five different places in the New Testament, and each has a slightly different emphasis (Matt. 28:18-20; Mark 16:15, 16; Luke 24:45-48; John 20:21; Acts 1:8). In all five of these accounts Jesus urges His followers to carry the gospel message to every corner of the globe, and He gives the formula for a successful implementation of His missionary enterprise.

SUBMIT TO THE RIGHT AUTHORITY

Jesus proclaimed to His disciples that He had been give total authority in Heaven and on earth (Matt. 28:18). The Commission He gave was based on this *authority* (John 20:21). When someone makes a demand of us, our obedience or lack thereof is based on the authority of the one who gives the order. When parents tell a young child what to do, the child will most often obey, because parents are invested with the necessary authority to make demands of their children. Teachers make certain requirements of their students, and those who comply do so because of the teacher's authority. If a man works for a company not his own, the boss has the authority to tell him what to do. Policemen are endowed with authority to arrest someone who is breaking the law. Referees have the right to penalize a team member that breaks the rules of the game. Authority is an important element in life.

The all-important point that Jesus emphasizes here is that He is in control of all things. He now has and wields authority over the entire order of creation both in Heaven and on earth. All creatures, nature, angels, and man, are at His disposal and under His authority. He is the One who has given us life and by the shedding of His blood, redeemed us from destruction (Ps. 103:4). What more is needed to qualify Him with the authority necessary to make whatever demands of us He chooses? We would not, nor should we, obey the command of a person who is not endowed with legitimate authority. Not only does Jesus have the right to tell us what to do, He has the power to enable us to successfully fulfill all aspects of the command.

GO WITH THE RIGHT MESSAGE

In the Matthew Commission (Matt. 28:19) Jesus commands His disciples to *go* and *teach all nations* (literally, *make disciples of all nations*). The Mark Commission gives a slightly different slant. Jesus states that His disciples are to go and *preach* the Good News of Christ's death, burial, and resurrection to all people everywhere (Mk. 16:15). The word *preach* means to "herald the message." It is the same word found in 2 Timothy 4:2, where Paul urges his young protégé Timothy to "*preach the word.*"

In ancient times a herald communicated momentous events. This was the King's personal messenger who would cry out the king's message as the people in the town eagerly assembled together to hear the latest news. The herald would not give his own message, nor would he add his own interpretation to the king's message. He would simply give the message word for word. It made no difference whether the herald liked the message or not. He was obligated to faithfully deliver it. Paul declared that he was compelled to preach the gospel, but if he failed to do so, or if he substituted another message, a "*woe*" would be on him (1 Cor. 9:16). It is a serious matter to fail to accurately announce the King's message of good news.

We are not to substitute our programs for Christ's Commission. Our primary calling is *not* to feed the hungry, clothe the destitute, or cure bodily illnesses. These humanitarian activities may be useful as door openers, permitting us to preach the gospel where otherwise it might not be possible, but they should not be considered an end in themselves. Our foremost calling is to *"preach the gospel."*

William Booth, the first general of the Salvation Army, said that the real objective of his organization "was not just the amelioration of social conditions, but first and foremost the bringing of men and women to repentance that their souls might be saved." J. W. Hyde declared, "If every person in the world had adequate food, housing, income; if all people were equal; if every possible social evil and injustice were done away with, people would still need one thing—Jesus Christ."

The Commission entrusted to us includes an element often overlooked by parachurch organizations: *the importance of baptism.* Baptism is one of the two ordinances of the local church, the other being the Lord's Supper. Converts are to be baptized in the name of the Father, the Son, and the Holy Spirit (Matt. 28:19). Baptism follows conversion but is not a part of the salvation decision. It is the immersion in water of one who has already trusted in Christ, and symbolizes the believer's death to the old life and resurrection to a new life (Rom. 6:1-11). It is an act of obedience, signifying to the church and to the world that he or she is now identifying with Jesus Christ and His people.

The message, however, is not to be *exclusive.* It is to be preached to *every* person in the world. Being a Jew, Paul felt compelled to take the gospel first to that ethnic group (Rom. 1:16); however, he confessed that the message was not for Jews alone. No one is excluded and no part of the world is to be neglected (Luke 24:47).

TEACH WITH RIGHT DOCTRINE

Baptized converts are to be taught whatever Jesus has commanded (Matt. 28:20a). Every church is a teaching center, not just an evangelistic center. Evangelism is to be done chiefly beyond the walls of the church building; obviously, this is where most lost people are to be found. In the world we should be *reaching* the unconverted; in the congregation we should be primarily *teaching* the converted. The saints need to be indoctrinated in the local church; the indoctrinated saints need to be evangelizing the world.

Jesus commanded His followers to *go* into the world. He did not command sinners to *come* into the church. He urged His disciples to go out into the highways and byways of the world and *"compel"* people to come in (i.e., evangelize them) that His house might be filled (Luke14:23). Once in the congregation, they were to be taught all the things that Christ commanded.

In saying this, it is in no way meant to discourage God's children from inviting lost people to the services of the church. That is one way to fulfill the Great Commission. We rejoice for every sinner who hears a gospel message in church and receives Christ as personal Savior. When the gospel is faithfully taught and preached, people *will* respond and be saved.

At the same time, we must not disregard the words of the Lord Jesus. A vital part of the Great Commission is to instruct members of the church so that they may be built up in the faith and be prepared to give an answer to unbelievers who may question them about their Christian beliefs (Jude 20a; 1 Pet. 3:15).

RELY ON THE RIGHT PROMISE

Jesus promised to be with us, not part of the time, but always— *"until the end of this present age"*—as we carry out His Great Commission (Matt. 28:20b). Paul reminded the Corinthians that a great door for effective work for Christ had been opened to him, but he added, *"there are many adversaries"* (1 Cor. 16:9).

No one has ever attempted to carry out the Commission of Christ without encountering opposition; but we are not asked to enter this mission in our own strength, armed with our own weapons (2 Cor. 10:3-5; Acts 1:8). In addition, the great Captain of our salvation has promised His abiding presence. Furthermore, Paul reminds us that we can do all things through Christ who strengthens us (Phil. 4:13).

David Livingstone, the great missionary pioneer in Africa, was once asked how he could keep going, considering he had encountered so many obstacles in his attempt to get the gospel to the people of

Africa. He replied, "The answer is simple. It is the promise of the Lord Jesus: *"Lo, I am with you always, even unto the end of the world."*

CONCLUSION

Implicit in the Great Commission is the necessity of church involvement. Because baptism, an important element in the Great Commission, is the prerequisite to the privileges of church membership, and the church is the *"pillar and ground of the truth"* (Note: Paul, 1 Timothy 3:15, does not intend to convey the thought that the church is the *source* of truth, as Catholics teach; he is simply affirming the crucial role of the church as the support and bulwark of God's truth), we may correctly assume that in order to fulfill Christ's Commission, churches must plant other churches if we are to reach a burgeoning world population.

Paul reminds us that no one can believe on someone about whom they have never heard, and they can never hear unless a preacher comes to them with the message; but how can anyone preach the message unless they are sent (Rom. 10:14, 15)? The New Testament pattern is that churches send messengers to those on mission fields who have never heard the gospel. The sober implication is, if there are no churches, no one will be sent. Few churches mean few will be sent. If there are many churches, many will be sent—a compelling reason why churches must reproduce themselves.

Churches are to be teaching centers so believers can be grounded in the truth, well equipped to articulate that truth to nonbelievers. Making disciples, baptizing them, and teaching them replicates the whole process. An important by-product is that churches will be birthing centers; new churches will spring up under their influence. Then and only then can the Great Commission be fulfilled.

BASIC BAPTIST BELIEFS

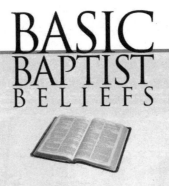

THE GRACE OF GIVING

Scriptural giving is one of the fundamentals of the faith.
We are commanded to bring our gifts into the storehouse
(common treasury of the church)
upon the first day of the week.

CHAPTER 41

HOW IS THE CHURCH TO BE FINANCED?

More than anything else, living a Christian life means *surrender*—a giving up of oneself completely to Christ. When we surrender all that we are and have to God—to whom it all belongs anyway (1 Cor. 3:21-4:2)—He accepts it, but then puts us back in charge of it, making us *stewards*, or *caretakers* of everything He has entrusted to us.

A very important part of the Christian life has to do with our use of money: how we make it, how we spend it, and how we invest it. A clear recognition that we are stewards of the possessions God has entrusted to us enables us to have a right attitude about money. Additionally, God promised He would open the windows of Heaven and pour out an abundant blessing on those who bring their tithes and offerings to Him, as faithful stewards are expected to do (Mal. 3:10).

THE MEANING OF STEWARDSHIP

The Bible teaches that we were purchased or redeemed at a high cost (1 Cor. 6:19, 20). We now belong to God. In one sense we belonged to Him from the beginning, for He created us and placed us on this earth that is rightfully His (Gen. 1:1; Ps. 24:1).

Now, in a special way, He has appointed His people, those who have received the gift of eternal life through His Son, to serve as stewards of His possessions. A steward is a person entrusted with the management of the household or estate of another.

To the Christian, stewardship means a person's responsibility for, and use of, everything entrusted to him by God—life, time, talents and abilities, material possessions, opportunities to be of service to others, and his knowledge of truth.

WAYS TO ACKNOWLEDGE GOD'S OWNERSHIP

Life can be divided into three basic areas, each a gift from God: abilities, time, and material possessions. We will consider each of these three gifts, but concentrate primarily on the stewardship of material possessions.

The stewardship of abilities.

Each person has special gifts or abilities. One may be talented in the musical realm, another in manual trades such as sewing or auto mechanics. Some may make friends easily and mingle well with others, while others may naturally tend toward more solitary pursuits. Every talent can be used to glorify either the one who possesses it or its original Bestower. A person can diligently perfect talent for God's glory or for personal selfishness. By cultivating the gifts the Holy Spirit gives each of us, we are enabled to multiply those gifts (Matt. 25:14-30). Good stewards use their gifts wisely and liberally in order to bless others and bring glory to their Master.

The stewardship of time.

As faithful stewards, we glorify God by a wise use of time (Col. 3:23, 24). The Bible admonishes us not to behave like fools, always wasting time, but to make the best possible use of time because these are evil days in which we live (Eph. 5:15, 16). Like Jesus, we must be about our Father's business (Luke 2:49). Because time is God's gift, each moment is precious. Faithful stewardship of time means using it to get to know our Lord better, to serve our fellowmen, and to share the gospel with others. The Psalmist prayed, and so should we, that the Lord would teach him to make the most of his time so that he might obtain a heart of wisdom (Ps. 90:12).

The stewardship of material possessions.

Because humanity needed a constant reminder that God is the source of every blessing in life (James 1:17), and that it is He who provides us with the power to get wealth (Deut. 8:18), He instituted a system of *tithes and offerings.* The system eventually provided the financial means for supporting the priesthood of the Israelite temple.

God has ordained that sharing the good news is to be dependent on the tithes and offerings of His people. He calls them to be unselfish co-laborers with Him by giving tithes and offerings to Him.

The word *"tithe"* means *"tenth."* Scripture tells us that the tithe is *"holy to the Lord,"* symbolizing God's ownership of everything (Lev. 27:30, 32). It is to be faithfully returned to Him. The tithing system is beautiful in its simplicity. Its equity is revealed in its proportional claim on the rich and on the poor. In proportion as God has enabled us to make money, so we are to return to Him a tithe or tenth.

When God calls for the tithe (Mal. 3:10), He makes no appeal to gratitude or generosity. Although gratitude should be a part of all our expressions to God, we tithe because *God has commanded it.* The tithe belongs to the Lord, and He asks that we return it to Him.

Tithing is an accepted practice throughout Scripture. Abraham gave Melchizedek, the priest of God Most High, a tenth of everything (Gen. 14:20). By doing so he demonstrated that he was well acquainted with this sacred institution. Apparently it was already an established custom at that early date. Jacob also understood the tithing requirement (Gen. 28:22).

Far from repealing this institution, the New Testament assumes its validity. Jesus approved of tithing and condemned those who refused to practice the custom (Matt. 23:23). The ceremonial laws regulating the sacrificial offerings symbolizing Christ's atoning sacrifice ended at His death, but the tithing requirement did not.

After the Crucifixion, when the divinely appointed role of the Levitical priesthood ended, tithes were still to be used to support the ministry of the church. Paul illustrated the principle underlying this by drawing a parallel between the Levitical service and the newly established gospel ministry (1 Cor. 9:11-14).

Church members, then, are to willingly bring their tithes to the church that all the needs of the congregation would be met (Mal. 3:10)—in other words, so that there are enough funds in the church's treasury to provide a living for its ministry and to carry forward the outreach of the gospel.

Offerings are also to be given in addition to the tithe. Grateful Christians cannot limit their contributions to the church to their tithes. In Israel, the tabernacle, and later the temple, were built from *"freewill offerings"* (Ex. 36:2-7; 1 Chron. 29:14). Special offerings also covered the maintenance expenses of these places of worship (Ex. 30:12-16; 2 Kings 12:4, 5; 2 Chron. 24:4-14; Neh. 10:32, 33).

Today, the Lord calls for liberal giving. Offerings are needed to build, maintain, and operate churches, and to support missionary personnel and projects around the world. In the New Testament, Christ laid down the principle of true stewardship—that *our gifts to God should be in proportion to the light and privileges we have enjoyed* (Luke 12:48). Nowhere does the New Testament repeal or relax this system. When Jesus sent His disciples on a mission He said, *"Freely you have received, freely give"* (Matt. 10:8).

THE BLESSINGS OF LIBERAL GIVING
It results in a personal blessing.

One reason God asks us to tithe and give offerings is to encourage our own spiritual growth and character development. Also, it assists us in gaining victory over covetousness and selfishness. Covetousness, one of our greatest enemies, is condemned numerous times in Scripture (Exo. 20:17; Mark 7:22; Luke 12:15; Rom. 13:9). Our giving on a regular basis helps to root out covetousness and self-centeredness from our lives. It leads to the development of habits of economy and efficiency. A deep satisfaction and joy comes from the assurance that our investment is resulting in the salvation of the lost.

It results in a blessing to the church and to the world.

Tithes and offerings are indispensable for the ongoing ministry of the church. Only then will the church have adequate funds to support the ministry, to expand God's kingdom in its immediate vicinity, and to extend it to the remote places of the earth. Think of the millions around the world who are followers of Christ as a result of effective missionary outreach. None of this would have been possible without the tithes and generous offerings of God's people.

BASIC BAPTIST BELIEFS

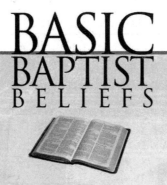

CIVIL GOVERNMENT

We believe that civil government is of divine appointment,

for the interests and good order of human society;

that magistrates are to be prayed for,

conscientiously honored and obeyed;

except only in things opposed to the will

of our Lord Jesus Christ;

who is the only Lord of the conscience,

and the coming Prince of the kings of the earth.

CHAPTER 42

WHAT SHOULD BE
THE CHRISTIAN ATTITUDE
TOWARD GOVERNMENT?

God has put in the world three institutions which He has ordained for the good of mankind. The first is the home (Gen. 2:18-25); the second is human government, and the third is the local church. God established the principle of maintaining law and order in society by means of the state. Governments are ordained of God. The first record of this provision is found in Genesis 9:6, where God gave society the right to enforce laws, even to make use of capital punishment when necessary.

GOD ORDAINED CIVIL GOVERNMENT

The Apostle Paul informs his readers that no governmental authority exists that God did not establish (Rom. 13:1). Twice in this same chapter he identifies civil rulers as servants of God (13:4, 6). To resist this principle is to resist the God who established government in the first place, and it means inviting His displeasure. The exception to this general rule is detailed later in this chapter.

The book of Daniel reveals that God sets up kings and removes them (Dan. 2:21). The writer of Proverbs declares that by God's permission kings reign, rulers make just laws, and princes govern. All nobles who rule throughout the earth do so with God's approval (Pro. 8:15, 16).

The most unjust and wicked rulers in the world have no power but what is given them from above. When Jesus refused to answer

Pilate's question about His identity, Pilate remonstrated with Him, claiming that he had power either to free or to crucify Him (John 19:8-10). Jesus' response to Pilate reveals that civil rulers receive their power from God (19:11). This does not mean that God condones or is responsible for the atrocities of tyrants. Nor does it imply that every decision governmental authorities make has God's approval. It serves only to establish that God has the power, if He so wills, to control a ruler's decisions, and that the authority to rule comes originally from Him.

RULERS ARE TO BE HONORED

Scripture commands that Christians are to *"honor the king"* (1 Pet. 2:17). To *"Honor the king"* means essentially the same as to honor the President, the Governor, the Senator, or the Mayor. All civil magistrates are to be respected. Surprisingly, Peter wrote these words during the time the corrupt Roman Empire controlled what was once the nation of Israel; and this was an Empire fiercely dedicated to stamping out the fledgling Christian movement.

While Christians may not agree with everything government does, in most situations they are not to be guilty of insubordination to governmental authorities. They are to submit to and honor those who exercise authority over them and to the laws they have instituted.

Jude speaks of those who reject authority and speak evil of dignities (Jude 8). God requires us to speak evil of no man (Titus 3:2), but it is an even greater evil when we speak disparagingly of magistrates, those whom God has set in authority over us.

Submitting to governing authorities is a visible way for Christians to show their submission to God. Those who refuse to honor their rulers or to submit to the laws of the land are refusing to obey God (Rom. 13:2). With that in mind, be sure to treat all government officials with respect—whether they are collecting your taxes or giving you a speeding ticket. It is especially important to honor policemen, state patrolmen, and military personnel. These people serve an important function in helping to maintain a peaceful society.

RULERS ARE TO BE OBEYED

On one occasion the Pharisees attempted to trap Jesus by asking

Him whether it was right to pay taxes to Caesar or not. The Roman Empire exercised authority over the Jews living in Israel during that time, and a prickly issue with them was the requirement to pay taxes to pagan Gentile rulers. If Jesus had said it was improper for Jewish people to pay taxes to Rome—and this is precisely what the Pharisees hoped He would say—they would turn Him over to the Roman authorities as a seditionist.

Jesus' answer took them by surprise; but it also teaches an important lesson to Christians about respect for authority. Jesus asked them for a coin. It was a Roman coin. When He asked whose portrait was on the coin, they answered, *"Caesar's."* Jesus then answers their question by instructing them to render to Caesar what belongs to Caesar, and to God what belongs to God (Matt. 22:15-22; see also Rom. 13:2; Titus 3:1; 1 Pet. 2:13, 14). These Scriptures clearly teach that Christians must obey those who rule over them, even though the ruler may have questionable ethical or moral standards.

However, *there are exceptions to the above rules.* When a government official is defiant towards God and His people, it is no sin to express disagreement or defy his orders. Several examples in Scripture bear this out. When certain Pharisees informed Jesus that Herod intended to kill Him, Jesus called Herod a "fox"—meaning he was the embodiment of deceit and cunning (Luke 13:32). It was the most contemptuous name ever given anyone by Jesus. John the Baptist told King Herod that it was unlawful for him to be living with his brother's wife. That put John at odds with the king and ultimately cost him his life. Nevertheless, John is not to be faulted for censuring Herod for his blatant immorality (Mark 6:18). Shadrach, Meshach and Abednego, three young Jewish captives in Babylon, refused to obey the command of King Nebuchadnezzar to bow down before the image of gold on the plain of Dura (Dan. 3). Daniel defied the decree of King Darius forbidding him to pray to his God (Dan. 6).

When the disciples were given strict orders by government officials not to teach anymore in the name of Jesus, they replied that they had a higher loyalty: they were to obey God rather than men (Acts 5:27-32). A command of God takes precedence over human commands. It is the price of being a Christian that one must at times be prepared to obey God rather than magistrates, and bear the cost of doing so.

The true Christian is not lawless; however, he recognizes that if human government makes demands on him contrary to the Word of God, it is permissible to resist such authority.

RULERS ARE TO BE PRAYED FOR

In 1 Timothy 2:1, 2, Paul exhorts Christians to be a praying people. Not only should we pray for *everyone*, we should especially pray for those in authority such as the head of state and other national and local leaders. And this includes those duly elected officials whom we voted against in the last election.

When Paul wrote these words, the heathen Emperor Nero ruled. A hostile enemy to Christianity, Nero used any excuse to persecute Christians. Yet Paul urged Timothy to have the church pray for him. We, too, must pray for our leaders. We need to pray that:

(1) They will be just (2 Sam. 23:3a);

(2) They will rule in the fear of God (2 Sam. 23:3b);

(3) They will punish evil-doers (Rom. 13:3a);

(4) They will exercise their prerogative to punish serious crimes by capital punishment (Rom. 13:4).

It is for our own good that we pray for those who rule over us. The purpose of such praying is that we might be enabled to live quiet and peaceful lives. Paul knew that prayer had the power to change things. Not in vain do godly people pray for national and world peace. God has control over national and international affairs, and it is in times of peace that followers of Jesus Christ can quietly pursue a life of holiness.

CHRISTIANS ARE TO BE LAW-ABIDING CITIZENS

We are to seek the good of our country and do nothing or join in nothing that tends to disturb or destroy the peace.

We are to do everything in our power to promote the welfare of our country. We are to teach our children to be law-abiding citizens, which is best done by example, not merely by precept. One of the best ways to promote a good and peaceful society is to be involved in the life of a church, because churches are the foundation of a sound, healthy community. In most cases, the community mirrors the churches. If the churches are weak, the community will be weak.

CONCLUSION

If you live in a country that allows freedom of worship, you should be especially grateful. However, it is still true that *"eternal vigilance is the price of liberty."* If you do not pray for your country, if you do not try to make it a better place, if you do not obey its laws, vote for candidates that best reflect your Christian values, you are joining hands with those who are seeking its overthrow.

BASIC BAPTIST BELIEFS

THE RETURN OF CHRIST AND RELATED EVENTS

We believe in and accept the sacred Scriptures upon these subjects at their face value. We believe that after Christ rose bodily "the third day according to the Scriptures," that "He ascended to the right hand of the throne of God;" that He alone is our "merciful and faithful High Priest in things pertaining to God;" that this same Jesus shall return in like manner as He was taken up into Heaven—bodily, personally and visibly; that the "dead in Christ shall rise first;" that the living saints "shall all be changed in a moment, in the twinkling of an eye, at the last trump;" that "the Lord God shall give to Him the throne of His Father David;" and that "Christ shall reign a thousand years in righteousness until He has put all enemies under His feet."

CHAPTER 43

CAN WE STILL BELIEVE IN THE SECOND COMING?

Our focus for the next few chapters will be the return of Christ and related events. One of the most prominent and foundational doctrines taught in the Word of God is the Second Coming of Christ to the earth. The Apostles held out the possibility of His returning in their day, and the next generation kept alive the *"blessed hope"* as an event that was imminent. In time, however, this truth began to be neglected and even rejected on the part of many. Centuries passed before this great truth was to be revived. In the past 150 years, we have witnessed renewed emphasis on it, even though there is still much indifference and opposition. The Apostle Peter predicted that in *"the last days"* scoffers would emerge asking why Christ had not returned as He promised (2 Pet. 3:4).

However, Christians are to love the appearing of their Lord (2 Tim. 4:8). They have spoken about Him, prayed to the Father in His name, and longed to see Him. And one day, perhaps sooner that many think, He will appear. We will *"see Him as He is"* (1 John 3:2).

THE IMPORTANCE OF THE SECOND COMING
Its prominence in the Scriptures.
While this truth is alluded to a number of times in the Old Testament, in the New Testament it is specifically mentioned more than three hundred times, or once in every twenty-five verses. Jesus' discourse on the Mount of Olives treats this theme exclusively and

takes up two whole chapters in the Gospel of Matthew (Matt. 24, 25). Other books deal primarily with this subject, such as First and Second Thessalonians and the Book of Revelation.

It is the hope of believers (Titus 2:13).

Throughout the ages of church history, true believers have found comfort in this great truth. Paul called the anticipation of the Lord's return *"the blessed hope."* While some aspects of the coming of the Lord should create a sober attitude about the issues of life today, yet this hope can lift Christians above the sorrows, disappointments, and uncertainties of this life. It creates within us the sense that a day of victory is coming when all wrongs and injustices will be made right, and Jesus Christ will be recognized for who He really is.

It is an incentive to Biblical Christianity.

Those who entertain a sincere belief in this doctrine seldom dispute the infallibility of the Bible or depart from the faith. The acceptance of this truth leads to holiness of life (1 John 3:3; 2 Pet. 3:10, 11). It inspires watchfulness and perseverance (1 Thess. 5:2-11; 1 John 2:28). It fosters patience and comfort in times of adversity (James 5:7; Heb. 10:35-37; 1 Thess. 4:16-18).

It results in more faithful service to Christ.

Those who hold to this truth are the ones most likely known for their personal faithfulness, generous giving, missionary zeal, and evangelistic endeavors. There is no greater stimulus to service than to believe that Christ may come at any moment.

THE TWO PHASES OF CHRIST'S COMING

The Second Coming of Christ is one event, but it develops in *two stages*. The first stage: He comes *for* believers; the second stage: He comes *with* believers.

His coming for believers.

Christ will return to meet the saints in the air (1 Thess. 4:16, 17). This is sometimes labeled *"the rapture,"* which means "to snatch away" or "to transport." Christians will be caught up to meet the Lord. This stage of Christ's coming may take place at any moment.

When the Lord returns, only believers will be caught up to meet Him. Those who are alive and have rejected Him will be left on earth to experience the sorrows of *"the great tribulation."*

His coming with believers.

After the Tribulation period, our Lord will return triumphantly to the earth to defeat the Antichrist and establish His kingdom. When He returns, His saints will be with Him (Jude 14, 15; Col. 3:4).

THE TIME OF CHRIST'S COMING

No one knows the exact time of Jesus' return (Matt. 24:36, 42). Occasionally people have ignored our Savior's warning and have set dates for His return. Informed Christians always maintain an attitude of anticipation, eagerly awaiting His return, but they are careful not to set dates.

While we must not be "date setters," devout Christians are not in the dark about such an important event and will not be caught by surprise when Jesus returns (1 Thess. 5:4). No doubt as the first phase of His coming approaches, God will give His people an awareness of the imminence of that great event.

As we study prophecy and relate that to current events, we cannot but conclude that the Lord's return may be near. We see that the nations of Europe are uniting for economic and military protection, Israel is back in her land, and that little slice of geography is the focal point of many of today's headlines. Militant Islam is on the march. They would like nothing better than for Israel to be driven into the sea, and much of Islamic terrorism today is linked to that issue. Furthermore, at the precise moment in history when the wealthy nations, and even the developing nations, need fuel for the burgeoning automobile, airplane, and manufacturing market, Arab (or Islamic) nations control a good portion of the oil supply of the world. All of these foreboding issues are *"signs of times."*

THE MANNER OF CHRIST'S COMING AT THE RAPTURE
He will return personally.

There is no need to look for another Messiah or prophet. *"This same Jesus"* will return in person as was prophesied by the angels and by our Lord Jesus Christ Himself (John 14:3; Acts 1:11).

He will return with a mighty shout (1 Thess. 4:16).

The Greek word for *"shout"* (*keleuma*) signifies a "war-shout." Jesus is represented as a victorious King who will deliver His people and defeat His enemies.

He will be accompanied by the voice of the archangel (I Thess. 4:16).

As angels came and ministered to Jesus at the time of His temptation (Matt. 4:11), they will accompany Him at the time of His future triumph.

He will return with the sound of the trumpet (1 Thess. 4:16b).

The trumpet was used to convene God's people to their solemn convocations (Num. 10:2, 10); here it is used to summon God's people together in preparation for their glorification with Christ (1 Cor. 15:52).

The above events depict the first phase of His coming, when both dead and living believers will be "caught up" or "raptured" to meet the Lord in the air (1 Thess. 4:16, 17), and be taken to Heaven.

The second phase of His coming is when He returns to earth with the angels and saints from Heaven to reign over the earth in His thousand-year kingdom. These entirely different events should not be confused.

CONCLUSION

Because the Lord's coming may be at any moment, it is vitally important that proper preparation be made. First, those who are lost should speedily make their calling and election sure. Today is the day of salvation (2 Cor. 6:2). Second, those who are saved should live in the light of that great expectation. No one is more likely to live an exemplary life than those who cherish this hope (1 John 3:2, 3).

In the mean time, Jesus said we are to be occupied in His service, doing His bidding, until He returns (Luke 19:13). The lesson Jesus is teaching in this parable is this: "Put your talents (*minas*) to good use while I am away (the *minas* or *talents* represent the different gifts the Lord gives to each individual). Do not sit back and complain that the world is getting worse and worse and do nothing. Get busy and invest what you have—your time, talents, and treasure—in my enterprise, for the night is coming when no one can work. At a time when most people least expect it, I will return; and after that will come a day of reckoning" (Luke 19:11-26).

CHAPTER 44

WHEN DOES THE GREAT TRIBULATION OCCUR?

Nothing could be more certain than the promise that Christ is coming back to the earth again. There may be differences of opinion as to exactly when certain key end-time events might occur, but the promise of His coming is so prominent in the New Testament, that to neglect it would not only be sin, it would deprive the one who chooses to disregard it of a rich storehouse of blessings; not to mention the strong incentive it provides for godly living.

The purpose of Christ's coming is made clear in the New Testament, as is information about one of the most talked about topics in prophecy—the Great Tribulation. These two important matters will be the theme of this chapter.

THE PURPOSE OF THE RAPTURE
Christ is coming to take believers to be with Him (John 14:3).

From henceforth we shall forever be with the Lord (1 Thess. 4:17). But because *"flesh and blood cannot inherit the Kingdom of God,"* it is evident that certain changes must take place before He can receive us to Himself. First, *the dead in Christ must be raised* (1 Thess. 4:16). This will no doubt include the bodies of all the saints who have ever lived. Second, *the believers who are alive when He comes must be changed* (1 Cor. 15:50-58; 1 Thess. 4:17). The exact nature of the change spoken of is nowhere revealed, but the possibility of being caught up without dying is illustrated in the translation of Enoch (Gen. 5:24; Heb. 11:5) and of Elijah (2 Kings 2:11-18).

Suffice it to say that we will be like Christ (1 John 3:2). This does not mean we will have a similar physical appearance; we will be like Him in the sense that we will be free from the possibility of defilement, sin, sickness, sorrow, and death.

Christ is coming to judge and reward.

Christ will come to judge the works of believers and to bestow rewards at the *Judgment Seat of Christ*. The believer will not be judged with regard to His sins (John 5:24). He was already judged for them in the person of Christ (John 3:18). When Christ returns, the believer will be judged as to the use he has made of the talents and opportunities that have been entrusted to him (Matt. 25:14-30; 20:1-16). It is with regard to these *"works"* that the believer will be judged (2 Cor. 5:10).

THE GREAT TRIBULATION

The period between the rapture of the saints and the triumphant return of Christ to the earth to establish His Kingdom will be fraught with peril for the inhabitants of the earth (Dan. 12:1). In Matthew 24:21 it is described as a time of *"Tribulation"* or *"Trouble"* beyond anything the world has ever seen. In the Old Testament it is referred to as *"the time of Jacob's trouble"* (Jer. 30:7). It will be particularly a time of intense suffering for Israel, but as other Scripture predictions make clear, the entire world will suffer anguish as never before.

The duration of the period.

We are nowhere told in so many words just how long the period will be. To many expositors, the seventieth week of Daniel is still future and it is the Tribulation period. If the seventy *"weeks"* of Daniel each represent seven years, and the seventieth week has not yet been fulfilled, the Tribulation can be expected to last seven years (see Dan. 9:24-27).

In harmony with this, the latter half of the period is elsewhere referred to as *"a time, times, and a half a time"* (Rev. 12:14); as *"forty-two months"* (Rev. 13:5); and as *1,260 days* (Rev. 12:6), or three and one-half years.

The nature of the period.

The first three and one-half years of the Tribulation will be a time of relative calm as the Antichrist disguises his true intentions, all the while strengthening his alliances and laying the groundwork for his assault on Israel. He will covenant with the Jews to restore their temple sacrifices, but after three and one- half years he will break the covenant, fulfilling Daniel 12:11, and 2 Thessalonians 2:3, 4.

During the latter half of the period there will be a federation of nations led by the "*Beast*" (another name for the Antichrist) and the "*false prophet,*" the chief aim of which will be to destroy Israel. In our own time, hatred for Israel (anti-Semitism) is becoming alarmingly widespread throughout the world.

The religion of that era will center around the Antichrist. His willing accomplice, "*the False Prophet,*" will use trickery and spectacular miracles to deceive the nations into giving their allegiance to the Antichrist. Those who do not worship the Beast will be persecuted and forbidden to buy or sell (Rev. 13:11-17). The possibility of governmental regulation and restriction of commerce has already been clearly demonstrated in times of war.

Revelation chapters 6 through 18 describe the horrible events (not necessarily in chronological order) of the last three-and-one half years of the Tribulation period. We see, then, that the Tribulation will indeed be *the hour and power of darkness.*

The chief actor of the period.

Not surprisingly, behind this rebellion is none other than Satan himself. The Bible reveals that he gives his power, throne, and great authority to the Antichrist (Rev. 13:2-4). Hence, this monarch, along with the False Prophet, will be Satan-energized and Satan-empowered, and no earthly ruler will be able to successfully make war with them. This triumvirate—Satan, the Beast, and the False Prophet—is often nicknamed "The Satanic Trinity."

THE PURPOSE OF CHRIST'S SECOND COMING
To judge the Beast, the False Prophet, and their armies (Rev. 19:19-21; 2 Thess. 2:8).

As the years of unprecedented tribulation draw to a close, the dragon, the beast, and the false prophet, go forth and gather together the governmental leaders of the world along with their armies (Rev. 16:12-16). They mass their forces under the pretext of capturing Jerusalem and defeating the Jews, but just at the moment when victory seems assured, Christ descends from Heaven with His armies (Rev. 19:11-16). The conflict is short and the outcome certain. The leaders of the rebellion are taken and cast into the lake of fire (2 Thess. 2:8; Rev. 19:19, 20).

To bind Satan (Rev. 20:1, 2; Rom. 16:20).

This binding of Satan signifies his removal from the sphere of his previous operation and his loss of opportunity and ability to continue his work.

The binding of Satan, however, does not include the removal of the carnal nature from those who will still be in their mortal bodies. Sin will still be present during the Millennium. Note that this binding is for the definite period of a thousand years.

To set up His kingdom.

This subject will be taken up more fully later on, but a few words must be said regarding it in this connection. God promised David that He would establish His Kingdom forever (2 Sam. 7:8-17).

Many Scriptures allude to a future, literal kingdom whose ruler will be none other than the Son of God Himself. The city of Jerusalem will become the capital, and all the nations will be obliged to come up to worship at Jerusalem (Zech. 14:16-19). It will be a time of unprecedented peace for the world.

CHAPTER 45

WHAT WILL THE MILLENNIUM BE LIKE?

The word *"millennium"* comes from the Latin *mille* (thousand) and *annus* (years), and means a thousand years. The doctrine of the Millennium holds that Christ will reign over an earthly kingdom for a thousand years. Implicit in the teaching is that Christ will return before the Millennium. This is known as the doctrine of Premillennialism. Those who believe that Christ will return after a thousand year period of universal peace and righteousness are called Postmillennialists. Those who deny a literal Millennial reign are called Amillennialists. The word *"millennium"* does not occur in the Bible, but the *"thousand years"* are mentioned six times in Revelation 20:2-7.

THE FACT OF A MILLENNIUM
The teaching of Scripture.

The hope and expectation of a future "golden age" has value only insofar as it is based on Scripture. In this instance we have ample warrant for such a belief.

"The day of the Lord" is an expression found often in both the Old and New Testaments (Joel 2:11; 2 Thess. 2:2). The *"morning star"* will herald the breaking of a new day (2 Pet. 1:19), and the "Sun of righteousness" will usher it in shortly thereafter (Mal. 4:2). This is the period of which prophets, poets, and sages have spoken; it is the earth's coming jubilee or Sabbath.

Furthermore, the God of Heaven will set up a kingdom that is never to be destroyed (Dan. 2:44; Rev. 11:15). In order to keep His covenant with David, God must restore the earthly kingdom (2 Sam. 7:11-16)

The revealed purpose of Christ in His return to earth is to set up His Kingdom (Luke 19:12, 15; Matt. 25:31ff). The disciples looked forward to the establishment of such a Kingdom. Jesus refused to reveal to them the time of its inauguration, but He never rebuked or corrected them for holding such a belief (Acts 1:6, 7).

The belief of the early churches.

The belief in a millennial kingdom on earth to follow the second advent of Christ was widely held by the early churches. It is found in the writings of such early biblical scholars as Justin, Irenaeus, and Tertullian. A. A. Hodge admits that this view "prevailed generally throughout the church from A.D. 150-250."

THE NATURE OF THE MILLENNIUM
As regards Christ.

Christ will be personally present on earth and sit on the throne of His father David. He will reign over all the earth (Jer. 23:5, 6). Two things will characterize His kingdom: universal peace (Isa. 2:4) and universal righteousness (Isa. 11:4, 5). Righteousness will be maintained by the "rod of iron" with which the King of Kings shall rule (Rev. 2:27; 19:15).

As regards believers.

Believers will reign with Christ over the Gentile world (Rev. 20:4, 6; 5:9, 10). It would seem that believers will have individual rather than collective responsibility in the kingdom (Luke 19:16-19).

As regards Israel.

Israel is to be re-gathered to her homeland (Isa. 11:10-13). The establishment of the State of Israel in 1948 is surely a forerunner of the ultimate re-gathering. We learn from Scripture that Israel is to repent and be converted (Isa. 66:8; Rom. 11:25-27). They will receive Him who came to be their Savior long ago, and their reception by the Lord will be *"life from the dead."*

As regards the nations.

They will form the nucleus of the Kingdom, together with restored and converted Israel. But it is evident that multitudes will be born during that age and these will need to be evangelized (Zech. 8:4, 5; Isa. 65:20). Finally, the Gentiles will go up to worship at Jerusalem, especially at the annual feast of Tabernacles (Zech. 14:16-19). One of the major features of the Millennium will be the temple, which will be the center of worship in Jerusalem. God gave Ezekiel the detailed architectural features of this future temple (Ezk. 40:1-46:24). Jesus Christ, sitting on the throne of His father David as King of Kings and Lord of Lords, will be the focal point of worship. As the waters fill the sea, so shall the earth be full of the knowledge of the Lord (Isa. 11:9).

As regards Satan.

At the beginning of this period Satan will be bound and banished into the bottomless pit for a thousand years (Rev. 20:1-3). Hence, his influence over earth will be restricted. He cannot carry on the deceptions and persecutions that previously occupied his time. Forced to view the results of his rebellion against God and His people, he now must contemplate the part he has played in the controversy between good and evil.

As regards nature.

This is the time that Jesus calls, *"the regeneration"* (Matt. 19:28). It is creation's rebirth. The nature of ferocious animals will be changed (Isa. 11:5-9). Nature will bring forth in great abundance (Joel 2:22-27). Human life will be prolonged; but there will be deaths during that period (Isa. 65:20).

As regards conditions in general.

The Scriptures represent this period as one of great joy and happiness. It will be a time of vast material prosperity and security (Micah 4:2-5). Friendly relations will exist among all nations, and men will no longer learn war (Isa. 2:4). The presence of Jesus Christ as the absolute ruler, and His activities in governing righteously, reveal a spiritual climate different from anything before it.

THE EVENTS AT THE CLOSE OF THE MILLENNIUM
Satan will be loosed from his prison (Rev. 20:7).

We are not told the reason for this. Some purpose of the divine plan calls for it. We can rejoice that it will only be for a brief period of time (Rev. 20:3).

Gog and Magog.

During this interim, Satan, now released from his long period of confinement, will go out to deceive the nations once again. It is after the *"many days"* of the millennium that the invasion of Gog and Magog occurs (Ezk. 38:8-23). Satan gathers together the nations, Gog and Magog, the number of whom is as the sand of the sea (Rev. 20:8). It could be that these terms refer symbolically to all nations that join Satan in this final rebellion against God. These nations will no doubt be primarily the Arabic or Muslim nations that surround Israel, all of which, even today, desire the destruction of the Jewish state.

Under Satan's leadership, these armies will proceed to the camp of God's people and the city of Jerusalem. But the contest is short and the issue decisive. Fire falls down out of Heaven and devours those armies (20:9). Thus the career of Satan and his followers will come to a dramatic and timely end; but they must yet appear before the Great White Throne for judgment with the rest of the lost.

CHAPTER 46

WILL EVERYONE BE JUDGED?

The Bible teaches that all who ever lived will give account of themselves to God (Rom. 14:12; Acts 17:31). The service of the saved will be judged at the Judgment Seat of Christ and the sins of unbelievers will be judged at the Great White Throne Judgment.

THE REASON FOR DIVINE JUDGMENT

Our heavenly Father is tender, compassionate and kind (Eph. 2:4, 7). He is *"love"* (1 John 4:8). Were it not for this attribute of God, all mankind would be lost. But those who think that God is *only* love are sadly mistaken. To ignore or reject His other characteristics is to deny many parts of the Bible. Because of who He is, it is impossible for God to ignore or minimize sin. These are the reasons why:

The justice of God.

He is *"the Judge of all the earth"* (Gen. 18:25). He is completely righteous and will not tolerate sin. Contrary to the way some picture Him, He is not a benign, grandfatherly type who never chastises and always overlooks sin.

The universality of sin.

All humans are both by nature and choice sinners (Rom. 3:9, 10, 23). There are no exceptions to the rule. We live in a day when sin is belittled; in fact, many deny there is such a thing as sin for which humans will be held accountable at some future judgment. Those who reject the plain teaching of Scripture on the subject of sin do so at their own peril. Because we are sinners, all may expect judgment.

THE METHOD OF JUDGMENT

It will be absolutely fair and just.

It is based on truth (Rom. 2:2). All of us have witnessed cases in modern law courts where the guilty party was acquitted. On the other hand, we have heard of innocent people who have been condemned and executed. However, the Judge of all the earth will do what is right. Never has He been biased in the past, nor will He be when we stand before Him on the day of Judgment. Paul reminds us that we should not be deceived regarding the actions of the Almighty. God cannot be mocked. Whatever a person sows, that is what he will reap (Gal. 6:7). No one will reap more in this life than they sow, nor will they reap more, or be falsely accused of sins they did not commit, in the next life.

It will be universal.

No one will escape being judged. God will render to each person according to what he has done (Rom. 2:6). Criminals often escape judgment in this life, but no one will escape or be exempt from judgment in the next.

It will be proportionate.

The degree of guilt and punishment will be based on the person's deeds (2:6). Paul is not teaching salvation by good deeds. He is making clear that God judges according to deeds, just as He judges according to truth. God will give to each one proportionately whatever his deeds deserve.

It will be impartial.

God does not show favoritism (Rom. 2:11). Not surprisingly, many guilty persons are acquitted today simply because of who they are. As the old saying goes, "Money talks," and sometimes it says, "Not guilty," when all the evidence indicates otherwise. It is well to remember that God cannot be bribed or influenced by a person's title or money.

It will be discerning (Rom 2:16).

Even the secrets of humans, their innermost thoughts and the deeds they have done clandestinely or in the dark, must be revealed and judged.

THE JUDGMENT AT CALVARY

On the cross the Lord Jesus bore our sins in His own body on the tree (1 Pet. 2:24). The Prophet Isaiah declared that the Messiah would suffer on our behalf—He would be wounded or pierced for our transgressions, crushed for our iniquities, chastised for our peace, and scourged for our healing (Isa. 53:5). The sins of believers were forever judged at Calvary. Therefore, they cannot come into judgment in the sense of being one day condemned and sent to Hell for some transgression (John 5:24).

The scope of the judgment.

All sins of believers—past, present and future—were borne by Christ (Acts 13:39). Their sins, past, present and future, were placed on the Son of God when He died on the cross.

The judgment was final.

It was once for all (Heb. 10:10, 12, 14). Humans must not seek to add to it or to subtract from it. When the Savior cried out on the cross, *"It is finished"* (John 19:30), He meant His death met all of God's requirements to the fullest. The sin debt had been paid once and for all. His death need never be repeated.

Its effects.

It is the basis of our forgiveness, justification, eternal life, and entrance into Heaven (Eph. 1:7; Rom. 5:9; John 5:24; Rom. 8: 1).

How to take advantage of its benefits.

Faith in Jesus Christ as one's Lord and Savior is the golden key (Rom. 3:26, 28). The moment one genuinely receives the Son of God as Savior and Lord, one is no longer under condemnation (judgment). He is saved and safe forever (Rom. 5:9; Eph. 2:8, 9; Heb. 1:3; 9:26).

THE JUDGMENT SEAT OF CHRIST

This judgment is also called the "Bema" judgment. In speaking to the believers in Corinth, Paul writes, "*we must all appear before the judgment seat of Christ*" (2 Cor. 5:10). *Bema* is the Greek word translated "*judgment seat*" in this verse.

The time.

Many scholars believe this judgment will take place immediately after the time of the Rapture when the Lord comes *for* His saints (Luke 14:14; 2 Tim. 4:8). However, the exact time of the judgment is not revealed in Scripture and is not the most important aspect of this event. Who will be judged and the standards by which judgment will be meted out are the more important considerations.

The participants.

All true believers will appear before this judgment seat. It is only reasonable that there should be a variety of rewards, considering the different types and length of service rendered by Christians while on earth. For every child of God there will be "*reward*" or "*loss*" (1 Cor. 3:14, 15); although, as a believer, he or she will be saved (1 Cor. 3:15).

The basis of judgment.

Believers will not be judged with regard to their sins as we have already observed. Believers will be judged on the basis of works they have done to the glory of God (Rom. 14:10; 2 Cor. 5:10). No one is saved by works they have performed, but by faith in Christ. However, they are saved to do good works (Eph. 2:10).

The rewards.

Only one foundation exists (1 Cor. 3:10-15), Jesus Christ. Those who build upon Him—His example, teachings, death, resurrection, intercession, and return—are building with gold, silver, and precious stones, and will have greater rewards. Those who build with selfishness, pride, covetousness,etc., in other words, with wood, hay, and straw, may expect their deeds to be of little value. The expectation of rewards should move us to greater zeal in Christian service (Matt. 5:12; 6:1; 10:41; Col. 2:18; 3:24; Heb. 11:26).

THE GREAT WHITE THRONE JUDGMENT

The time.

It will occur after Christ's thousand-year reign on earth and after the rebellion at the end of it. Also, it follows the doom of Satan (Rev. 20:1-11).

The judge.

The Bible reveals that Jesus Christ is the one who will be the Judge of the living and the dead (Matt. 25:31-33; John 5:22; Acts 10:42; 2 Tim. 4:1). The right to act as judge over the whole universe is an entitlement the Father has granted to the Son (John 5:26-27). The Bible reveals that Christians will assist in the process of judgment (1 Cor. 6:2, 3).

The participants (Rev. 20:11-13).

The dead in verse 13 refers to unbelievers. It is clear from these verses that all unbelievers will stand before this judgment seat.

As we have already seen, the sins of believers were judged at Calvary and the works of believers will be judged at the Judgment Seat of Christ. When a believer dies, his spirit goes at once to Heaven to be with Christ (2 Cor. 5:8; Phil. 1:23). The body will be resurrected and reunited with one's spirit at the return of Christ.

The Scriptures make plain that the wicked dead who die before this judgment go to Hades or Hell, a place of the dead and a place of torment. This is illustrated in the experience of the rich man who died (Luke 16:19-31). The spirits of departed unbelievers are left in Hades until the Great White Throne is set up.

The verdict.

Without exception, all who appear before this judgment will be found guilty. All will be eternally separated from God in the lake of fire (Rev. 20:14, 15; 21:8). However, this judgment of unbelievers will include degrees of punishment, for we read that the dead were judged on the basis of what they had done (Rev. 12:13; see also Luke 12:47, 48).

CONCLUSION

The fact that there will be a final judgment for every human assures us that ultimately God's universe is fair, that there is equity after all. The naysayers—those who have stubbornly insisted that there is no God, or if there is a God He is indifferent to human suffering and inequality—will not have the last word. God is in control; He keeps accurate records and renders to each one impartially what is due them (1 Pet. 1:17; Rom. 2:11). No one will be able to claim injustice. When all is said and done, all accounts will be settled and all will be made right.

BASIC BAPTIST BELIEFS

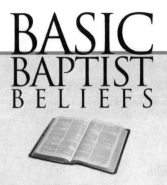

THE FINAL STATE

We believe that there is a radical and essential difference
between the righteous and the wicked; that such only as
through faith are justified in the name
of the Lord Jesus and sanctified by
the Spirit of God are truly righteous in His esteem;
while all such as continue in impenitence and unbelief are
in His sight wicked, and under the curse,
and this distinction holds
among men both in and after death, in the everlasting
felicity of the saved in Heaven, and the everlasting
conscious suffering of the lost in Hell.

CHAPTER 47

HOW CAN A LOVING GOD SEND PEOPLE TO HELL?

As we have already observed, the entrance to Heaven will be closed to the wicked. The Bible reveals that the wicked will be turned into Hell (Ps. 9:17). If there is one biblical concept more odious to people than any other, it is the teaching of Scripture on the subject of Hell. Agnostic Bertrand Russell said anyone who threatens people with eternal punishment, as Jesus did, is inhumane. The word *"Hell"* is actually a very popular word in our modern culture—used frequently as an expletive—and people are often derisively told to go there.

There are four modern views of Hell:
- *It is a literal place.* Hell is actual fire and punishment forever. Bible-based Christians hold to this position.
- *It is figurative.* The only hell is the hell people experience in this life. It is merely a state of mind. This tends to be the Liberal view of Hell.
- *It is mythological.* Hell is nothing but a myth like Aesop's Fables. It is a ploy to frighten the gullible into circumspect behavior. Agnostics and Atheists believe this.
- *It is the grave.* It is annihilation. The person burns up immediately and does not suffer eternal torment. Jehovah's Witnesses and others believe this.

One of the earmarks of most false religions is a denial of the reality of eternal punishment for unbelievers. Even among those in mainline Christian groups, Hell has become a moot subject. Polls have been taken in major denominations, and it is usually less than twenty percent who believe in a place of eternal punishment.

The Greek word *hades*, most often translated Hell in the New Testament, means the same as the Hebrew word *sheol* in the Old Testament. It refers to the grave, the pit, or the place of the dead. But make no mistake: it often refers to a place of retribution for those who persist in wickedness and unbelief. Another word translated Hell in the Bible is *gehenna*. It is related to a place called "the Valley of Hinnom," a valley immediately southwest of Jerusalem where garbage was burned and the bodies of criminals were thrown. The Jews associated this place with the everlasting punishment of the wicked.

God's justice demands a place of punishment.

Because God is just, the existence of a place of punishment for the wicked after this life is necessary to maintain His justice (Rom. 2:1-3). Indeed, there would be no real justice were there no place of punishment for evil people like Hitler, Stalin, Mao Tse-Tung, Saddam Hussein, and other such heartless and cruel dictators.

Surprisingly, Jesus said more about Hell than any other person in the New Testament. In fact, He said far more about Hell than about Heaven. Whenever Jesus spoke of Hell He did so in compassion, to warn people away from this ultimate tragedy. He wished to call people to conversion, and to warn that those who deliberately persist in unbelief will come to total ruin.

In Luke 16:19-31 *Jesus reveals six facts about Hell*:

IT IS A LITERAL PLACE

If the Bible cannot be relied on in its description of Hell, one might well question other concepts taught in Scripture. If there is no Hell, how can we be sure there is a Heaven? In Luke 16 Jesus told about the rich man in Hell. There is no suggestion that this is a parable as some have intimated; and because actual names are used, the reasonable conclusion is that Jesus intended for Hell to be understood as an actual place, not as a figurative place or state of mind.

IT IS A PLACE OF SUFFERING

Four times in Luke 16 Hell is revealed as a place of torment. Jesus said it was a place of torment (vs. 23). Twice the rich man said it was a place of torment (vss. 24, 28). Abraham said the same (vs. 25).

Other verses in the Bible echo a similar belief. In the Parable of the Marriage of the King's Son, Jesus told of an uninvited guest spotted by the King at the wedding. When asked why he was there without being properly attired for the occasion, the man was speechless. Then the king told the servants to bind the man's hands and feet and cast him into outer darkness, where there will be *"weeping and gnashing of teeth"* (Matt. 22:1-14). The suffering of the improperly attired guest is a picture of those who spurn God's invitation to be clothed in the righteousness of Christ and the ultimate punishment for such unbelief (2 Cor. 5:21).

The Devil's final end is described in Revelation 20:10. Indeed, Hell was prepared for the Devil and his angels (Matt. 25:41). The Devil is cast into *"the lake of fire and brimstone,"* where the Antichrist and False Prophet are already confined (Rev. 19:20), and will be "tormented" day and night forever. Revelation 20:15 reveals that all whose names were not written in the Book of Life were cast into *"the lake of fire."*

ITS INHABITANTS WILL EXPERIENCE
DEGREES OF PUNISHMENT

Just as there are degrees of reward in Heaven, there will be degrees of punishment in Hell. Because the rich man was often exposed to the believing beggar, Lazarus, his punishment becomes greater than those who have experienced no such exposure. The basis used to determine the degree of punishment is the opportunity a person had in this life to accept Christ. Jesus denounced the citizens of Chorazin and Bethsaida, telling them that if the miracles performed there had been performed in Tyre and Sidon, they would have repented long ago. Then He adds that it will be more tolerable for Tyre and Sidon on the Day of Judgment than for them. About Capernaum, Jesus said it will be more bearable for Sodom on the day of judgment than for them (Matt. 11:20-24).

The principle here seems to be, the greater one's knowledge, the greater one's responsibility, and the greater will be one's punishment if one fails in that responsibility. It may well be that the different degrees of punishment in Hell are not only a matter of physical suffering, but the awareness of one's eternal separation from God.

IT IS A PLACE WHERE MEMORIES
WILL HAUNT INHABITANTS

This account of the rich man shows that the lost in Hell are conscious and possess full use of their faculties and memory. The rich man cried out to Abraham and asked that he might have mercy on him, dip the tip of his finger in water and cool his tongue, for he was tormented by the flames. Abraham admonished him to remember how things were in his lifetime, that he lived in comfort while Lazarus laid at his gate full of sores, hoping to be fed crumbs from his table. Now the circumstances are reversed: Lazarus is comforted and the rich man is tormented (Luke 16:23-25). The memory of a person's lost opportunities to trust Christ and do good to others will haunt a person in Hell.

IT IS A PLACE OF CONCERN

The rich man passionately urged Abraham to go to his five brothers and warn them not to come to *"this place of torment"* (vss. 27-28). Those who are now in Hell are concerned for their loved ones. They do not want them there. Sometimes people jestingly say, "I want to go to Hell because that's where all my friends are." The rich man, however, did not want those close to him to come to that place.

Just as the rich man was concerned that his brothers not join him in Hell, so Christians who are still living should be interested in reaching those who are lost, lest they should end up in Hell.

IT IS AN EVERLASTING PLACE

Abraham told the rich man that an impassable gulf was fixed between the two of them so that those who want to go from where he is to where Lazarus was would be out of the question (Luke 16:26). Nor could anyone cross over from where Lazarus was to Abraham. There is no passing back and forth. In other words, there was no way to escape.

Three times in Mark 9 Jesus spoke of Hell as being a place where their worm does not die and the fire is not quenched (vss. 44, 46, 48). Imagine dying and yet never dying—eternal death. In Matthew 18:8, the word the Greek word translated *"eternal"* or *"everlasting"* (*aionios*), is the same Greek word used in John 3:16. The same word is found in Matthew 25:46; Mark 3: 29; 2 Thessalonians 1:9; Hebrews 6:2; and Jude 7. *Aionios* is the strongest word found in Greek for never-ending duration.

These verses rule out a second chance after death. There will be no reincarnation, affording people additional chances to be born on this earth for as many times as it takes to become cleansed of all impurities. There will be no opportunity for restitution, no purgatory where one may be purged of sins committed and finally made suitable for Heaven. One seals one's eternal destiny in this life.

CONCLUSION

Revelation 20:14 speaks of death and Hell being cast into the lake of fire, which is *"the second death."* The *"second death"* and the *"lake of fire"* are identical terms and are used to denote the eternal state of the wicked.

It is an illusion to reject something simply because we wish not to believe in it. We are not free to accept one doctrine and reject the other simply because one is contrary to our way of thinking or is difficult to understand. A refusal to believe in Hell is a refusal to take God seriously.

The Bible does not reveal in detail how such punishment will be possible; for instance, how there can be fire that does not consume, or how humans are able to remain alive and conscious under such grim circumstances. We know that God is just in all His dealings, and has everything well planned. We must leave the imponderables to Him. It is not for us to speculate.

It should be made clear that Lazarus did not go to Heaven because he was poor; nor was the rich man condemned to Hell because of his wealth. Although we are not told that Lazarus was a true believer, we may rightly assume that he was, because Scripture never says that God accepts a person simply on the basis of his poor economic circumstances. On the other hand, the rich man was not punished because of his affluence or for his lack of compassion for the poor. He was condemned for refusing to accept God's offer of pardon for his sins. There is only one way to Hell and that is the way of unbelief (John 3:18). God does not "send" people to Hell. People end up in Hell because of their refusal to take God at His Word. The only way to avoid Hell is to believe in the Lord Jesus Christ, and make that decision in this life (Acts 16:31).

CHAPTER 48

WHAT IS HEAVEN LIKE AND WHO WILL GO THERE?

Not only is there a noticeable difference between the righteous and the wicked in this life, there will be a vast difference between their destinies in the next. According to the Bible, the righteous are those who, by faith, have been justified in the name of the Lord Jesus and by the Spirit of God; the wicked are those who have willfully chosen to reject Christ as Lord and Savior (1 Cor. 6:9-11).

According to the Word of God, only two destinations are spoken of in the Bible: Hell for those who have rejected Christ, and Heaven for those who have believed on the Lord Jesus. Jesus spoke only of these two destinies in the afterlife (Matt. 7:13, 14; John 14:1-3). No mention is made in the New Testament of Purgatory or reincarnation.

HEAVEN IS A REAL PLACE

The longing for a place of rest and joy after this life is almost universal in the human heart. The fact that humans could even conceive of such a place and long for it is not without significance. Jesus gave voice to our deepest longings in John 14:2, 3 when He told His disciples that He was soon to leave them, but He would prepare a *place* for them in His Father's House. He assuaged their fears by assuring them He will come again one day and take them to live with Him in that place. Many deny that Heaven is an actual place, insisting, rather, that it is nothing more than a state of mind. To deny that Heaven is an actual place is to contradict the emphatic words of Jesus in John 14:2, as well as other passages in the New Testament.

Christ came from Heaven (John 6:38).

Almost all of Jesus' contemporaries believed He was the son of Joseph who was born in the little town of Bethlehem. But on a certain occasion in Galilee, Jesus made a claim that profoundly stunned his listeners. He declared that He was the living bread that *came down from Heaven* (John 6:51). He contrasts Himself with the manna that miraculously fell from Heaven to nourish the Israelites in the wilderness. To the astonishment of His audience, Jesus revealed publicly that Heaven is His original home, the place He lived before His birth in Bethlehem. This claim not only proves that He is more than a mere human being; it also attests that He acknowledged Heaven to be a real place.

Christ returned to Heaven.

Forty days after His resurrection, Jesus gathered His disciples together for a final word of instruction. He commanded them not to leave Jerusalem until they had experienced what the Father promised, meaning the coming of the Holy Spirit (Acts 1:1-5). Soon after completing His instructions, He began to move up into the sky and disappeared into a cloud (1:9).

While they were staring up at the cloud with bewilderment, two angels appeared and chided them for their failure to comprehend the significance of the event. The angels assured them that Jesus had been taken up from them into Heaven (Acts 1:10,11; see Heb. 4:14). He came from Heaven; He went back to Heaven. One day He will return from Heaven to this earth.

Some day—either at the time of our death or when Christ comes back again—Christians will be taken to Heaven to be forever with the Lord. He assured the believing thief on the cross that on that very day they would meet again in *paradise* (Luke 23:43). Paul's words, *"to die is gain,"* imply that a Christian who dies goes immediately to a better place (Phil. 1:21). Again, Paul affirmed that to be away from the body is to be at home with the Lord (2 Cor. 5:8). Jesus promised His disciples that He would come again for them, so that where He was, they could also be there to enjoy the blessings and benefit of that beautiful and enduring place (John 1:14).

It is called the "third Heaven."

According to Biblical teaching, the first heaven is the atmosphere where the birds fly; heaven number two is the stratosphere, and the third Heaven is God's dwelling place where His throne is located (2 Cor. 12:2-4). In these verses Paul recounts in the third person, an experience in which he was taken up into the third Heaven, into *Paradise*, where he heard remarkable and mysterious things not permissible for a human to relate. We may assume that he also *saw* things he could not describe with ordinary human words.

HEAVEN IS A PLACE OF INDESCRIBABLE BEAUTY

The first two chapters of the Bible tell of God's creation of a perfect world as a home for the human beings He created. The original home of the first two humans was called *"the Garden of Eden,"* or *"Paradise."* As we have noted, the third Heaven is also portrayed as *"Paradise."* When humans use the term *"paradise,"* it usually suggests a place of extraordinary beauty.

The last two chapters of the Bible speak of God's creating a perfect world for redeemed humanity (Rev. 21-22). The apostle John gives a brief but vivid glimpse of the holy city, New Jerusalem, in these chapters. He observed it coming down from God out of Heaven, prepared as a bride adorned for her husband (Rev. 21:2). His portrayal of that city defies description and staggers the imagination. Unlike all earthly cities, it is filled with *"the glory of God."* When Christians think of Heaven they often think of *glory* and sometimes call it "glory land" (as in "I've got a home in glory land that outshines the sun").

The brilliance of the city is like that of a precious jewel, clear as crystal. The wall is made of jasper; the city is pure gold, clear as glass; the foundations of the walls are decorated with all manner of precious stones. The twelve gates are twelve pearls, each gate made of a single pearl. The street of the city is pure gold, like transparent glass. It is a city of immense size. Its length, breadth, and height are equal, measuring approximately 1400 miles (2,250 kilometers) each. The river of the water of life, clear as crystal, flows from the throne of God and of the Lamb. On each side of the river is the tree of life, the leaves of which are for the healing of the nations. The city has no need of sun or moon, for the glory of God provides illumination. There will be no night there. It will be a world of unsurpassing splendor. It citizens will live forever and enjoy the highest conceivable happiness.

Scripture locates the Father's throne and heavenly headquarters in the New Jerusalem, which will descend to the renovated earth (21:2, 3). The New *Jerusalem* is the capital city of this new earth. In the Hebrew language, Jerusalem means "city of peace." How different the New Jerusalem will be from the earthly Jerusalem, which seldom has lived up to its name. The New Jerusalem is the city for which Abraham looked (Heb. 11:10). Within that vast city Christ is preparing a dwelling place for each believer (John 14:2).

HEAVEN IS A PLACE OF HAPPY ASSOCIATION

The redeemed of all the ages will be there (Rev. 21:24). In Heaven we will fellowship with the truly important people who have graced our planet. Imagine seeing Enoch, Noah, Abraham, Sarah, Moses, David, Peter, Mary, Lydia and Paul face to face. How long will it take to hear their story? No matter, we have eternity.

Our loved ones will be there and will be recognized as such. On the Mount of Transfiguration Moses and Elijah were identified and even had their same names. After Christ's resurrection His disciples had no trouble recognizing Him. Mary knew His voice (John 20:11-16). Thomas recognized His physical appearance (John 20:27, 28). We may safely assume that in the heavenly world we will continue our relationships with those we know and love.

Will there be marriage in Heaven? Jesus plainly said that in the resurrection people will neither marry nor be given in marriage. We will be like the angels in Heaven (Matt. 22:29, 30). The question arises: will the redeemed be deprived of the benefits now associated with marriage? In Heaven, the redeemed will not be deprived of any good thing. The quintessence of marriage is love. The epitome of joy is in the expression of love. We may be confident that in the heavenly world no one there will lack for either love or joy or pleasure. No one there will feel lonely, empty, or unloved. We can trust that the loving Creator who designed marriage to bring joy in this present world will have something far better in the next.

HEAVEN IS A PLACE OF ACTIVITY

Although Heaven will be a place of rest, it will be rest from toil and mental stress, not rest from activity or work. We sing,

O Land of rest for thee I sigh!
When will the moment come
When I shall lay my armor by
And dwell in peace at home?

It is appealing to think of not having to punch a clock or work hard for eight or ten hours a day. Heaven will be a place of rest from that kind of labor. At the same time, our new-earth existence will offer many activities in which we can be engaged. What these activities may involve, we can only speculate. Adam and Eve had plenty of work assigned to them before the fall and the subsequent curse that turned it into toil and stress (Gen. 3:17-19). Our new life will present endless challenges to grow in our knowledge and understanding not only of God but also of the entire universe. How exciting to think of exploring this vast universe that was spoken into existence by our Creator God.

HEAVEN IS A PLACE OF BLESSED EMANCIPATION

Some of the most striking aspects of the heavenly city have to do with what is *not* there. In the Book of Revelation are a number of *"no mores:" "no more pain"* (21:4); *"no more sorrow"* (21:4); *"no more tears"* (7:17); *"no more death"* (21:4). Death, man's last and most feared enemy, will no longer strike terror into hearts as it has for thousands of years of human history. It will be cast into the Lake of Fire, and we will be in a world beyond its reach (Rev. 20:14).

CONCLUSION

Only the righteous, those whose names are written in the Lamb's Book of Life, will enter into that holy city (Rev. 21:27). Only the names of those who have been washed clean in the blood of the Lamb will be inscribed in the Lamb's Book of Life. The door will be closed to all the unrighteous who refuse to enter through the one and only door—Jesus Christ.

More important than the physical beauty of the heavenly city, more important than the fellowship we will enjoy with the saints of all the ages, more important than the freedom we will experience from pain, sorrow, and death, will be the fact that we will be in the very presence of God enjoying the beatific vision (seeing God face to face). The blessed Trinity—Father, Son, and Holy Spirit—will be there to welcome us. Each will be the object of our adoration, and we will enjoy unbroken fellowship with them throughout eternity (21:3, 4; 22:3, 4).

APPENDIX 1

OTHER NOTABLE BAPTIST DISTINCTIVES

Three key issues not discussed in previous chapters, *the separation of church and state, religious liberty*, and *the priesthood of the believer*, are principles Baptists have cherished and defended for centuries. No other religious body has done more to advance these vital causes.

THE SEPARATION OF CHURCH AND STATE

In America, separation of church and state originally meant the exclusion of civil authority from religious affairs and the independence of organized religion from government sanction or support. In other words, there was to be no state-sponsored church as was the norm in England and other European countries. This represented a bold experiment unparalleled in human history. Not until the twentieth century would other countries follow in America's footsteps and institute this principle.

After the Revolutionary War, religious dissenters throughout the states sought to bring an end to religious establishment. Religious and political leaders alike argued that religion should be free of the state, and government should be denied the right of jurisdiction over religion, a view championed by the Founding Fathers. The Baptist, Isaac Backus (1724-1806), said: "The free exercise of private judgment, and the unalienable rights of conscience, are of too high a rank and dignity to be submitted to the decrees and councils, or the imperfect laws of fallible legislators."

From dissenters, especially Baptists, came the demand in the form of a Bill of Rights to guarantee the separation of church and state and to provide assurance of the free exercise of religion. Consequently, on September 25, 1789, Congress expressly prohibited an establishment of religion with the adoption of the First Amendment, which begins with the familiar words: "Congress shall make no law respecting an establishment of religion or prohibiting the free exercise thereof." It was ratified in 1791.

The downside of this issue is that in recent years secularists have tried to give the separation of church and state a meaning never intended by the Founders. Whenever religion is mentioned today within the confines of government, secularists vigorously protest and base their objections on the separation of church and state. However, the separation of church and state does not mean the separation of religion and politics, or the denial of the right of churches to be involved in the body politic.

Some are surprised to hear that the phrase, "separation of church and state," does not even appear in the Constitution. In a letter dated January 1, 1802, Thomas Jefferson made the statement about "a wall of separation between church and state" to the Danbury Baptist Association of Connecticut. The Baptist group had heard a rumor that the Congregationalists were to become the national religion. Jefferson clearly stated in his letter that the new government would not establish a national religion, or dictate how people were to worship God.

Under the old regime in England, people were required by law to attend the state sponsored Anglican Church (Church of England). No other churches were allowed, and mandatory attendance was compelled under the Conventicle Act of 1665. Failure to comply could mean imprisonment and torture. The people in the new American Republic did not want freedom *from* religion but freedom *of* religion.

Today, Christians are often considered the enemy by liberal social engineers. These misguided people want to achieve a new, humanistic America where children in school and citizens in general will be protected from outmoded Christian standards of morality and justice. The separation of church and state is being shamelessly perverted to advance their humanistic agenda.

It must be remembered that neutrality on this issue is impossible. Some authority, whether it be God or humans, will be used as the reference point. If a government rejects one system, it adopts another. Our United States Constitution was founded on Biblical principles, and it was the intention of the authors of this document for the new nation to be sustained by these principles. No thought was ever given to separating the state from religion; the intent was to prevent government from establishing a state religion.

To insist that Biblical principles should not be allowed in government and in schools is to be either ignorant of the historic intent of the founding fathers or to be blatantly prejudiced against Christianity.

RELIGIOUS LIBERTY

Baptists have long been known as exponents of religious liberty. Seventeenth-century English Baptists were among the first advocates of religious toleration. In America, Roger Williams (1603-1683), the founder of Rhode Island, was the first champion of religious liberty. After being banished from Massachusetts for advocating separation from the Church of England, he fled with his family and a few like-minded friends to the uninhabited regions to the south, outside the limits of Massachusetts, and founded a settlement there in 1636, which he named Providence. It was there that Williams established what some believe to be the first Baptist church in America.

In Providence Williams adopted the principle that "God requireth not an uniformity of Religion" and saw to it that all individuals and religious bodies enjoyed what he called "soul liberty," that is, religious freedom. On a trip to London he was able to procure a charter from Parliament on March 14, 1644, uniting the various towns into the colony of Rhode Island, guaranteeing its independence, and for the first time in

American history granting complete religious liberty to all of its inhabitants.

Religious liberty guarantees the ability of every congregation to regulate its own internal life, its doctrine and discipline, in accordance with its own perception of divine truth. It requires that there be no external political intrusion into its internal affairs.

THE PRIESTHOOD OF THE BELIEVER

The priesthood of the believer infers that every Christian has direct access to God the Father through Jesus Christ, our great High Priest, the sole mediator between God and humans (1 Pet. 2:9; Rev. 1:6; 1 Tim. 2:5). This is one of the great New Testament principles recovered by John Wycliffe in the fourteenth century, and given particular prominence in the sixteenth century by Martin Luther and other Reformation leaders, including the Anabaptists. When joined with justification by faith alone and the authority of Scripture, it untangled the complex web of medieval Catholicism that placed impenetrable barriers between the individual Christian and God.

First, it meant that laypeople could pray directly to God through Jesus Christ without going through a human intermediary (priests, saints, etc.), the result being that laypeople became more involved in private and public worship.

Second, it meant that God communicated directly to the individual Christian through His Word, hence, encouraging vernacular versions of Scripture and personal Bible study.

Third, it meant a new sense of liberty for ordinary Christians who no longer felt restricted by tradition or ecclesiastical hierarchies.

On the negative side, some have hijacked this cherished belief and forced a meaning into it that was never intended. The teaching has been used to justify the attitude that a Christian may interpret the Bible "in any way I choose" and still be considered a Christian. A root doctrine of the priesthood of the believer is soul freedom. However, we are free only under the authority of Scripture; we are not free outside of that authority. In no way does this doctrine give license to misinterpret or explain away the great, foundational truths of the Bible. Such triumphant subjectivism often leads to the neglect of the Bible altogether.

Others have used this principle to undermine pastoral authority in the local church. This revered truth does not grant permission to those, like Diotrephes, who seek to usurp the pastor's role and foment dissension in the church (3 John 9, 10; cf. Heb. 13:17). The emasculation of this doctrine often manifests itself in a lack of reverence and respect for the local church.

While few would deny the importance of the doctrine of the priesthood of all believers, we should be careful not to trivialize its meaning by equating it with theological liberalism, or the freedom to believe as one pleases, regardless if it contradicts Scripture. Far from providing a cover for individual doctrinal error, it is a stimulus for defending the church against those forces which would weaken and destroy it.

APPENDIX 2

SELECTIVE GLOSSARY OF TERMS

Abraham's Bosom—Term used by Luke (Luke 16:22) to describe the abode of the just persons who died during Old Testament times. Upon His ascension, the Lord Jesus took the inhabitants of Abraham's Bosom with Him to Heaven (Eph. 4:8). Today, believers who die do not go to Hades (that is, to the place called "Abraham's Bosom") but go directly to be with Jesus in Heaven (Luke 23:43; 2 Cor. 5:8; Phil. 1:23).

Adoption—God's act of making estranged human beings part of His spiritual family. The act takes place when a person receives the Lord Jesus Christ by faith (Rom. 8:15; Gal. 4:5; Eph. 1:5).

Advent—Literally means "coming" or "arrival." The first advent refers to the coming of Jesus Christ to earth to provide salvation to all who would trust in Him. His second advent refers to His return to earth to establish His earthly kingdom.

Advocate—A title of Christ who is said to be our "Advocate" with the Father (1 John 2:1). Also the title of the Holy Spirit, whom Christ promised to send to His followers (John 14:16). Christ is our Advocate who defends believers against their accuser, the Devil.

Age of Accountability—The time of life at which a person is assumed to be morally responsible and able to distinguish between right and wrong, hence, accountable for sins.

Agnosticism—The belief that either knowledge or certitude about ultimate realities (e.g., "God exists") is impossible.

Alexandrian Theology—Dominant theology in the early church of Alexandria (Egypt), led by Clement (A.D. 190) and Origen (A.D. 202). It favored a mystical or allegorical interpretation of the Bible in contrast with the literal and historical approach of the Antiochene theology.

Almighty—All-powerful, referring to God. The title is used many times in the Bible in combination with God (*El, theos*) and Lord (*Kurios*).

Alpha and Omega—The first and last letters of the Greek alphabet. Used in reference to Christ, the expression witnesses to His deity (Rev. 1:8).

Amen—From the Greek *amen* and means, "It is so" or "so be it." Used after a prayer or other solemn pronouncement to express ratification or agreement. It was often spoken by Christ and is given as one of His names (Rev. 3:14).

Amillennialism—The belief that the thousand-year reign is figurative, not literal. Amillennialists usually interpret Revelation 20 as referring to Christ returning at the end of history and that the church is presently in the final era of history.

Anabaptist—A term referring to several movements during the 16th century Reformation period. Anabaptists rejected infant baptism and urged their followers to be baptized (immersed) upon receiving Jesus Christ as Savior.

Annihilationism—The belief that all non-Christians will be judged by God and thrown into the lake of fire where they will be "annihilated" rather than suffer eternal punishment.

Antichrist—Literally means "against Christ." Anyone who is against Christ is an "antichrist;" but the Bible teaches that there will be a future world-wide leader whose rule will signify the nearness of Christ's second coming (1 John 2:18).

Antinomianism—The conviction that a person's faith in God and in the person of Christ frees him from the moral obligations of the law (thus *anti* "against" + *nomos* "law"). It is rejected by most Christian groups on the basis that although keeping the law does not save Christians, they still have a responsibility of living an upright life. Paul clarified that God's grace brings liberty from sin, not liberty to sin (Rom. 6:1-11).

Antiochene Theology—The dominant theology of the early church at Antioch. In contrast to the Alexandrian school of interpretation that emphasized an allegorical approach to Scripture, the Antiochene school practiced a method of scriptural interpretation that emphasized the literal meaning of the text.

Apocrypha—From the Greek *apokrypto*, "to hide, conceal." Composed by Jews during the two centuries before Christ and the early centuries of our era, the books of the Apocrypha are considered canonical by the Roman Catholic and Orthodox Churches but not by Jews or non-Catholic churches. These books were included in all early English Bibles, including the KJV, but were inserted between the books of Malachi and Matthew, usually with the explanation that, though the books were profitable for inspirational and historical purposes, they were not to be regarded as authentic Scripture.

Apologetics—(Greek *apologetikos*, a defense). The formal defense of the Christian faith. Apologists appeal to such methods as rational argumentation, empirical evidence, and fulfilled prophecy to defend such beliefs as the existence of God, the deity of Christ, miracles, and the authority of Scripture.

Apostles Creed—A statement of faith composed of twelve articles used by both Roman Catholic and many Protestant churches, but not generally repeated in non-creedal groups such as Baptists. Although ascribed to the Apostles, no conclusive evidence exists that they actually authored the Creed.

Aramaic—A Semitic language spoken by most Jews during and after the Babylonian exile (606-536 B.C.). Christ and the Apostles spoke Aramaic, since in New Testament times Hebrew was spoken mostly by those educated in Rabbinical schools.

Archangel—A chief or ruling angel. The term occurs twice in the New Testament (1 Thess. 4:16; Jude 9). They are messengers of God to humans in matters of great significance. Gabriel was the angel that announced the birth of Christ; Michael is the leader of the heavenly host who fought and won against the rebellious angels, led by the Devil.

Arianism—A fourth century heresy that denied the deity of Jesus Christ. Its chief spokesman was Arius (256-336), a priest of Alexandria, who in 318 began to teach the doctrine that now bears his name. According to Arius there are not three distinct persons in the Trinity, co-eternal and equal in all things, but only one person, the Father. The Son is only a creature like all other created beings, though the highest of all the creatures. The Council of Nicaea was convened in 325 to meet the Arian crisis. The Council affirmed the deity of Christ and condemned Arius as a heretic.

Arminianism—A system of theology named after Dutch theologian Jacobus Arminius (1560-1609). At first a Calvinist pastor, he came to question some of the teachings of Calvinism. He and his followers opposed John Calvin's teaching that grace benefits only the elect, that Christ died for the elect only, and the doctrine of selective salvation and absolute predestination, independent of human merit. Arminius taught that predestination was based on God's foreknowledge in seeing whether an individual would freely accept or reject Christ. Because salvation is freely chosen, it could also be freely lost. This is the theological system held by the majority of those in the Methodist, Pentecostal, and Free-will Baptist traditions.

Ascension—Term used to refer to Christ's going up to Heaven forty days after His resurrection from the dead. The souls of the just from the pre-Christian era went with the Savior into the glory of Heaven.

Atheism—Denial of a personal God who is totally distinct from the world He created.

Baptismal Regeneration—The teaching that baptism is a necessary part of salvation.

Baptism for the Dead—Vicarious baptism practiced by Mormons for those who died unbaptized, based on Paul's words in 1 Corinthians 15:29. Some teach that certain believers in Corinth were being baptized on behalf of friends or relatives who had professed faith in Christ but died before baptism. If Paul is referring to vicarious baptism, as some believe, he does not appear to condone the practice ("what will *they* do who are baptized for the dead"), but uses it for the sake of argument. He simply mentions the practice as taking place, and asks what meaning it can possibly have if the dead do not rise. Some commentators deny that there is any reference at all to vicarious baptism in this passage. They see in it as a reference to newly baptized people taking the place in the church of those who had died. Others see it as a reference to those who had been inspired by the martyrdom of saints to receive Christ and profess Him in baptism, thus filling up their vacant places in the church.

Bible—From the Greek *biblos* ("book"), meaning the inspired Book or Word of God; the written record of revelation.

Born Again—Spiritual rebirth commanded by Christ (John 3:5). The spiritual change effected by divine grace, by which a person who believes on the Lord Jesus Christ is regenerated into a new creature, a child of God and heir of Heaven.

Calvinism—The theological system based on the work of John Calvin (1509-1564), the celebrated Reformation theologian. The traditional summary of the major tenets of Calvinism is depicted in the acronym TULIP (total depravity, unconditional election, limited atonement, irresistible grace and the perseverance of the saints). The basic principles of Calvinism are set forth in John Calvin's famous work, the *Institutes of the Christian Religion.*

Canon—(of the Bible)—Literally "standard" or "rule," it refers to the official list of the inspired books of the Bible (39 Old Testament Books and 27 New Testament books) that the church has recognized as the written word of God. Together these books function as the "rule" or "standard" of faith and practice in each church.

Capital Punishment—The death penalty imposed by the state for the punishment of serious crimes. Scripture clearly teaches that civil authorities may lawfully put certain criminals to death (Rom 13:4). The state is much like a body composed of many members, and as a surgeon may cut out a cancerous growth to save the other parts of the body, so the civil authority may lawfully put a criminal to death. By so doing he provides for the common good of the rest of society.

Catechism—A manual of instruction in Christian doctrine, used mostly in Roman Catholic and other liturgical churches.

Catholic—A Greek word (*katholike*) which means "general" or "universal." The term has come to be associated primarily with Roman Catholic, Anglican, and Orthodox churches. However, in the beginning, the word "catholic" suggested that the gospel message the early churches proclaimed and church membership are universal in scope; that is, it is not restricted to one ethnic group or geographical location but is open to Jew and Gentile, slave and free, male and female living anywhere (Gal. 3:28).

Charismatic—A movement spanning several denominations that stresses the "gifts" of the Holy Spirit, especially the "sign" gifts, such as speaking in tongues, healing and miracles.

Cherub—(plural, *cherubim*)—Heavenly creatures (angels) mentioned in the Bible as guardians and protectors. Cherubim were the sentinels stationed at the Garden of Eden (Gen. 3:24); they were golden figures erected on the Ark of the Covenant (Exo. 25:18). The Almighty mounted a cherub to rush to the rescue of David from his enemies (2 Sam. 22:11). More than any other creatures, cherubim reveal the power and majesty of God.

Chiliasm—From the Greek *chilioi*, "thousand." The view, based on Revelation 20:1-5, that Christ will reign on earth for a thousand years following His second coming. Chiliasm can be traced through church history to the very early days of Christianity.

Christ—From the Greek word *Christos*, translated in English as "Christ." It is the equivalent of the Hebrew word *Messiah*; a significant title of Jesus meaning "the anointed one."

Christology—The specialized study of the person of Jesus Christ and especially the mystery of the union in Christ of the divine and human natures.

Church—From the Greek *ekklesia*, meaning "a local assembly of people" gathered together for a specific purpose. In the New Testament sense, it is a "called out assembly" of baptized believers in Jesus Christ, who have covenanted together for a common purpose, and whose chief goal is to fulfill the Great Commission.

Church fathers—The leading theologians and pastors of approximately the first six centuries of the Christian era.

Circumcision—The cutting off of the foreskin of the penis as a sign of the covenant between God and Abraham. Every male, God ordered, was to be circumcised when he was eight days old (Gen. 17:12). Under the New Covenant, Gentiles were not required to submit to circumcision (Acts 15:28).

Codex Sinaiticus—A late fourth-century manuscript of the Greek Bible, sold by the Soviet Government to the British Museum in 1933. Written on vellum, it contains part of the Old Testament, all the books of the New Testament along with the Epistle of Barnabas and part of the Shepherd of Hermas. Its name comes from the fact that the manuscript was discovered in 1844 by Constantin von Tischendorf (1815-74) in the Orthodox monastery of St. Catherine on Mount Sinai.

Codex Vaticanus—A fourth-century manuscript of the Greek Bible, now in the Vatican Library. It contains most of the Old Testament and all the New Testament except Hebrew 9:14 to the end. The codex is known to have existed in the Vatican library since at least 1475 when it was listed in a catalogue. Being in the Vatican library does not mean Roman Catholics produced it. Some believe the manuscript was brought to Rome from Constantinople as a gift by the Greek delegation to the Council of Ferrara-Florence in 1438-39. Others claim Greeks could have been brought it to Rome after the defeat of Constantinople by Muslim Turks in 1453. The New Testament formed the basis for Westcott and Hort's Greek text published in 1881.

Communion of Saints—The entire community of Christians—those on earth and those in Heaven.

Confessions of faith—Formal statements of doctrinal beliefs.

Confirmation—One of the sacraments of the Roman Catholic Church in which the person confirms the faith testified to in baptism. A few other groups also practice confirmation.

Conservatism, biblical—The conviction that all the accounts of Scripture are to be taken at face value, its supernatural sections as well as its historical accounts.

Consubstantiation—The Lutheran belief that in the Lord's Supper the bread and wine do not become the actual body and blood of Christ, but that the molecules of the flesh and blood are present "in, with, and under" the molecules of the bread and wine.

Covenant ("testament")—An agreement (contract) God made first with the Israelites and then second with all people everywhere who have trusted in the Lord Jesus Christ. The agreement includes a promise to bless those who trust and obey Him.

Creatio ex nihilo—Literally, "creation out of nothing," the idea that God created without the use of previously existing materials.

Creationism—The belief that the universe and life itself originated from a divine Creator rather than from chance factors.

Dead, Prayers for the—The practice of praying for the dead, found mostly in Roman Catholicism, and based in large measure on the apocryphal text of

2 Maccabees 12:44.

Day of the Lord—A biblical phrase pointing to a future series of events during which God, through Christ, will visit judgment on the world in preparation for the establishment of the millennial kingdom.

Decrees of God—Decisions of God, made in eternity, that make certain all that occurs within time.

Deism—A belief system that flourished in England from the mid-17th century until the mid-18th century. It accepts the existence of God, that He created the world, but He has no continuing involvement with it or the events within it. Those who held this view denied the supernatural element in Christianity.

Demonology—The study of demons.

Depravity, Total—The idea that the whole of one's nature is affected by sin and impacts all one does.

Dispensationalism—A system of biblical interpretation that divides God's dealing with humans into different periods that He administers on different bases. It involves a literal interpretation of Scripture, a distinction between Israel and the church, and a premillennial, pretribulational eschatology.

Doctrine (teaching)—A body or system of teachings relating to a particular theological topic in Scripture.

Dogma—A system of principles or tenets of a church. In Roman Catholic tradition, a church doctrine issued with the highest authority and solemnity; a core teaching of the church.

Double predestination—The belief that God has chosen some to be saved and others to be lost.

Dualism—The belief that there are two divine powers or spiritual principals set against each other: one good, the other evil.

Eastern Orthodoxy—Designation of the Eastern or Greek churches that separated from the Western churches (Roman Catholic) in A.D. 1054.

Ebionism—An early heretical group that thought of Jesus as human but not divine.

Ecumenism—The movement that seeks Christian unity throughout the world

Election—God's decision, based on His foreknowledge, in choosing a special group or certain persons for salvation or service.

Elohim—A very common Hebrew name for God.

El Shaddai—A name for God that emphasizes His power.

Emmanuel (also "Immanuel")—A name for Jesus that means "God with us."

Episcopacy—The system of church government that places primary authority in the office of bishop.

Eschatology—Teaching about last things—death, judgment, Heaven, Hell, the second coming and the resurrection of the body.

Eternal death—The permanent separation of the sinner from God.

Eternal destruction—The endless future punishment of the wicked.

Eternal security—The doctrine that truly regenerate believers will never lose their salvation.

Eucharist—From the Greek word meaning "thanksgiving." In the Roman Catholic Church it refers to the Mass. Some Protestant churches use the term to refer to the Lord's Supper.

Euthanasia—("good death")—An attempt to prevent the process of death from being unduly prolonged and painful.

Evangelical—One who holds to the beliefs and practices of evangelicalism.

Evangelicalism—A movement in Christianity emphasizing personal conversion through faith in Jesus Christ, and affirming orthodox doctrines.

Evolution, Theistic—The belief that God began the creation and then used the process of evolution to produce the desired results.

Exegesis—Obtaining the meaning of a passage by drawing the meaning from, rather than reading it into, the text.

Expiation—The cancellation of sin, whereas "propitiation" is the appeasing of divine wrath.

Extrabiblical—Pertaining to material not found in the Bible.

Extreme unction—Also known as "last rites," it is a sacrament of the Roman Catholic Church, and consists of an anointing with oil at the time of death.

Faith—One of the three theological virtues. Faith refers to (1) assent of the mind to truths God has revealed in His Word; (2) the truths themselves (the content of faith); and (3) the lived witness of a Christian life (living faith).

Fideism—The view that the great doctrines of Scripture must be accepted by faith rather than proved by reason.

Firstborn—The oldest legitimate son. In ancient times the firstborn received a special inheritance (sometimes everything; at other times a double portion). In the New Testament, Christ, "the firstborn of all creation," is designated as the heir of the Father (Col. 1:15; Heb. 1:6).

First fruits—An offering from the first harvestings of the year, in recognition that the land and all that it produces come from and belong to the Lord.

Foreknowledge—God's knowledge of events prior to their occurrence, including free human actions.

Foreordination—God's rendering an event certain before it occurs.

Free churches—Churches that are not aligned with any state entity and have traditionally opposed such alliances.

Free will—The idea that human beings have the voluntary power of moral and psychological choice.

Fundamentalism—A theological movement that began in the United States in the late nineteenth century and remains influential today. It stresses certain basic doctrines or "fundamentals," such as the inspiration of Scripture, the virgin birth of Christ, His sacrificial death, resurrection, and second coming.

Fundamentals, The—A twelve-volume series of articles published between 1910 and 1915 by leading conservative theologians. The fundamental doctrines of the Christian faith were set forth in those publications, and from them were derived the terms "fundamentalism" or "fundamentalist."

Gap theory—The belief that an indeterminate period of time or "gap" exists between Genesis 1:1 and Genesis 1:2. Virtually all of geological time is placed in this gap between God's original creative act in verse one and His subsequent re-creation of the world in verses two and following.

Gehenna—Transliteration of the Hebrew (*ge-hinnom*) meaning "valley of Hinnom" (2 Kings 23:10). Located southwest of Jerusalem, it was where some of the kings of Judah engaged in forbidden religious practices, including human sacrifice by fire (2 Chron. 28:3; 33:6; Jer. 7:31; 32:35). Subsequently, it became the city's garbage dump, where dead animals were thrown and refuse burned. Because of these associations and the smoke that continually ascended from it, the word "Gehenna" came to be a symbol of Hell and eternal punishment (Matt. 10:28; Mark 9:43).

Gifts, Spiritual—Special endowments granted by the Holy Spirit to Christians, whether unusual abilities, spiritual qualities, or gifted individuals (Rom. 12:6-8; 1 Cor. 12:4-11; Eph. 4:11; 1 Pet. 4:11).

Glorification—The final step in the process of salvation; it involves the completion of sanctification and the removal of all spiritual defects.

Gospel—Literally, "good news." Gospel refers to (1) the good news preached by Jesus Christ; (2) the good news of salvation won for us in the person of Christ (He is the good news proclaimed by Christians); (3) the four written records of the good news—the gospels of Matthew, Mark, Luke and John.

Grace—A free gift, something to which we have no right. In the biblical sense, it is the free and unmerited favor of God bestowed on unworthy, guilty sinners, enabling them to become adopted into His family through faith in His Son, the Lord Jesus Christ.

Hades—Greek word used in the Septuagint for the Hebrew *Sheol*, the place of the dead. In the New Testament it represents the place of punishment of the wicked (Matt. 11:23; Luke 10:15; 16:23).

Hallelujah—Hebrew word meaning "praise the Lord."

Heaven—The future eternal home of believers, a place of complete happiness and joy, distinguished especially by the presence of God.

Hell—The place of future punishment for the wicked or unbelieving persons. In the New Testament, Hell is pictured as a place of unending fire and the undying worm (Mark 9:43ff.); outer darkness with weeping and gnashing of teeth (Matt. 8:12); a lake of fire (Rev. 19:20); the second death (Rev. 20:14). It becomes the destiny of people only because they have refused their true destiny which God offers them in Christ.

Heresy—Any false teaching that denies an essential doctrine (teaching) of the Bible.

Hermeneutics—The science of interpretation of Scripture.

Homoousios—("of the same substance")—Greek term used by orthodox Christians, especially Athanasius and his followers, to establish that Jesus is of the same nature or substance as the Father.

Hope—One of three virtues (along with faith and love) often linked together in Scripture. Hope is the expectation of the believer that God will fulfill promises made in the past.

Hosts, Lord of—Name for God that depicts Him as the head of the angelic forces of Heaven.

Humanism—A philosophy that makes humans the highest of all beings, in which case it becomes a form of atheism.

Humanism, Christian—The idea that, on the basis of the teachings of Christianity, human beings are to be highly valued.

Hypostatic union—From the Greek, *hypostasis*, meaning "substance" or "nature." It is a term used to denote the union of Jesus' divine and human natures in one person.

Ideology—The ideas that influence a whole group or society and motivate their conduct.

Immaculate Conception—The Roman Catholic teaching that Mary, the mother of Jesus, was free from sin from the very first moment of her conception. She alone, of all people who have ever lived, apart from Jesus Christ, did not need a redeemer. The Immaculate Conception is sometimes confused with the virgin birth of Jesus.

Immutability of God—Absolute changelessness. Every creature changes, but God does not change.

Imputation—In theology it refers, negatively, to the *transfer* of the sin and guilt of Adam to the rest of mankind. Positively, it refers to God's act of transferring (crediting) the righteousness of Christ to sinners who believe on Him for salvation.

Incarnation—A key theological term for the teaching that the Son of God, without giving up His deity, became man in Jesus Christ, born of the Virgin Mary. (The term literally means "taking on human flesh.")

Inerrancy—The belief that Scripture is entirely free from error.

Infallibility—A reference to the doctrine that Scripture is the inspired word of God, it is free from error, authentic in all its claims, and reliable in its revelation. In Roman Catholic theology, infallibility is extended to the teaching of the church under the authority of the pope.

Inspiration—(of the Bible)—The guidance of the Holy Spirit, which enabled the writers of the Bible to record exactly what God wanted written.

Inspiration, Plenary—The view that all of Scripture, not just certain parts, is inspired. In other words, the Bible is the word of God in its entirety; it does not merely contain the Word of God.

Inspiration, Verbal—The doctrine that the Holy Spirit so guided the biblical writers that even the words are precisely what God intended them to be.

Judaizers—In the New Testament era, people who attempted to impose the standards and laws of Judaism upon Christianity. Paul's letter to the Galatians refutes this position.

Justification by faith—A legal term relating to the divine act whereby a holy and righteous God makes sinful humans, worthy of condemnation, acceptable to Himself. The sinner is justified and brought into relationship with God by faith in Jesus Christ.

Koinonia—A Greek word for "fellowship."

Landmarkism—A view held by some Baptists, particularly in southern United States, that only the local visible church fits the New Testament model. The concept of a universal, invisible church is rejected. The Lord's Supper is restricted to members of the local assembly (called "close" or "closed" communion). It also maintains that there is an apostolic succession, especially as regards believer's baptism, from the time of the apostles to modern Baptist churches.

Law—A reasonable norm of conduct given by proper authority for the common good. In the Hebrew Scriptures, the law is summarized in the Ten

Commandments. Jesus affirmed that all the law could be condensed into two propositions: loving God with all your heart, soul, and mind, and loving your neighbor as yourself.

Legalism—The idea that keeping the law is meritorious, a necessary element of salvation.

Legalist—One who puts an undue emphasis on cultural standards that are not necessarily forbidden in Scripture.

Lent—The period of forty fast days from Ash Wednesday to the Saturday preceding Easter is intended to be a time of abstinence, prayer, and works of charity. Observed by most liturgical churches.

Liberalism—A movement that is open to redefining or changing the traditional doctrines and practices of Christianity.

Limbo—A term used in two ways by Roman Catholics: first, it is a place where the Old Testament saints awaited Christ's descent into Hades to lead them into Heaven (*Limbus Patrum*); and second, it is the place where all unbaptized infants go after death, their suffering consisting solely in the lack of the "beatific vision" (*Limbus Infantum*).

Logos—A Greek term for "Word" used in the prologue to the Gospel of John to refer to Christ.

Love feast—A common meal shared by the members of the early church.

Man of sin—A reference to the Antichrist (2 Thess. 2:3).

Mercy seat—A slab of gold on top of the ark of the covenant, symbolizing God's forgiveness of sins. The blood of atonement was sprinkled on the mercy seat.

Millennium—From the Latin word for "thousand," the millennium refers to the thousand year reign of Christ (Rev. 20:1-8).

Monotheism—Belief in and worship of one God, as opposed to polytheism, the belief in many gods.

Mystery of iniquity—A phrase in 2 Thessalonians 2:7 that refers to Satan's work in the world. The Holy Spirit is restraining the work of Satan, but will be removed at the time of the Rapture.

Neo-orthodoxy—A system of theology associated particularly with the Swiss theologian, Karl Barth (1886-1968). Although emphasizing divine transcendence as well as human sinfulness and the centrality of Christ, many of the elements of the old liberalism were still present, such as a denial of the Bible as the very word of God. Parts of the Bible may *become* the word of God to the individual believer, but exactly which parts is a cause for dispute.

New covenant—The Christian dispensation and the economy introduced by Christ and the apostles.

Nihilism—A rejection of tradition, morality, and authority; it is philosophical skepticism with respect to both truth and morality.

Nirvana—The goal of Hindus. The cycle of reincarnation ceases, and the individual is absorbed into the Brahma.

Nonconformity—Unwillingness to comply with the established religion or the state church.

Omnipotence—The almighty power of God. He can do whatever does not deny his nature or that is not self-contradictory.

Omnipresence—God's ability to be present everywhere simultaneously.

Omniscience—God's knowledge of all things.

Open theism—The belief of a small group in the evangelical tradition that immutability and omniscience are not necessarily attributes that can be ascribed to God. They hold that God grows in knowledge, discovers things he did not know, and changes His mind. He cannot necessarily foreknow the actions of humans.

Ordinance—A practice established by Jesus Christ with the command that it is to be carried out. Most non-Catholics, such as Baptists, refer to baptism and the Lord's Supper as *ordinances* rather than sacraments.

Original Sin—The expression often used (though not found in the Bible) to describe the state or condition of sin into which all generations of people are born since the time of Adam's transgression.

Orthodox—Literally "straight" or "proper," that which is in harmony with correct doctrine or practice as set forth in Scripture. Or it may refer to the Greek Eastern branch of Catholicism that separated from the Latin Roman Catholic Church in 1054.

Pacifism—The doctrine that all war is inherently wrong and that warfare is forbidden by the Gospels. While war is undesirable, and sinful passions often give rise to war, not all armed conflict is necessarily sinful, and Christians may engage in a just war.

Pantheism—The belief that everything is divine, or that God and the universe are really identical.

Parable—A short story based on a familiar life experience used to teach a spiritual lesson.

Parachurch—Generally refers to an organization or group that operates outside the jurisdiction of a church or denominational body.

Paradise—A synonym for Heaven. Jesus spoke of it in His promise to the believing thief on the cross (Luke 23:43). Only two other places in Scripture mention the term in connection with Heaven (2 Cor. 12:2-4; Rev. 2:7).

Parousia—A Greek word meaning "advent," specifically the second coming (advent) of Christ which will usher in the full establishment of God's kingdom on earth.

Pedobaptism—The practice of baptizing infants.

Pelagianism—A theological system named after Pelagius (c.360-420), which emphasizes human ability and free will as opposed to depravity and sinfulness. Human nature is essentially good and unbaptized infants are not necessarily condemned.

Perfectionism—The view that it is possible to attain a state of sinlessness.

Perpetual virginity—The belief of Roman Catholicism that Mary not only was a virgin at the time of the conception and birth of Jesus, but remained so throughout her life.

Perseverance of the saints—The belief that those who are truly converted will persevere to the end. Once saved, they are eternally secure.

Polytheism—Belief in more than one God.

Postmillennialism—The belief that Christ's second coming will occur after the millennium.

Postmodernism—An extreme left-wing movement that developed in the late twentieth century in architecture, literature, philosophy, economics, theology, music, and popular culture, and represents a reaction against the correspondence concept of truth, as well as the traditional view of objectivity, rationality, and progress. The capitalist economic system is blamed for most of the evils of the modern world, hence socialism is regarded as the only equitable economic system. The missionary attempt of Christians to save the "heathen" is looked upon as an unnecessary invasion of peoples whose religion is just as valid as Christianity. It is especially an assault on the doctrines and practices of biblical Christianity.

Prayer—Conversation with God. Joining one's thoughts and love to God in adoration, confession, thanksgiving, and supplication (petition).

Predestination—The decision of God in choosing who will be saved and who will be lost. Some, including Arminians, believe God foresees the faith of those who will believe and then elects them. Calvinists hold that the faith of the believer results from rather than causes God's choice.

Premillennialism—The belief that the return of Christ precedes the millennium (the earthly reign of Christ). Jesus will then rule the earth for one thousand years, followed by a final rebellion led by Satan. Christ will crush the rebellious, judge unbelievers, and establish the new heavens and the new earth.

Preterists—Those who hold that the prophetic events spoken of in Scripture, particularly in the book of Revelation, had already taken place or were shortly to take place.

Pretribulationism—The belief that Christ will rapture or remove the church from the world prior to the tribulation.

Process theology—A view which sees everything still in the process of becoming what it will be, but nothing really is. It is a form of evolutionary pantheism which postulates a finite god who is becoming perfect, but is not infinite and all-perfect from eternity. It is called "process" because it claims that the universe (including God) is moving toward completion, without identifying when or whether this completion will be reached. There are no determined moral laws and no absolute norms of conduct. Everything, including the thinking mind, is ever becoming what it was not and ceasing to be what it was.

Prophet—One who serves as a channel of communication between humans and God. This may or may not involve the foretelling of future events. Every preacher or teacher who speaks of future events revealed in the Bible is assuming the role of a prophet. On the other hand, faithfully proclaiming any truth of Scripture certifies one as a prophet. In one sense all Christians are called to be prophets, that is, to testify in word and action to the truths of God's Word.

Propitiation—An offering that turns away the wrath of God. In sending His Son to be the propitiation (or atoning sacrifice) for sin, God has provided the offering that removes or turns away His divine wrath (see 1 John 4:10).

Protestantism—The system of faith, worship, and practice derived from the principles of the Reformation in the sixteenth century. The name comes from the *Protestatio* of the Reformers at the Diet of Speyer (1529) against the decisions of Catholics who were present, that no further religious innovations were to be introduced. Protestants are known for three premises primarily: namely the Bible as the only rule of faith and practice, excluding tradition; justification by faith alone, excluding meritorious works; and the universal priesthood of believers, excluding a priesthood divinely empowered to teach, govern, forgive sins, and sanctify the people of God.

Purgatory—According to Roman Catholic teaching, purgatory is the abode in the afterlife for those who die in a state of grace, but are not yet free from all imperfection. By making expiation (the blotting out or removal of sin and renewal of communion with God) they will eventually be purified and admitted into Heaven.

Rapture—The belief that the church will be caught up from the world (1 Thess. 4:16, 17) to be forever with the Lord. Controversy exists as to whether it will be before (pre-), during (mid-), or after (post-) the Great Tribulation.

Real Presence—The teaching of the Roman Catholic Church that Christ is present truly or actually in the "Holy Eucharist" and not only symbolically.

Reconciliation—The bringing together of two parties that are estranged; particularly, Christ's bringing God and sinful humans together, the result of which is salvation.

Redemption—Literally, to free or buy back. Because humanity was held captive, enslaved by sin, kept in bondage by the Devil, the only ransom payment acceptable to God that would free mankind from captivity was the death of His son Jesus Christ. Christ rendered satisfaction, not by giving money, but by spending what was of the highest value. He gave Himself, and therefore His death resulted in humanity's redemption.

Reformed theology—The branch of theology that emphasizes Calvinism, especially with respect to the matter of salvation.

Regeneration—Another name for being "born again." Jesus plainly said that no one would enter the kingdom of God without being regenerated, or born again. Jesus spoke to Nicodemus about being born of "*water*" and the "*Spirit*" (John 3). His statement implies that there are two kinds of generation: physical and spiritual, one as a human being at physical birth, the other as a child of God at the new (or spiritual) birth.

Revelation—God's self-communication of Himself to us through creation, His written Word, and His Son Jesus Christ.

Rule of faith—The norm that enables the faithful to know what to believe. The revealed Word of God in Sacred Scripture is the only rule of faith for the believer.

Sabaoth—A title of majesty applied mainly to God. The Hebrew word means "armies" or "hosts" and is found mainly in the expression "Lord of hosts," which occurs over 200 times in the Old Testament, and mostly in the prophetical books. In the New Testament the term is used twice (Rom. 9:29; James 5:4)

Sabbatarianism—Strict observance of one day of the week as a day of worship and rest.

Sacrament—In the liturgical churches such as Roman Catholicism, an outward sign instituted by Christ to confer grace (salvation). There are seven sacraments in the Catholic church: baptism, confirmation, Eucharist, reconciliation, anointing of the sick, marriage, and holy orders.

Sacramentalism—The belief that grace is conveyed through certain religious rites.

Salvation—The act whereby God's forgiveness and grace are extended to us through acceptance of Christ's sacrificial death on our behalf. Salvation brings about union with God and fellow believers through the work of our Savior, Jesus Christ.

Security of the believer—The view that Christians are preserved by the power of God and kept from forfeiting their salvation. The doctrine is also referred to as the "perseverance of the saints."

Secularism—The philosophy which attempts to achieve human betterment without belief in or commitment to God or religion. It is expressed in the human's preoccupation with this world rather than the next.

Semitic—A group of people that in ancient times included Babylonians, Assyrians, Aramaeans, Canaanites, and Phoenicians, but in more recent times has come to represent Jews; hence the term, "Anti-Semitic."

Septuagint—(abbreviated LXX, Roman numeral for 70)—Earliest Greek translation of the Hebrew Old Testament. Produced by 70 (or 72) Jewish translators brought to Egypt by Ptolemy II Philadelphus (285-246 B.C.), it was completed about two and a half centuries before Christ.

Sheol—The Hebrew word for Hell, corresponding to the Greek *Hades*.

Signs of the times—The signs predicted by Christ foretelling His second coming and the end of the world (Matt. 24:3-44)

Situation ethics—The belief that any action, including the most heinous crime, may be right and permissible in a given situation. The situation determines the rightness or wrongness of a given action.

Sola Fide—By faith alone, the basic principle of Reformation Protestantism. It declares that humanity is justified only by a confident trust in God through the saving merits of Jesus Christ.

Sola Scriptura—In Scripture alone. One of the cardinal principles of Protestantism; it declares that all of divine revelation is contained in the Bible, not in the Bible *and* tradition.

Soteriology—That part of theology which treats of Christ's work of salvation. It covers the study of man's fall in Adam and the sins of mankind, which needed a Savior, the doctrine of grace by which the guilt and consequences of sin are removed, and especially the twofold mystery of Christ as Redeemer and Mediator of the human race.

Soul sleep—The idea that between death and resurrection the person is in a state of unconsciousness. Two of the most vocal proponents of this idea are Jehovah's Witnesses and Seventh-Day Adventists.

Sovereignty—The concept that God, by virtue of creation, is King over all the earth and has supreme authority over the entire universe.

Supralapsarians—Followers of John Calvin who hold that God's decree of reprobation of some people to Hell is absolute, and not conditioned by the Fall. God would have condemned these people to Hell even though Adam had not sinned.

Tetragrammaton—The four letters in Hebrew for the name of Israel's God: YHWH, or Jehovah.

Theism—Belief in a personal and provident God. Theism is commonly distinguished from atheism, which denies the existence of a personal, transcendent deity.

Theocracy—A form of government in which God, acting usually through His priestly or prophetic representatives, is the ruler.

Theodicy—Natural theology, or the study of God's existence and attributes as known by the light of natural reason and apart from supernatural revelation.

Theology—Greek *theos*, "God," and *logos*, "word;" the systematic study of the being, attributes, purposes, and works of God.

Theophany—A visible appearance or manifestation of God, particularly in the Old Testament.

Tradition—(something "handed over")—Originally (in the biblical sense) meant the revelation of God made known to people through the prophets and apostles. In the Roman Catholic Church it eventually came to mean Scripture, as well as creeds and the accumulated explanations of the faith and the wisdom of the church through history. Hence, Catholics regard tradition as being equal in authority to Scripture.

Transubstantiation—The official Catholic Church teaching that the substance of the bread and wine is changed ("transubstantiated") into the substance of the blood and body of Jesus Christ at the consecration of the Mass.

Trinity—The Christian teaching that holds that there are three persons in one God: Father, Son and Holy Spirit. Although the word "Trinity" does not occur in the Bible, the concept is clearly revealed in the New Testament, and hinted at in the Old. There are passages in which all three persons of the Trinity are mentioned in the same context. The most important of these are the Apostolic Benediction of 2 Cor. 13:14, and the baptismal formula of Matt. 28:19.

Universalism—The view that all persons will be saved, and there will be no eternal punishment.

Unlimited atonement—The doctrine that Christ's atoning death was for all people everywhere.

Unpardonable sin—Blasphemy against the Holy Spirit (Matt. 12:31-32; Mark 3:28-29; Luke 12:10). The unpardonable sin is often thought of as a persistent denial of God's offer of mercy through Christ, resulting in a hardness of heart that prevents the individual from recognizing the truth, repenting of sin, and believing on Christ.

Vicarious atonement—Vicarious means "in place of." Because Jesus died *for* us, it means He took on Himself the consequences of our sin; hence His death was a sacrificial, substitutionary death, a *vicarious* atonement.

BIBLIOGRAPHY

Ankerberg, John, John Weldon. *Protestants & Catholics: Do They Agree?* Eugene, Oregon: Harvest House Publishers, 1995.

Bancroft, Emery H. *Christian Theology*. 2nd ed. Grand Rapids: Zondervan Publishing House, 1976.

Bauman, Michael. *The Creed: What You Believe and Why.* Nashville: Thomas Nelson, Inc., 2002.

Cairns, Alan. *Dictionary of Theological Terms*. 2nd. Ed. Belfast/Greenville, S.C.: Ambassador Emerald International, 1998.

Cassels, Louis. *Christian Primer.* Garden City, NY: Doubleday & Company, 1964.

Catechism of the Catholic Church. Liguori, Missouri, 1994.

Chafer, Lewis Sperry, rev. by John F. Walvoord. *Major Bible Themes: 52 Vital Doctrines of the Scripture Simplified and Explained.* Grand Rapids: Zondervan Publishing House, 1974.

Coffey, Tom. *Once A Catholic: What You Need to Know About Roman Catholicism.* Eugene, Oregon: Harvest House Publishers, 1993.

Cole, C. Donald. *Basic Christian Faith.* Westchester, Ill.: Crossway Books, 1985.

Cottrell, Jack. *The Faith Once for All: Bible Doctrine for Today.* Joplin, MO: College Press Publishing Company, 2002.

Elwell, Walter A., ed. *Evangelical Dictionary of Theology.* Grand Rapids: Baker Books, 1984.

Erickson, Millard J. *Christian Theology.* 2nd ed. Grand Rapids: Baker Books, 2000.

Evans, William. *The Great Doctrines of the Bible.* Chicago: The Bible Institute Colportage Association, 1912.

Ferguson, Sinclair B., David F. Wright, J. I. Packer, eds. *New Dictionary of Theology.* Downers Grove, Illinois: InterVarsity Press, 1988.

Geisler, Norman L. *Baker Encyclopedia of Christian Apologetics.* Grand Rapids: Baker Books, 1999.

Grudem, Wayne. *Systematic Theology: An Introduction to Biblical Doctrine.* Grand Rapids: Zondervan Publishing House, 1994.

Henry, Carl F. H. *Basic Christian Doctrines.* New York: Holt, Rinehart and Winston, 1962.

Hobbs, Herschel H. *Fundamentals of Our Faith.* Nashville: Broadman &

Holman Publishers, 1960.

Jastrow, Robert. *God and the Astronomers*. New York: W. W. Norton & Company, 1978.

Kenyon, Frederic, rev. by A. W. Adams. *Our Bible and the Ancient Manuscripts*. 5th ed. New York: Harper & Row, 1962.

Kreeft, Peter & Ronald K. Tacelli. *Handbook of Christian Apologetics: Hundreds of Answers to Crucial Questions*. Downers Grove, Ill.: InterVarsity Press, 1994.

Lewis, C. S. *Mere Christianity*. New York: The Macmillan Company, 1957.

Lindsell, Harold, Charles J. Woodbridge. *A Handbook of Christian Truth*. Old Tappan, New Jersey: Fleming H. Revell Co., n.d.

Lockyer, Herbert. *All the Doctrines of the Bible*. Grand Rapids: Zondervan Publishing House, 1964.

McDowell, Josh. *The New Evidence That Demands a Verdict*. Nashville: Thomas Nelson Publishers, 1999.

Micks, Marianne H. *Introduction to Theology*. New York: The Seabury Press, 1964.

Mueller, John T. *Christian Dogmatics: A Handbook of Doctrinal Theology for Pastors, Teachers, and Laymen*. St. Louis: Concordia Publishing House, 1951.

Neff, LaVonne, Ron Beers, Bruce Barton, Linda Taylor, Dave Veerman, Jim Galvin, eds. *Practical Christianity*. Carmel, NY: Guideposts, 1987.

Nevins, Albert J. *Answering a Fundamentalist*. Huntington, Indiana: Our Sunday Visitor Publishing Division, 1990.

Reid, Daniel G., Robert D. Lindner, Bruce L. Shelley, Harry S. Stout, eds. *Dictionary of Christianity in America*. Downers Grove, Ill.: InterVarsity Press, 1990.

Spong, John Shelby. *Rescuing the Bible from Fundamentalism: A Bishop Rethinks the Meaning of Scripture*. San Francisco: Harper, 1991.

Sproul, R. C. *Essential Truths of the Christian Faith*. Wheaton, Ill.: Tyndale House Publishers, 1992.

Strobel, Lee. *The Case for Christ*. Grand Rapids: Zondervan Publishing House, 1992.

Strong, Augustus H. *Systematic Theology*. Valley Forge, Pa.: Judson Press, 28th printing, 1972.

Swindoll, Charles R., Roy B. Zuck, eds. *Understanding Christian Theology*. Nashville: Thomas Nelson Publishers, 2003.

Taylor, Richard S., J. Kenneth Grider, Willard H. Taylor, eds. *Beacon

Dictionary of Theology. Kansas City, Mo.: Beacon Hill Press, 1983.

Thiessen, H. C., rev. by Vernon Doerksen. *Lectures in Systematic Theology.* Grand Rapids: William B. Eerdmans Publishing Company, 1989.

Walvoord, John F. *Major Bible Prophecies: 37 Crucial Prophecies That Affect You Today.* Grand Rapids: Zondervan Publishing House, 1991.

Wilson, Bill. *The Best of Josh McDowell: A Ready Defense.* Nashville: Thomas Nelson Publishers, 1993.